Of Others Inside

Of Others Inside

Insanity, Addiction, and Belonging in America

Darin Weinberg

Foreword by
Bryan S. Turner

Temple University Press
Philadelphia

Temple University Press
1601 North Broad Street
Philadelphia PA 19122
www.temple.edu/tempress

⊗ The paper used in this publication meets the requirements of the American
National Standard for Information Sciences—Permanence of Paper for Printed Library
Materials, ANSI Z39.48-1992

Library of Congress Cataloging-in-Publication Data

Weinberg, Darin.
   Of others inside : insanity, addiction, and belonging in America / Darin Weinberg ;
foreword by Bryan S. Turner.
      p.   cm.
   Includes bibliographical references and index.
   ISBN 1-59213-403-3 (cloth : alk. paper)—ISBN 1-59213-404-1 (pbk. : alk. paper)
   1. Mentally ill—United States—Social conditions.   2. Addicts—United States—Social
conditions.   3. Homeless persons—Mental health—United States.   4. Homeless
persons—Mental health services—United States.   5. Homelessness—United States.
6. Marginality, Social—United States.   I. Title.

HV3009.W45 2005
362.2'0973—dc22
                                                                                    2005044007

2 4 6 8 9 7 5 3 1

To my family

The type of social science ... we wish to put forth is an *empirical science* of concrete *reality*. We wish to understand the reality that surrounds our lives, in which we are placed, *in its characteristic uniqueness*. We wish to understand on the one hand its *context* and the cultural *significance* of its particular manifestations in their contemporary form, and on the other the causes of it becoming historically so and not otherwise.

—Max Weber, *The Methodology of the Social Sciences*, 1922

Contents

Foreword

SOCIAL SCIENCE, and specifically sociological, approaches to health and illness have been typically bifurcated around a dichotomy between what, for convenience, we might call *naturalism* and *social constructionism*. Naturalistic explanations seek physical causes of health and illness on the assumption that disease can be effectively controlled or eliminated by targeted medical intervention. This approach historically involved treating the human body as a machine that could be manipulated by medical science without the distractions of such dubious entities as "mind" or "subjectivity." The spectacular treatment of the infectious diseases of childhood in the late nineteenth and early twentieth century provides the ideal model of medical science and its therapeutic potency. Of course, critics of this vision of medical history argue that these treatments were successful only after the social and physical environment had been improved by the introduction of sewerage, clean water, and an adequate food supply. Perhaps more importantly in the present context, while the physical etiology for example of measles has been successfully identified, there is far less scientific consensus as to the physical "substance" that produces alcohol addiction or mental illness. Similarly, the quest to discover genes that explain specific forms of social deviance is like a fable from Don Quixote in the sense that deviancy, because it is paradoxically a product of law or moral convention, does not lend itself to such explanations. The classic sociological argument is that the search for a genetic explanation of deviancy involves a category mistake. As Emile Durkheim argued, social facts can be explained only by social facts. Is homosexuality a genetic disorder, a socially constructed category, or a lifestyle choice? Is there a gene to explain the prevalence of divorce in modern society? Perhaps, but first we need to find the gene that will explain the prevalence of matrimony. We tend to assume that matrimony needs no explanation simply because it is a "normal" relationship between men and women that has the blessing of the Law. We tend to look for naturalistic explanations in the social sciences only when phenomena appear to be untoward.

The naturalistic research strategy looks particularly unpromising if our effort is to explain the link between mental disability and patterns of social exclusion such as homelessness. At least some aspects of homelessness will be a function of macrosocial and economic changes—including interest rates, property prices, the rental market, availability, local governmental policies, and so forth. The complex causal processes behind the housing market do not allow for simple biological explanations of aggregate homelessness. Moreover at the individual level, the social reality of alcoholism is profoundly shaped by local circumstances. The consumption of whisky among middle-class Scots may be addictive from some perspectives, but we know that middle-class resources (income, education, and connections) typically act as a buffer against negative labeling, permitting them to manage such dispositions or preferences without coming to the attention of the authorities. Homeless men consuming alcohol in public spaces in Britain are by contrast very likely to come to the attention of the police. In the everyday world, my consumption preferences may very well constitute someone else's addiction.

These arguments are well known, and possibly taken for granted by social scientists. In order to avoid these pitfalls of naïve naturalism, social constructionist sociologists have contested clinical labels, arguing, for example from the standpoint of symbolic interactionism, that pathology is in the eye of the beholder. Alcoholism exists if a professional person can deploy expert knowledge to secure the social efficacy of the label. I am mad if a label of insanity can be successfully attached to me or, in the famous words of W. I. Thomas, definitions are real if they are real in their consequences. Social constructionist critics of the naturalist position have drawn attention to the social processes by which "troubles" in some very broad sense get translated into recognizable medical "conditions" that professional groups can diagnose and if necessary treat. Constructionist epistemologies have many and diverse origins—including the pragmatism of Richard Rorty and the poststructuralism of Michel Foucault. These approaches at one level demonstrate that, insofar as conditions have a history, they can be shown to be context-dependent and hence determined by a welter of social and cultural variables. Foucault's classical accounts of the history of psychiatry, penology, and criminology in such influential studies as *Discipline and Punish* or *Madness and Civilization* have had an important general impact on the study of professional groups and institutions and their systems of knowledge. In his powerful and commanding study of mental illness, Foucault explored the social history of folly in Shakespeare's *King Lear* to the interventions of Pinel and Tuke. Whereas in Tudor times folly was associated with a creative and superior imagination, the rise of the science of psychiatry ruled out any contamination of reason by folly, and the mentally unstable required restraint and seclusion. The effect of Foucault's social constructionist history of insanity was to show the arbitrary nature of the categories that are mobilized to describe and manage troublesome people or threatening social groups. The history of madness illustrates the ways in which scientific labels function to bring about an exclusion or seclusion of individuals and groups that do not fit easily or comfortably in regimes for the social and political administration of populations. In short, through the concept of "governmentality," Foucault was able to demonstrate the close relationship between a system of power and an order of knowledge.

Foucault's analysis of insanity has been deeply influential in shaping attitudes toward the development of psychiatry in Western societies and in molding historical inquiries into the role of the state in the general management of populations. This approach has more recently had a major impact on the study of physical disability and old age as well. Disability is often regarded as a consequence of social exclusion through the denial of social rights in a culture that promotes "able-ism" as a dominant ideology rather than as the consequence of a debilitating physical condition. Similarly, "old age" is seen to be a product of powerful social forces that have the effect of marginalizing the elderly and converting them, with the assistance of gerontology and geriatric medicine, into a tangible and recognizable social group of "old people." Despite Foucault's significant contribution to the critical history of insanity, sexual deviance, and crime, this approach is in many respects unsatisfactory.

Although the Foucauldian perspective has been productive in research terms, the approach has difficulty in accounting for the growth of social rights. In particular, the Foucauldian perspective on "power/knowledge" has problems accounting for the fact that new rights (or claims on the state) are often predicated on findings or proof of disability. Disability as a condition is plainly not just a matter of social rights denial, since being successfully defined as disabled can be necessary in acquiring rights to some forms of welfare entitlement. The analytical limits of a Foucauldian (or otherwise strict social constructionist) perspective are further illustrated when we consider the phenomenology of physical disability. Social constructionism has not fully succeeded in explaining the very real performative impediments associated with disability status. We might contrast the Foucault-inspired sociology of mental illness as a system of governmentality with the rich ethnographical accounts of the performative peculiarities of Tourette's syndrome by Oliver Sacks in his essay "A Surgeon's Life" in *An Anthropologist on Mars*. The macrosociology of governmentality tells us nothing about the phenomenology of the everyday world of involuntary swearing, twitching, and mimicry of the Tourette's syndrome victim.

Attempts to deconstruct the hegemonic paradigms of social control typically ignore as irrelevant or reject as misleading the subjective experiences of the individuals who get labeled as mad or neurotic or incompetent. Critical theories of insanity, because they concentrate on the study of the conditions that produce interpretation or knowledge (such as the history of psychiatric labels), do not address the phenomenological character of madness—or addiction, or illness, or deviance. They ignore the question (which we might express in Heideggerian terms) "What is this *thing* called madness?" in favor of other questions—under what conditions can untoward behavior get successfully labeled as a case of insanity? Those who treat the social world as socially constructed, that is, as a text that can be read and critically interpreted by sociologists or cultural analysts, often miss the performative aspects of the human condition. We may without doubt agree that the disabled child suffers from a loss of rights, but what is the phenomenology of the thalidomide child's experience? And furthermore, how shall we promote the rights of those with disabilities or special needs if we are not prepared to acknowledge the obduracy of those disabilities or special needs? The strict constructionist argument sometimes seems to imply that if we can simply persuade ourselves and our significant others that our disabilities are unreal then so they will be. This is not a happy conclusion for those of us who know that overcoming affliction very often amounts to much more than changing our beliefs.

It has been a common theoretical strategy of medical sociology to support cultural relativism with respect to a variety of conditions that can be regarded as "disability." In many tribal societies, any condition that reduces one's chances in the marriage market (such as small stature or disfigurement) is a "disability." However, it is not enough to argue simply that because impairments vary between societies, we need not consider their materiality, only their social constitution and consequences. For example, it is unlikely that a "small person" could become a successful basketball star, but it is not merely social conventions that prevent small people entering such sporting professions. They simply cannot perform the tasks that confront star players. A person of slight stature simply does not have the potentialities that are necessary for performance at that level. It may indeed be conceivable that a small but powerful monarch might influence the exchange value of people of small stature in elite marriage markets. But in the case of basketball, this kind of relativism is not so easily applied. Changing the rules of basketball so that stature did not count would in fact totally transform the game; it would no longer be basketball. There are certain social institutions—in this case, basketball—that, while being amenable to some reforms within a finite spectrum of possibilities, cannot be amenable to an infinite range of reforms without threatening their very abolition.

In the perspective of writers like Pierre Bourdieu and Richard Shusterman, we need as researchers to be attentive to the social practices of everyday life and what I would call the phenomenological conditions and circumstances of skill, performance, and action. Performing as a successful classical ballet dancer is not merely a function of social construction; it needs to be accomplished as a performance. There is of course a democratic politics behind social constructionism that encourages us to believe that, if only the social definition of the situation were to be changed, then I too could become a Nureyev, but such forms of idealism typically come up against the laws of gravity. We must as sociologists, again employing a language that could be derived from Heidegger, attend to what I want to call the "stuffness" of life or its quiddity. Often social constructionism appears to miss the thing-ness (quid) of a condition or what Heidegger might call the "throwness" of phenomena.

Darin Weinberg has addressed this traditional contradiction or tension between naturalism and social constructionism in an area that has been particularly prone to unhelpful arguments about the objective versus the constructed relationship between homelessness, addiction, and insanity. His arguments, which are systematically embedded in his ethnographic research, offer a way out of the conundrum by showing how these positions represent false alternatives. The arguments that he deploys, to use his own words, to advance a novel sociological understanding of the relationship between social exclusion and mental disability, should be carefully followed by the reader. It is not my intention here to produce a glib summary of his thesis; it provides its own compelling arguments, and the reader should be attentive to his text. It seems to me more useful in this short foreword to consider his exploration of the multiple meanings of the phrase "others inside." It conveys a sense of the strangeness of addiction and insanity to those presumed to be afflicted, and the problems of explaining that strangeness from the outside. A disease can often be best described by metaphors of an invasion of our inner world. Cancer may be experienced as such an invasion and no strictly constructionist account can fully grasp the "thing-ness" of such an alien and disturbing occurrence. Addiction in these terms might be conceptualized as one way in which people sometimes experience alienation from their sense of control over their lives. It was Karl Marx who in his *Paris Manuscripts* first explored the possibility that the subjectivity of social life can be alienated in just this sense by the overwhelming pressures exerted upon us by the capitalist mode of production. People cease to experience society as a collection of fellow human beings and begin to experience it as an anonymous, objective, and unforgiving thing. This kind of alienation implies a phenomenological transference of the agency we once found in our selves and each other to nonsubjective forces like the market system or conditions like insanity or addiction. The alienation that attends a dis-ease is also fundamentally a profound dis-comfort. We need also to explore the objective social conditions that may produce an addiction or mental illness, of which homelessness may be a poignant feature. To be homeless is to be discomforted, and in need of fortification.

Sociology is at its best a critical discipline that produces its own type of discomfort, inviting us to see the world as an alien place by breaking down taken for granted assumptions. The social constructionist argument, which is clearly a powerful vision of the world, is also discomforting; it helps us to question what Bourdieu has called the "doxic," or unquestioned, qualities of our objective realities. It often as a result appears to place sociologists and clinicians in opposite and opposed camps, by calling our attention to the negative as well as the therapeutic consequences of medicalization. Medical interventions are often understood by sociologists to obfuscate the material circumstances of homelessness by focusing undue attention on the individual characteristics of the alcoholic and naturalizing their personal incapacity to deal with social life. Weinberg takes a refreshingly open approach to the professional competences of both clinicians and sociologists by taking us beyond the critique of medicalization to suggest a more just, fruitful, and compassionate deployment of the medical devices that are to hand. In the last analysis, doctors like sociologists are only practitioners attempting to make sense of contradictory and uncertain evidence; both require hermeneutics. Clinicians, psychiatrists, and sociologists are not necessarily in opposite camps. As an illustration of this shared world, I often use a personal experience as a teaching device with my students to illustrate the notion of interpretative sociology and investigative medicine. During an investigation of a painful episode of pancreatitis, an attendant nurse tried to reassure me that my condition was not necessarily life-threatening or pathological—to which I exclaimed, "That's good news!" The clinician hovering over me thoughtfully responded, "There is no such thing as 'good news'; there is only interpretation." As an interpretative sociologist I could only agree, but I might also have said that a professional interpretation did not fully or effectively address the quiddity of my pain. Weinberg provides us with a method by which these two dimensions of human problems can be compassionately explored. In short, he shows how hermeneutics also needs phenomenology.

Of Others Inside is a study of social problems, but it contains a powerful philosophical and methodological conclusion, namely that the conventional analytical dichotomy between objectivism and subjectivism turns out to be a false opposition. Weinberg has transformed a debate that has become increasingly unproductive by showing that while we need to understand how mental disability is constructed, we also need to understand its clinical reality, not least from the victim's point of view. If the naturalistic paradigm has sought to demonstrate the physical determinacy of the world, the sociologist wants also to identify just how social and historical causality works, and interacts with those forces that are presumed to be natural. In sociology as in life, deeply divided camps often turn out to be not only highly compatible, but also mutually sustaining positions. In resolving this conundrum between objectivism and subjectivism in the sociology of mental health, *Of Others Inside* is a remarkable, original, and timely achievement.

BRYAN S. TURNER

Acknowledgments

OVER THE COURSE of writing this book I have incurred many intellectual debts. Thanks are due first and foremost to Mel Pollner. His intellectual sensitivities and investigations of the variegated nature of personal being, the ultimate fluidity of social forms, and the social boundaries of reason have been both foundational to my scholarly development and a personal inspiration. Next, to Bob Emerson who taught me virtually everything I know about fieldwork and ethnography. Without his painstaking cultivation of my incipient (and insipid) insights in the field, this project would have never left the ground. To Harold Garfinkel for his passionate regard for the "what more" there is to social life and its study, and the "what more" there might be to my own capacity for insight. To Stuart Kirk for coming to UCLA in the nick of time and for his interest in my project and willingness to let it germinate as it has. To Paul Koegel for getting me into this project in the first place, for his many, many hands-on contributions to the fieldwork and the thinking that is its basis, and for his early faith in me. To Jim Holstein and Jay Gubrium for forging much of the path that I have taken, and to Jay for his generosity and guidance during the three years I spent with him at the University of Florida. To Bryan Turner for refining my thinking on so many topics but in particular those on the interface of medicine and social inclusion. I would also like to thank Doni Loseke, Spencer Cahill, Gale Miller, Joel Best, John Heritage, Jack Katz, Ivan Szeleyni, Steve Clayman, Manny Schegloff, Peter Kollock, Jeff Prager, Jeff Alexander, Rogers Brubaker, Mike Lynch, David Bogen, Dusan Bjelic, David Goode, John A. Hall, Peter Ibarra, John Kitsuse, and Bennett Berger for teaching me and for their help along the way. This project has also benefited immensely from the countless conversations and debates I have shared with my friends: Geoff Raymond, Byron Burkhalter, Larry King, Dana Rosenfeld, Patrick Baert, Eric Hanley, Marc Smith, Christine Morton, Eric Rivera, Benita Roth, Susan Markens, Dave Grant, Margie Zamudio, Andy Roth, Nick Wolfinger, Eric Magnuson, Gil Eyal, Stavros Karageorgis, Manali Desai, Eleanor Townsley, and Dylan Riley. Thanks as well to Doug Anglin, and everyone at the Drug Abuse Research Center, for expanding the scope of my intellectual horizons well beyond the boundaries of sociology and compelling me to think more seriously about the relationship between the social and clinical sciences. To everyone on the "Course of Homelessness" and "Treatment Options" studies at Rand, but particularly Audrey Burnam and Elizabeth McGlynn for bringing me aboard and Bud Hayes for his generosity of time and spirit. The bulk of my data collection and some of the analysis were funded by NIAAA Grant 1 VO1 AA08821 and NIDA Institutional Training Grant No. DA07272. I would also like to thank Micah Kleit, my editor at Temple University Press, for his enthusiasm and thoughtful advice. It has been an absolute pleasure to work with him. No words can repay the debt I owe the many people who allowed me into their lives and who graciously helped me try to understand their worlds. Finally, I want to thank Diana for giving me a place to call home through all of this and my little boys Ethan and Tristan for making that home an infinitely more beautiful place to live.

1 Introduction

Beyond Objectivism and Subjectivism
in the Sociology of Mental Health

THE OBJECTIVE of this book is to advance a novel sociological understanding of the relationship between social exclusion, specifically homelessness, and mental disability. Current research leaves little doubt that homelessness, mental illness, and addiction are empirically linked, but the particular nature of this relationship is anything but settled. In fact, debate in this area has fallen into something of a theoretical stalemate. While clinically oriented studies argue that the rise of homelessness in the eighties was caused primarily by the deinstitutionalization of people with mental illnesses, alcoholism, and rising rates of drug addiction (cf. Baum and Burnes 1993), sociologically oriented studies argue that homelessness was caused by social structural processes like deindustrialization, racial and economic segregation, dwindling social services, and dwindling low-income housing stocks (cf. Rossi 1989; Snow and Anderson 1993; Wagner 1993; Wright 1989). Social scientists have generally argued that even if there is some truth to findings of mental disability among the homeless, these findings must be interpreted in light of their social structural contexts. While some suggest that homelessness (and severe poverty more generally) is less a result than a cause of mental disabilities, others argue that the epidemiology and clinical assessment of mental disorder are themselves social context sensitive and prone to produce false positives (cf. Horwitz 2002; Snow et al. 1986).

Moreover, in critical contrast to clinically oriented research, sociological research often suggests that findings of mental disabilities among dispossessed peoples reflect a pervasive tendency in Western societies to unjustly attribute personal pathology to the poor and other outsiders. Critical sociologists generally base their condemnation of what is often called the *medicalization* of poverty and marginality on four specific complaints. The medicalization of poverty and marginality (1) blames victims, (2) obfuscates social structural sources of misery and injustice, (3) wrongly exalts the medical profession, and (4) by casting problems

1

in individualistic terms, exonerates the better-off from the duties of citizenship. Several eminent members of this research tradition including Peter Conrad, Michel Foucault, Roy Porter, Nikolas Rose, David Rothman, and Andrew Scull have made absolutely indispensable contributions to our sociohistorical understanding of medicine and psychiatry as technologies of social control and of why culturally marginalized populations are so often held to suffer from mental disabilities. Nonetheless, this body of research suffers a rather profound limitation. One searches the critical literature in vain for analyses that in any way provide for the terrible reality that mental illnesses and addictions seem to possess for those who claim to suffer from them. Moreover, despite a broad historical validity, critical analyses of the medicalization of poverty and marginality simply fail to capture much of the complex micropolitics of actual clinical work involving homeless, impoverished, or otherwise culturally dispossessed people.

This can be demonstrated by counterposing the four critiques I've just mentioned to the work that I observed take place in my own ethnographic research settings. These settings were treatment programs state-mandated to serve homeless clients "dually diagnosed" with both serious mental illness and alcohol or drug addiction. As such, we should have every reason to suspect them to exhibit the problems suggested by critics of the medicalization of poverty. However, they did not do so. First, as to blaming victims: the diagnosis of mental disability was used in my programs to facilitate people's disowning of behaviors they found troubling or blameworthy. Hence the recipients of this label were not so much blamed as morally purified through the attribution of mental disability. Second, as to obfuscating social structural injustices: claiming mental disability and following a medicalized regimen of personal recovery did not discourage people from recognizing their victimization by economic, racial, or masculine oppression. Indeed, several counselors quite actively sought to politicize clients and in one of my programs successfully installed racial, gender, and sexual awareness segments into the program's clinical regimen. Third, as to exalting the medical profession: despite trading on the concepts of disease and recovery, these settings were not staffed by medical doctors but by self-described recovering addicts committed to a fairly nonauthoritarian image of their own roles as clinicians. Lastly, as to the duties of citizenship and social inclusion: far from reducing their entitlement to public benefits, diagnoses of mental disability were, sadly enough, the most promising access to entitlement that many of these people knew. A diagnosis could entail a move from no shelter or short-term shelter to a long-term program bed. It usually entailed state-sponsored provision of more intensive casework and a reduction of the chores associated with accessing benefits, housing, meals, shower, laundry, transportation, legal assistance, etc. And if one doggedly persevered, it could also mean a fairly significant increase in income. One might jump from no benefits, or meager General Relief benefits, to the more generous Supplemental Security Income, or Social Security Disability Insurance. In these various ways, claiming mental disability entailed certain modest entitlements for the people I studied and hence modest reentries back into their communities rather than exclusion from them.

Stated very briefly, then, my effort in this book is to reconcile the macrohistorical insights of the medicalization literature to the micropolitics of mental illness and addiction as these took form in two contemporary treatment programs state-mandated to serve homeless clients. More specifically, I have sought to analyze the sociological dimensions of why, and specifically how, mental illnesses and addictions came to be socially constructed or, as I prefer, socially *activated*, as manifest causes of human behavior and experience in these programs. In undertaking this project I eventually ran up against some rather serious theoretical limitations in the social scientific literature on mental health. These limitations became apparent to me when I discovered the very basic fact that though members of my programs regarded mental illnesses and addictions as genuine causal agents that overtly interfered with their lives, they nonetheless very plainly exercised discretion over whether, when, and how they invoked mental illness and addiction to account for their own and each other's troubles. None of the extant approaches to theorizing the nature of mental illness and addiction can provide for this basic fact.

THE LIMITS OF OBJECTIVISM AND SUBJECTIVISM IN THE SOCIOLOGY OF MENTAL HEALTH

Since its inception, sociology has been caught between two seemingly antithetical analytic projects. The first, which may be called the objectivist project, is reflected in Durkheim's famous insistence that social facts be regarded as *things*—that is, as determinate objects with characteristic properties that exist as such beyond the consciousness of social actors (Durkheim 1982). This theoretical project has yielded research that attends to the social structures that ostensibly cause human actions but which usually ignores the understandings human actors themselves have of their lives. Likewise, the objectivist project has encouraged biological and psychological researchers to postulate the very same ontological status for mental illnesses and addictions (cf. American Psychiatric Association 1994). Mental illnesses and addictions are thus regarded as biological or psychological things—determinate biological or psychological objects with characteristic properties, which exist as such independently of the actions and perceptions of the human actors who are said to be influenced by them.[1]

Medical research concerning the genetic origins of mental disability, its neurological characteristics, or the biochemistry of mental disorder may consider issues of subjective meaning and practice to the extent they are regarded as symptomatic of underlying biological problems. But the idea that subjective processes must figure in the very conceptual linkage of behavior with biology is generally ignored. This is equally true of psychological researchers who claim to have discovered objective intrapsychic processes underlying certain constellations of experiential and behavioral symptoms (Chodorow 1999). Though these processes may be variously interpreted, their characteristic properties are construed as objective and largely independent of people's interpretations of them. Sociologists interested in mental health issues often predicate their research on objectivist biological and psychological theories of mental disorder as well. Many seek to theoretically link *social factors* like race, class, gender, age, or sexuality, and particular categories of mental disorder (cf. Dohrenwend and Dohrenwend 1975; Eaton and Muntaner 1999; Faris and Dunham 1939; Hollingshead and Redlich 1958; Mirowsky and Ross 1999; Rosenfield 1999; Williams and Harris-Reid 1999). Though primarily interested in stress processes and psychiatric epidemiology, such theorists usually allow that mental disorders are not "mere social constructions," but they are genuine entities with objective intrapsychic, anatomical, or physiological components.

While the objectivist approach allows us to abstractly model mental disorders as discrete objects capable of causing human behavior, it does nothing to illuminate the temporal processes through which their meaning and practical relevance emerge and evolve for people over the course of history or situated social interaction. To put this more precisely, objectivist models of mental disorder do not themselves describe,

---

1. This includes the various "imbalances." Dysfunctional chemical or intrapsychic imbalances are uniformly cast as objectively embodied causal agents lying behind the experiential and behavioral problems that constitute their putative symptoms.

nor do they explain, how people come to subjectively perceive mental disorders as influential causal agents in the course of their daily lives. While a small amount of important research has been done with respect to how different objectivist models of disorder arise in history or are actually applied in clinical practice (cf. Barrett 1996; Hacking 1995; Lynch 1984; Peyrot 1995; Sass 1992; Young 1995), we must be careful not to assume that these models are necessarily operative in all cases of putative mental disorder. Indeed, the vast majority of cases wherein people infer the causal influence of mental disorders do not entail the methodical application of formal scientific models at all.

The second theoretical enterprise, which may be called the subjectivist project, is captured by Weber's injunction to treat the topical objects of the social sciences (i.e., people) as ontologically different in kind from the topical objects of the natural sciences. Whereas the objects of the natural sciences are regarded as relatively immutable, inanimate, and responsive only to ahistorical or fixed laws of nature, Weber (1978) proposed that social objects be regarded as eminently mutable, self-animating agents actively and meaningfully engaged in the world (see also Blumer 1969; Collins 1994; Giddens 1993). This theoretical project has yielded research that attends to the ways in which human *subjects*, through their own creative actions and interpretations, constitute themselves and the locally meaningful characteristics of the worlds in which they live.

Psychosocial theorists of mental disorder like Gregory Bateson (1972), R. D. Laing (1969), and Theodore Lidz (1958) boldly followed this analytic project to its logical conclusion by theorizing even the severest mental disorders exclusively in terms of people's dysfunctional social relationships with each other. They thereby reduced the entire spectrum of human behavior, no matter how self-destructive or seemingly unintelligible, to self-governed and intrinsically meaningful adaptations to the troubling social conditions under which people believe they must live. In brief, the universe of these psychosocial theorists is populated only by better and worse functioning human subjects. The main difficulty with this approach is this. Given that the inference of severe mental disorder tends to arise in response to just those problems that obstinately defy understanding in straightforwardly subjectivist terms (cf. Barrett 1996; Jaspers 1963), the project of deciphering the distinctive personal logic presumed to underlie symptoms of severe mental disorder has been a singularly elusive one. Hence, radically subjectivist theories have largely remained articles of ideological faith rather than clinically valuable or empirically grounded scientific analyses. Most subjectivist theorists have not been so strident in their efforts to reduce *all* human behavior to quasi-rational, adaptive coping techniques. In other words, they have allowed that in some instances human behavior is properly understood to reflect the causal influence of nonhuman (or nonsubjective) forces (Horwitz 2002). However, where they have endeavored to theoretically provide for these forces, subjectivist social scientists have so far been unwilling or unable to resist uncritically objectivist references to historically and culturally invariant psychic or biological structures or processes.[2]

Such theories suffer from the same analytic limitations that I raised with respect to the more strictly objectivist approaches. They invoke biological processes as causes of human action and experience at an abstract level but tell us absolutely nothing about when, why, or how the people we study might be inclined to do so themselves. Furthermore, if our effort is to understand how or why people infer the influence of mental illness or addiction we must recognize that the bases of their inferences almost never include scientific evidence of biological and/or psychodynamic dysfunction. Much more commonly, the empirical evidence held to support these inferences is composed of manifest difficulties in attributing certain distressing and disruptive behavior to the movements of human subjectivity. Finally, this kind of theorizing can also be criticized for what Woolgar and Pawluch (1985) once called "ontological gerrymandering," or arbitrarily moving back and forth between objectivism and constructionism without sound analytic grounds for doing so.

In short, then, virtually all theorizing in the sociology of mental health and illness is predicated on an *a priori* analytic distinction between the *objective* causes and characteristics of the human condition, on the one hand, and the *subjective* interpretation and enactment of the

2. Subjectivist social scientists have contrived ingenious theoretical models in efforts to combine an analytic appreciation for the sociocultural determinants of insanities and addictions with a respect for their putative power to influence human experience and conduct. Since Lindesmith's pioneering work on opiate addiction (Lindesmith 1938), this has invariably been accomplished by insisting on a social *component* to the experience of insanities and addictions but nonetheless invoking objectivist versions of biological or psychic processes and conceptually positioning these processes, as it were, beneath human action and interpretation in order to invest them with a capacity to influence peoples' experiences and conduct (for classic restatements of this model, see Becker 1953, 1967; Lindesmith 1968; Schacter and Singer 1962; Thoits 1985, 1990). For critiques of this manner of theorizing, see Weinberg (1997a, 1997b, 1998, 2002).

human condition, on the other. Ultimately, as I have said, such distinctions are epistemologically limiting (Bourdieu 1990; Hacking 1999; Hazelrigg 1986; Pollner 1987; Woolgar and Pawluch 1985). Objectivist researchers must acknowledge that actual empirical instances of mental health and illness are inextricable from the locally meaningful activities in and through which social actors perceive them (cf. Barrett 1996; Coulter 1973; Gubrium 1992; Holstein 1993; Lynch 1984). However, subjectivists must themselves acknowledge that to the extent they are understood to influence human behavior and experience in any way at all, mental disorders must be understood to exist beyond the boundaries of human subjectivity. That is, those segments of behavior and experience we regard as symptomatic of mental disorder must be traced to causal agents distinct from both the human subjects who ostensibly suffer from them and those human subjects who endeavor to categorize, control, or cure them (Weinberg 1997a).

Hence, an interesting analytic problem arises as to how we might sociologically provide for the fact that mental disorders are at once realized only through the temporally emergent and situationally embedded practices of human subjects *and* often experienced by those human subjects as nonhuman objects that obdurately resist the efforts of both sufferers and health care providers to understand or control them. In the next section I describe how one avenue of research in the sociology of scientific practice may hold advantages for social scientists who would hope to overcome this analytic problem.

On the Status of Objective Forces in the Sociology of Scientific Practice

Over the last couple of decades, a number of sociologists, anthropologists, and historians of science have been working to develop the idea that science and technology are dynamic zones of encounter between human and nonhuman agencies (cf. Ashmore, Wooffitt, and Harding 1994; Callon and Latour 1992; Haraway 1991; Pickering 1995). These researchers have radically respecified the relationships that obtain between subjective and objective forces in ways that may be appropriated to overcome the limitations I have shown to afflict mental health research.

Social studies of science have shown time and again that scientific discoveries are temporally situated social constructions rather than revelations of a timeless and uniform natural order (cf. Ashmore, Wooffitt, and Harding 1994; Bloor 1991; Callon and Latour 1992; Garfinkel, Lynch, and Livingston 1981; Haraway 1991; Latour and Woolgar 1979; Lynch 1993; Pickering 1995; Shapin 1994). However, despite their rejection of orthodox realism, or what Hilary Putnam (1987) calls "seventeenth century objectivism," many of the intellectual leaders in this field have nonetheless found it necessary to acknowledge that scientists are not wholly uninfluenced by the ostensive phenomena they seek to understand. These researchers have concluded that some form of agency must be conceptually ceded to the objects realized in the course of scientific practice as well as to the human subjects who experience and endeavor to cope with those objects.

The best-known version of this theoretical position is the actor-network theory proposed by Bruno Latour and his colleagues (cf. Callon and Latour 1992). Latour recommends a semiotic approach wherein agency is ascribed to nonhuman "actants" when they are categorically represented by one's research subjects as doing things in the world. Pickering (1995) argues, I think rightly, that while actor-network theory invaluably brings the "natural" world back into sociological theorizing regarding scientific practice, it sometimes seems to overemphasize intellectual processes and underemphasize the logic of embodied practical action. Furthermore, by positing a symmetry between human and nonhuman agents, actor-network theory de-emphasizes the fact that only human agents seem to behave intentionally—or with respect to their own goals. As an alternative, Pickering suggests we conceptualize the objects realized by scientists as not only semiotically, but also practically emergent and influential (see also Hacking 1983). That is, he suggests they be understood as material as well as semiotic products that in turn influence both human thought and embodied human practice in empirically identifiable kinds of ways. He also recommends foregoing the symmetry actor-network theory postulates between human and nonhuman agents. While there are at times good sociological reasons for attributing causal agency to nonhuman objects, there are apparently no good reasons for attributing intentions to them in the sense that we attribute intentions to human subjects.

Pickering's ideas may be usefully appropriated to theorize the effects and identities of mental illnesses and addictions. In opposition to orthodox objectivism, Pickering's approach confers no properties on the phenomenal world that need be regarded as occurring independently of human action and experience. Instead he suggests the phenomenal world influences us only in the sense that it often *resists* our efforts to formulate its character, to predict what it will do, or to cope with the practical challenges it places before us. Our formulations, predictions, and efforts to cope are in every respect socially constructed but they are socially constructed in part to accommodate the *resistances* the world has presented toward former formulations, predictions, and coping strategies. Formulating the processes through which people perceive and engage their own or other people's mental disabilities in this way appears to overcome the limitations of extant theoretical approaches in the sociology of mental health.

Under a wide spectrum of social conditions, particular features of particular people's personal behavior and experience may be observed to *resist* recognition as the effects of the distinctive human subjects they take themselves, or are taken by others, to be. The empirical form taken by this resistance is not socially invariant but intimately related to the social contexts within which it is observed. It would therefore appear that an exciting, and as yet underdeveloped, research program for social scientists might be to investigate exactly how such episodes emerge and are managed in the variety of circumstances under which they occur. This research program would be predicated on an acknowledgment that social actors do in fact install nonhuman agents as surrogates for human selves for a wide variety of reasons. But in contrast to biomedical models of disorder, it would remain vigilantly agnostic as to the objective characteristics those surrogates are said to possess. Rather than positing such characteristics from outside the social worlds under investigation, we would seek to understand how and why members of those worlds attribute characteristics to these surrogates themselves. It is precisely such a project that I have undertaken in this book.

A Note on the Concept *Others Inside*

In what follows I use the concept *others inside* in place of the variety of concepts now used to construe insanities and addictions. Let me begin to explain my partiality to this concept by noting that it possesses a double entendre. On the one hand, it may be read to connote intrapersonal agents other than one's self. Writing of *others inside* preserves the idea that people diagnosed with serious mental health problems often feel profoundly alienated from the thoughts, behaviors, and experiences they and others diagnose as symptomatic of those mental health problems. By using this terminology I also hope to periodically remind the reader that my focus in this study is not scientific models of insanity and addiction per se. Instead I am concerned with how putative mental health problems have been *experienced* and *managed* when they have been found to afflict homeless, impoverished, and/or otherwise culturally marginalized members of the community. While there can be absolutely no doubt that clinicians and researchers trained in the medical sciences have played core roles in shaping how Americans orient to putative mental health problems, they have never possessed a monopoly of influence over either caregiving itself or how insanities and addictions are understood. This is particularly true of settings mandated to treat poor and culturally marginalized Americans. By using the concept *others inside* I hope to give credence to the idea that people genuinely suffer from manifestly intrapersonal afflictions without thereby having to adopt any particular theory regarding the nature of those afflictions.

The concept "other" has already been used in similar ways by important scholars concerned with the phenomenology of disability. Arthur Frank (1997) has come to write of people's disabilities as "others within" in his analyses of illness narratives (see also Desjarlais 1997; Hacking 1999; Klienman 1988). Robert Barrett (1996) effectively draws upon the anthropological legacy of the concept "other" to highlight both the fact that people often experience schizophrenia as a distinct entity quite separate from themselves and the rich affinities between contemporary scientific theorizing regarding the nature of schizophrenia and the more general history of Western thinking about the nature of peoples different from ourselves. But the concept *others inside* also possesses a second connotation. It may also be read to connote the difficult relationship felt by homeless people seeking recovery from mental disabilities to those of us who share their communities but who are not homeless and diagnosed as mentally disabled. To what extent does recovery for them amount to a project of forging and fortifying a place for themselves *among* others inside—we who are housed, employed, and ostensibly free of the mental disabilities by which they are presumed afflicted?

As I have indicated, my fundamental objective in this book is to advance a novel sociological understanding of the relationship between social exclusion and mental disability. More specifically, I am concerned to closely scrutinize both the relationship between symptomology and alterity, on the one hand, and the relationship between clinical recovery from insanities and addictions and the assimilation of sufferers into their communities, on the other hand. My central argument is that throughout American history considerations of community solidarity and exclusion have consistently figured centrally in assessments of whether, and how, the diagnosis and treatment of mental illness or addiction should be undertaken. The concept *others inside* allows me to more effectively emphasize the conceptual proximity of my discussion of mental disability and recovery to debates about social exclusion and community solidarity than is afforded by received biological and psychological concepts like disease or disorder. In sum, by writing of insanities and addictions as others inside those who are presumed to suffer from them I simultaneously emphasize both my agnosticism with respect to their basic nature and the enduring conceptual and institutional relationships that continue to exist in the United States (and elsewhere) between insanity, addiction, and cultural otherness more generally.

So how does this book improve upon the existing critiques of the medicalization of poverty and marginality? It does so by incorporating the following insight: even when it is construed as drenched in social structure, culture, and meaning, there is overwhelming evidence to suggest there is a depth to what Heidegger called human being-in-the-world of which we as selves, subjects, or egos are at best only dimly aware, and at best only partially able to control. My research suggests that the extreme material and emotional hardships of homelessness quite seriously intensify the tendencies we all sometimes have to find the *other*, the "not-us" and "not-me," in our very own personal actions and experiences. Though we may sometimes wish to relish such mysteries, we may sometimes also find them profoundly disturbing and yearn for therapeutic assistance to secure for ourselves a more intelligible and socially integrated personal being. In this sense, the work of recovery from insanity or addiction may be seen as a simultaneously collective and personal project of *self* (or social being) empowerment—one among many types of struggle for redemption from the jointly psychic and social spaces of otherness with which we cannot or do not want to identify. We should not, then, merely oppose the medicalization of poverty and marginality so much as strive to make more just, more sensible, and more compassionate use of the medical devices that history has bequeathed.

THE SUBSTANTIVE CHAPTERS IN BRIEF

The study is divided into two parts, the first of which attends to the broader genealogy of my ethnographic research settings, and the second, to their immediate local histories, administrative structures, and distinctive modes of therapeutic practice. Chapters 2 and 3 make up Part I. Chapters 4 and 5 make up Part II. Chapter 6 is my concluding chapter.

In Chapter 2 I describe the rise of the American mental health, alcohol, and "narcotic" drug addiction fields. I show that modern concepts of insanity and addiction were first forged to preserve the moral integrity of certain kinds of otherwise respectable troublemakers, and to serve as resources for their redemption. However, concepts of insanity and addiction (and techniques for their control) evolved in considerably more punitive directions as they came to be more routinely applied to troubles involving poorer and culturally marginalized Americans. I tell how these processes variously unfolded in the fields of mental health, alcohol, and "narcotic" drugs. Particular emphasis is given to how these events shaped the types of clinical services available to homeless Americans today.

In Chapter 3 I follow the continuing evolution of the state-sponsored mental health, alcoholism, and drug abuse treatment industries into the late twentieth century. Though certainly separate in many respects, these fields have developed parallel to one another, often competing for public funding, and for the authority to name, explain, and manage the *others inside* to which they consensually, and with widespread popular support, insist human beings are heir. I describe how these fields grew into more or less discrete national systems, each of which was focally organized around the understanding and management of human troubles as products of distinct types of *others inside* their clients. Due primarily to the proliferation of what Gusfield (1989) calls "troubled person professionals" concerned with such matters (and increased pressures on these professionals to recognize each other's efforts), I show that there has been a vast expansion of the professionally acknowledged antecedents, identities, and consequences of insanities and addictions among the American poor. However, despite increasing professional appreciation for their profound variety and complexity, the management of insanities and addictions in state-sponsored settings is becoming ever more strictly formulated in terms of tenably integrating sufferers into their respective communities. Hence, as I will show, more than merely rendering poor and marginalized Americans more vulnerable to insanities and addictions, or less capable of securing adequate treatments, it is precisely their putative social, economic, and cultural deficits that increasingly constitute the *empirical evidence* of their respective disorders themselves.

Chapter 4 is divided into three sections. In the first section I describe the origins of Canyon House,[3] nesting the particulars of the program's emergence in the wider processes discussed in Part I. In the second section I describe the structural specifics of Canyon House administration. I begin this section by very briefly discussing the referral sources and economic parameters of residents' admission into the program. I then touch upon the backgrounds from which most residents and staff were drawn. The bulk of this section, however, is devoted to delineating the regimen of activities in which residents were required to participate, and the stages through which they were required to pass in order to graduate from the program. In the third section I specify the dynamics of therapeutic practice at Canyon House. Most fundamentally, therapeutic practice at Canyon House consisted in efforts to empower residents as agents of their own recoveries. I first demonstrate that this work consisted fundamentally in fostering and exhibiting what I am calling *right living* among program residents and outline the basic characteristics of *right living* as it was understood at Canyon House. Next I indicate how insanities and addictions were invoked primarily as resources for a retrospective assessment of troubles residents had either caused or experienced in the past. Finally, I demonstrate how insanities and addictions were made to figure not only as accounts for past troubles but as tangible entities in their own right, or, to put it more precisely—consensually present nonhuman contributors to the ongoing organization of Canyon House affairs.

Chapter 5 contrasts the emergence, organization, and operation of Twilights with that of Canyon House. It, too, is divided into three basic sections. In the first section I discuss the origins of Twilights, once again nesting the particulars of the program's emergence within the wider processes discussed in Part I. In the second section I discuss the specific trials that were encountered over the course of implementing the program in the image of Canyon House.[4] In the third section I address the dynamics of therapeutic practice at Twilights, specifically contrasting these dynamics with those at Canyon House. As at Canyon House, therapeutic practice at Twilights consisted fundamentally in efforts to empower clients as agents of their own recoveries. However, in contrast

---

3. The names of the programs and all research subjects are pseudonyms.

4. Twilights was a nonresidential program expressly modeled on the design in place at Canyon House (an established residential program serving dually diagnosed clients). This was to facilitate rigorous comparisons of the outcomes achieved through residential and nonresidential interventions with dually diagnosed homeless clients.

to Canyon House, I show how this work was carried out primarily in fostering *tenable community living* among program clients rather than *right living*. When insanities and addictions were invoked at Twilights, it was generally in the course of realistic planning for the immediate future rather than as resources for retrospectively assessing past troubles. Finally, I describe how the contrasting dynamics of therapeutic practice at Twilights systematically altered the patterns according to which insanities and addictions were made to figure as consequential worldly agents.

Taken together, these chapters trace the sociohistorical emergence, evolution, and contemporary deployment of various concepts of insanity and addiction to understand and manage homeless and other marginalized Americans. They empirically demonstrate the folly in regarding insanities and addictions as sociohistorically invariant natural pathogens that exist beyond the scope of social history and socially situated human activity. They show, in both historical and ethnographic detail, just how insanities and addictions are genuinely *social* products. But beyond this, these chapters show how despite being thoroughly products of human manufacture, insanities and addictions remain eminently real, and causally influential, for those invested in their discovery and management. In Chapter 6 I summarize and discuss the theoretical conclusions of the analysis offered in the substantive chapters.

I A History of Insanities and Addictions Among Marginalized Americans

THE FOLLOWING two chapters describe how particular concepts of insanity and addiction have been incorporated into state-sponsored regimes for the management of homeless, impoverished, and culturally marginalized Americans.[1] The net has been thusly cast for the simple reason that for most of American history, insanities and addictions have been found to afflict poor and culturally marginalized Americans in ways that are systematically different from the ways they have been found to afflict more prosperous Americans. However, they have been found to afflict poor and culturally marginalized Americans

1. A word concerning terminology. In the next two chapters I often refer to the following three related conditions: economic dependency, cultural marginality, and homelessness. Admittedly, these terms are drawn from my own time and place and are, in some sense, superimposed upon the activities of those who I discuss. This is particularly true of Chapter 2. In the eighteenth and nineteenth centuries, people empowered to administer the fates of very poor, deviant, and unattached Americans tended to make indiscriminate reference to the "defective, delinquent, and dependent classes," or simply the "rabble" or "dangerous classes," and to arrange public provision for them on an equally indiscriminate basis (Katz 1986; Monkkonen 1993; Rothman 1990). By and large, being assigned to this category required only having been found somehow disreputable and undeserving of the community's collective forbearance (Matza 1966). This, in turn, has always been intimately related to assessments of moral solidarity and difference (Katz 1989). Hence, the images of vagrant, transient, and tramp, all of which bear the stigma of social "disaffiliation," have been historically salient in descriptions of the rabble or undeserving poor. It is in this very general sense—of putative kithlessness—that homelessness has borne its enduring affinity with economic dependency, pathology, and cultural marginality more generally. The legacy of commingling poverty, cultural marginality, criminality, and pathology has endured, indeed thrived, despite the proliferation of taxonomic fads and their attendant designs for managing the variously described

in essentially the same ways whether they were currently housed or not housed. Thus to have attended exclusively to those we would now call *homeless* Americans would have created a badly distorted image of their particularity. Likewise, my analysis is cast largely at the national level because procedures for diagnosing and treating insanities and addictions among poor and culturally marginalized Americans evolved according to processes that unfurled nationally. To have focused exclusively on the state or local level would have prevented my giving adequate attention to the fact that changes occurring at the state and local levels were largely dictated by nationwide social movements and/or federally articulated public policies.

By and large my descriptions focus on the emergence, growth, and evolution of three relatively distinct social fields: the mental health industry, the alcoholism treatment industry, and the field of illicit drug control. To the extent these social fields have produced methods for managing those we would now call homeless Americans, their growth and development have been powerfully directed, though by no means determined, by public policy makers at the federal, state, and local levels. Thus, of course, my social history of these fields cannot be adequately told without earnest attention to the ways they have related to, and figured in, broader state agendas. Most commonly, these agendas have concerned how *membership* in communities subject to a government's administrative authority has been specified. Hence, as I show, considerations of collective identity, solidarity, and cultural otherness have always been paramount in determining if, when, and specifically how concepts of insanity and addiction have come to figure in the public government

---

categories of "other" thought to comprise this most alien segment of the American population (cf. Hopper 1991; Grob 1994; Irwin 1985; Polsky 1991; Scull 1984; Simon 1993). In its contemporary sense, the expression "homeless" has encouraged some to think only in terms of certain very narrowly circumscribed manifestations or consequences of severe poverty—in a word, shelterlessness. However, the best research indicates there is very little that distinguishes shelterless Americans from the broader category of extremely poor, but housed, Americans (Burt 1992; Jencks 1994; Kusmer 2002; Rossi 1989; Snow and Anderson 1993; Wright 1989). Myopic attention to the literally shelterless, then, overlooks the much deeper and more enduring social processes at work here. Hence, the task I have set myself in Chapters 2 and 3 is to show how concepts of insanity and addiction have figured in the work of managing and accounting for that population that Hopper (1991) aptly describes as "a poor apart." And, as will be evident, I wholeheartedly agree with Hopper (1991, p. 130) when he writes, "[t]he real alternative to homelessness, then, is not shelter but solidarity."

of poverty and homelessness in the United States. This demonstration, then, affords sturdy historical foundations for my formulation of insanities and addictions as *others inside* members of my ethnographic research settings.

It must be emphatically underscored that the following two chapters are not in any way intended to be comprehensive accounts of the American mental health industry, the American addiction treatment industry, or the American welfare, public health, or criminal justice systems. They have been written for the specific purpose of providing a genealogy of the settings in which I did ethnographic fieldwork (Foucault 1977). Therefore they address only those features of these various social fields that ultimately gave shape to my ethnographic research settings. And while I certainly hope there are elements of this account that historians will find interesting and useful, neither of these chapters have been written to engage debates of specific interest to historians. Historians are primarily engaged in the work of casting new light upon the past. These chapters have been written in the interest of integrating historical insights into the *ethnographic* work of illuminating those particular fragments of the present that were Canyon House and Twilights.

2   Setting the Stage

THIS CHAPTER is divided into five sections, each of which attends to a different aspect of the early genealogy of my ethnographic research settings. The sections are organized topically but presented in a more or less chronological order. I first describe how insanities and addictions were perceived in colonial North America. I tell how they came to be conceptualized as (a) somatic pathologies, or disease agents, (b) amenable to human influence, and (c) resources for the management of poor and culturally marginalized Americans. In the next section I describe the rise of moral treatment. In particular, I note how this process established two major conceptual elements of the modern regard for insanities: (a) that they are often amenable to *social* therapies, and (b) that the ostensibly afflicted might be enlisted as key collaborators in their own recoveries. In the third section I indicate three enduring products of the rise of asylum psychiatry: (a) the enrollment of the state as a major player in American mental health care, (b) the decisive medicalization of American orientations to insanity, and (c) the return of social exclusion to the ascendant regimes for managing madness, especially among the poor. In the fourth section I demonstrate how temperance boosters popularized the claims that alcohol addiction is (a) either a genuine disease or disease-like, (b) the main cause of poverty and moral decay among the urban poor, and (c) amenable to management through mutual help groups. I then show how practices of social exclusion were reinstated into the ascendant regimes for managing drunkenness, especially among the poor. In the fifth section I show how concepts of "narcotic" drug addiction (a) first emerged in efforts to redeem well-off opiate users, and (b) eventually became favored resources for promoting a racist and classist xenophobia in the late nineteenth and early twentieth centuries.

INSANITIES AND ADDICTIONS IN COLONIAL NORTH AMERICA

Historians agree that colonial Americans were not particularly concerned with those they considered "distracted" or drunkards (Grob 1994; Jimenez 1987; Levine 1978; Rothman 1990; Scull 1989). Though they acknowledged their presence in the community, colonials did not have systematic techniques for dealing with madness or drunkenness specifically. Grob (1994, pp. 5–6) writes of the early American orientation to the insane,

> The behavior of "distracted" persons might prove a threat to their own safety or that of others, and the inability to work meant that others would have to assume responsibility for their survival. Nevertheless, the proportionately small number of "distracted" persons did not warrant the creation of special facilities. Nor had insanity come under medical jurisdiction; concepts of insanity in that period were fluid and largely arose from cultural, popular, and intellectual sources. Mentally disordered persons, therefore, were cared for on an ad hoc and informal basis either by the family or community . . . Before the American Revolution mental illnesses posed social and economic rather than medical problems.

Likewise, those considered drunkards were the focus of public attention only if they became social and/or economic burdens but were left to their ways if they were self-supporting and nonthreatening. Levine (1978, p. 147) notes that with few exceptions,

> drunkards as a group or class of deviants were not especially problematic for colonial Americans. If they had property, or were able to support themselves, they were treated much like anyone else of their class. And those that could not support themselves were grouped among the dependents in every community . . . colonials did not make major distinctions among the poor and deviant: The fact of need was the important issue, not why someone happened to be needy.

As for other drugs that would later elicit concern as drugs of potential abuse, in colonial America, to the extent they were used at all, they were seen in uniformly medicinal terms and provoked almost no concern in the community (Courtwright 2001; H.W. Morgan 1981; Musto 1987). This does not mean, however, that there were no ascendant orientations to the nature and treatment of distraction or habitual intoxication. It only means that these orientations did not inform full-scale societal responses. Instead they figured only in the private remedies sought and undertaken by wealthier colonials for the difficulties presented by friends and family members. What is important to keep in mind is that insofar as the plight of poor people was concerned, little public effort was made at this point in American history to conceptualize or address what would become *their* insanities and addictions independent of efforts to address their generally troublesome conduct and/or their economic need.

Though they were not yet often turned onto poor Americans, a bit of background regarding colonial concepts of "distraction" provides a useful foundation for my discussion. In important respects the modern regard for insanities and addictions among homeless Americans derive from these early times. Then, as now, people held that distraction strikes with various degrees of severity. Many ostensibly distracted people were more or less capable of supporting themselves, and where they could contribute to their own, their family's, or their community's livelihood they were allowed and expected to do so (Jimenez 1987). In such cases distraction was met with fasting and prayers for the afflicted, and was regarded as something of a nuisance, but was normalized as much as possible. Where cases of distraction became more troublesome, however, they were met with decidedly different responses. For present purposes, the crucial difference between modern and colonial approaches to managing the more severely disabled is the status that was ascribed to the ostensibly afflicted. According to the clerical and medical wisdom of the day, insanity was an affliction that effectively deprived the sufferer of his or her very humanity (Foucault 1965; Rothman 1990; Scull 1989; Tomes 1984). By way of madness, one came close to assuming the status of a demon or a beast.

This comparison, dramatic though it may sound, is not intended as hyperbole. Puritans often regarded extreme, or "furious," madness as an expression of demonic possession or witchcraft (Jimenez 1987, p. 14). It was widely thought the sufferer had been effectively overtaken by Satan. And according to the science of the day, extreme madness consisted in the loss of reason—the one faculty that separated mankind from the brutes (Scull 1989, pp. 86–8). As Foucault (1965, p. 75) wrote in *Madness and Civilization*, so far from being considered a function of disease, madness was thought to shield the madman from disease:

> Madness, insofar as it partook of animal ferocity, preserved man from the dangers of disease; it afforded him an invulnerability, similar to that which nature, in its foresight, had provided for animals. Curiously, the disturbance of his reason restored the madman to the immediate kindness of nature by a return to animality...This is why, at this extreme point, madness was less than ever linked to medicine; nor could it be linked to the domain of correction. Unchained animality could be mastered only by *discipline* and *brutalizing*.

Generally speaking, then, concepts of insanity were applied only to troubles exhibited by members of one's own moral community.[2] But, among colonial Americans, the ascription of insanity was a technique by which the boundaries between "us" and "others" could be made permeable. While those judged insane might once have been familiar and/or honored community members, insanity rendered them *others*. During this period in American history, ascriptions of otherness did not merely indicate personal or cultural difference. The ascription of *otherness* placed one completely beyond the province of humanity (McGrane 1989). It was thus that *others*, including native Americans, slaves, vagabonds, and sometimes even women and children, were viewed as heathens and/or savage brutes—beings that were each in their own way decidedly less than human. This same sensibility was expressed in the severity with which even the most minor infractions of Puritan law were punished (Erikson 1966; Rothman 1990). To become deviant, or simply to be *others*, was to fail to partake of the natural order of God and was thus deserving of all the brutality one could anticipate from hell. Furthermore, the motive for treating *others* brutally was not in reforming them, or recalling them to humanity, but merely in taming them as one would wild beasts (Erikson 1966, pp. 202–203). The only consideration that spared *some* of the more seriously distracted from the wrath levied upon criminals, native Americans, slaves, vagabonds, unruly beasts, and demons was the sense that they were not so much the minions of Satan as completely deranged by demonic or divine intervention.

During the seventeenth and early eighteenth centuries, the forces thought capable of deranging human reason were largely considered supernatural and beyond human control (Grob 1994; Jimenez 1987). This was consistent with Puritan beliefs in predestination and the involvement of God and Satan in the most minute details of worldly existence (Erikson 1966; Weber 1958). Hence, the prospect of successful *human* intervention into the course of the malady was considered extremely limited (Dain 1964; Grob 1994; Jimenez 1987). By the early eighteenth century, however, the spread of Enlightenment thought to American

2. I use the expression *moral community* only to denote the presence of some corrigible sense of *we* that is sustained and sometimes lost between members of a human aggregate. I use the expression in this admittedly vague fashion so that I might sketch a genealogy of my research settings that is sensitive to both the different levels at which the boundaries of moral community are negotiated and to historical changes in the consequences of this kind of work.

shores brought madness within the purview of human influence. Grob (1994, p. 11) writes,

> Enlightenment thought . . . led to more naturalistic ways of explaining human behavior. God and Satan, hitherto central elements in popular perceptions of madness, were now relegated to a more remote position. A naturalistic interpretation of insanity merged with a moral component. Insanity no longer followed divine intervention, but rather was a penalty for the willful violation of natural law. Admittedly, natural law was of divine origin, but not beyond human comprehension. All individuals, precisely because they were endowed with rational minds and free will, could understand the moral imperative that constituted its central core. . . . If moral irregularities and excessive passions hastened the onset of insanity, then at the very least the illness was amenable to human intervention.

The Enlightenment ushered in three momentus historical changes that profoundly shaped how insanities and addictions were regarded in my ethnographic research settings. Prior to the Enlightenment, human beings could be afflicted by madness but could do little (other than pray to God) to personally affect whether someone became or remained afflicted. However, *since the early eighteenth century, people and insanities have become widely conceptualized as entities capable of interacting with one another directly rather than through the mediation of otherworldly, or supernatural, wills.* During the eighteenth century, Americans began to feel they could take direct measures, independently of God or Satan, to both precipitate and prevent insanity, and to both exacerbate and alleviate the sufferings caused by madness once it had ensued. Conversely, insanities ceased to be regarded merely as worldly *symptoms* of otherworldly agents and came to be seen as natural agents in their own right. That members of my ethnographic settings did indeed *interact* with their own and each other's insanities and addictions as discrete natural agents (i.e., as things-in-themselves whose shape is marked by the distinctive ways in which they interact with other things) is a fundamental feature of my thesis. This interaction was first made possible by the rise, and enduring popularity, of Enlightenment ideas regarding the nature and treatment of insanities.

The second important effect of Enlightenment thought was that habitual drunkenness began to appear as in some instances quite possibly beyond the wills of habitual drunkards (Levine 1978; Porter 1985; Valverde 1998; Warner 1994). It was at this point in American history that the concept "addiction" began to develop its long-standing affinity with insanity. If madness was a possible outcome of particular kinds of human activity, then perhaps the sufferings and troublesome conduct of chronic drinkers might be fruitfully understood as just such a form of madness. For many, this view provided epistemological gains over the received view that drunkards simply harbored a profound and incomprehensible "love" of drink that eclipsed their regard for anything else. Levine (1978) suggests that the idea that chronic use of intoxicants might indicate addiction, a disease akin to other forms of insanity, was first worked out for alcohol in the late eighteenth century and was only later applied to other drugs:

> The idea that drugs are inherently addicting was first systematically worked out for alcohol and then extended to other substances. Long before opium was popularly accepted as addicting, alcohol was so regarded. (Levine 1978, p. 144)

Alcohol addiction eventually became an exemplar, providing precedent for the fundamental schemas of perception and appreciation necessary to distinguish deeds people undertake voluntarily from those caused by their enslavement to nonhuman substances. With this heuristic at hand it became possible to think about other drugs as potentially addictive as well. The importance of this historical precedent to the work that was done in my research settings can scarcely be overemphasized. While ideas regarding the relationship between people and addictions would undergo a variety of important changes, it was in the late eighteenth century that addiction emerged in North America as a credible cause of human behavior and experience.

Lastly, in addition to facilitating interaction between people, insanities, and now addictions, the Enlightenment fostered a third change that was crucial to the founding of my research settings. It catalyzed the systematic application of the concepts insanity and addiction to troubles associated with poor and marginalized Americans. It did so in two ways: First, by making possible the claim that insanities and addictions result from irresponsible, or vicious, living and are thus the just deserts of those who suffer from them. In this way, concepts of insanity and addiction became amenable to rhetorical use by those concerned to blame the victims of poverty for their own sufferings (cf. Rothman 1990, pp. 162–4). Second, it did so by giving social reformers a method by which they might attribute the manifest wretchedness of certain segments of the lower classes to *diseases* endemic to the squalid conditions under which they were forced to live, rather than their intrinsic depravity as moral agents. In this way, reformers justified their attribution of basic human rights to members of socially marginalized groups without thereby legitimizing the beastly manner in which some of them were observed to behave. Ethnic minorities and the urban poor were thus cast as beings which, though fundamentally human and therefore deserving members of the American moral community, were nevertheless in desperate need of further humanizing (Boyer 1978; Schmidt 1995).

Without depreciating the importance of theological, scientific, or otherwise ideological themes, there were also important social structural changes taking place in American society at this time that put heavy pressures on colonials to adopt new approaches to madness. Grob (1994) suggests these changes issued primarily from the urbanization of colonial North America, which made the older traditions of taking care of one's own and "warning out" strangers unpracticable. New policies were required that did not draw so fine a line between dependent insiders and dependent outsiders. Similarly, Rothman (1990) argues that increasing migration, urban growth, and the erosion of traditionally local methods of dispensing welfare produced pressures to redraw the boundaries between the "deserving" and the "undeserving" poor. The new boundaries placed greater emphasis on people's personal responsibility for their circumstances and slowly came to place less importance on the legitimacy of their membership in the local community.

Scull (1977, 1984, 1989) insists these events be set within the context of expanding free-market capitalism, which drove the urban growth and increasing migration to which Grob and Rothman refer. Furthermore, the increasing emphasis on self-control and personal responsibility witnessed during this period (and which colored changing colonial perceptions of madness) are most adequately understood as responsive to changes taking place more generally in the relationship between the upper and lower classes (Thompson 1967).[3] Scull (1977, p. 340) writes:

> Prior to the emergence of the capitalist market system, economic relationships did not manifest themselves in purely market relationships. Economic domination was overlaid and fused with personal ties between individuals. But the market destroyed the traditional connections between

3. While I am largely persuaded by arguments that highlight the immense impact the transition from feudalism to industrial capitalism had on community life (Sennett 1976), it is important not to overstate the importance of capitalism itself to these transformations. As Elias (1978) has shown, the movement toward increasingly elaborate social controls on personal conduct was well under way long before industrial capitalism began to take hold.

rich and poor, the reciprocal notions of paternalism, deference, and dependence characterizing the old order, producing profound shifts in the
relationships between superordinate and subordinate classes, and of upper class perceptions of responsibilities toward the less fortunate.

In addition to changing the upper classes' views toward their responsibilities for poor people in their own communities, the emerging capitalist market system also affected changes in their views of those once
considered outsiders. Stark distinctions between poor neighbors and
poor strangers eventually collapsed and poor people came to be viewed
overwhelmingly in terms of their potential as wage laborers. While this
served to mitigate some of the scorn once levied upon transient and
impoverished strangers, it fused "the poor" into one great mass that
was seen as both potentially exploitable and potentially threatening by
wealthier members of society. In the wake of these developments, insanities and addictions came to be viewed as obstacles to the economic ex-
ploitation of the poor, catalysts to their becoming dangerous, scapegoats
for their apparent sufferings and intransigence, and, perhaps most importantly, explanations and justifications for their continuing treatment
as *others*. It was in response to these social structural developments that
the insanities and addictions of marginalized and impoverished Americans first began to attract serious public attention in the United States.

THE IMPACT OF MORAL TREATMENT

Before moral treatment, the medical management of insanity amounted
to little more than a collection of methods for enforcing docility. No
one sought to enlist the collaboration of patients in their own treatment
because to do so would have entailed ascribing to them the human,
moral,[4] aptitudes they were presumed to have lost to madness. Instead
of refusing to ascribe human aptitudes to the insane, advocates of moral
treatment insisted that to do so was the very essence of their method.
As Scull (1989, p. 88) writes:

> For them, the lunatic was no longer an animal, stripped of all remnants of
> humanity. On the contrary, he remained in essence a man; a man lacking
> in self-restraint and order, but a man for all that. Moreover, the qualities
> he lacked might and must be restored to him, so that he could once more
> function as a sober, rational citizen.

4. During the eighteenth and early nineteenth centuries the expression *moral* did not
merely indicate issues related to judgments of good and bad, right and wrong, or entitlement and obligation. It indicated everything that is distinctively human—i.e., every
aspect of humanity that sets human nature apart from physical nature (cf. Hume [1739]
1978).

As a point of departure, it is crucial to recognize that moral treatment began as a method for coping not with *others*, but with members of one's own moral community. William Tuke, the main source of moral treatment in the Anglo-American world, did not begin with a concern to manage vagrants, or other sorts of strangers, who had become insane, but fellow Quakers, indeed, "friends" with whom he shared a sense of religious solidarity (Tuke 1813). Similarly, when moral treatment was imported from Tuke's York Retreat to the United States it was put into service first among Quakers and then more generally on behalf of people who shared a privileged background with those who sought to cure them (Grob 1994; Mechanic 1989; Scull 1989; Tomes 1984).[5]

The recognition of an element of the mad person that remained human (and could be enlisted in the recovery effort) was crucially reliant upon some sort of identification between counselor and client. Only if they somehow identified with one another might counselor and client foster a shared sense of *we* opposed to the *it* that was the afflicted individual's disorder. It is thus little wonder that moral treatment first emerged as a method for reclaiming members of Tuke's own clan and encountered formidable obstacles as efforts were made to implement it among more culturally diverse populations. Despite its originally limited scope, though, moral treatment radically broke with prior conceptions of the relationship between people and insanities. Whereas insanity was priorly understood to effectively extinguish the whole of an individual's humanity, by the lights of moral treatment it was understood to corrupt only a fraction of the sufferer's personal being. Though it has weathered changing fortunes over the years, the idea that the afflicted might strive to overcome their own insanities was a fundamental precedent for the ways in which insanities and addictions were identified and managed at Canyon House and Twilights. It was only insofar as program members learned to distinguish behaviors caused by

---

5. To the extent they accepted state support, the early American hospitals that championed moral treatment of the insane were pressured to accept indigent clients. Rather than accepting this mandate, however, most struggled to resist admitting poor and minority clients. Though some made token efforts, the type of indigent clients served tended to be those who were, despite their poverty, honored members of the community. Addressing the social characteristics of client populations in these early hospitals, Grob (1994, p. 38) writes, "[A] homogeneous and affluent patient body ... was not merely a function of economics. Americans, like most peoples, tended to live within the relatively narrow parameters of a cohesive and clearly defined ethnic or economic group. The arrival in the United States of minority ethnic groups in the early nineteenth century only accentuated the process of group identification and solidarity. Affluent families sent their members to private hospitals with the expectation that they would not mix with ethnic or racial minorities."

insanities and addictions from those authored by sufferers themselves that insanities and addictions could take form as discrete *others inside* people rather than rendering them *completely other* and beyond the pale of moral community. This possibility emerged along with the historical emergence of moral treatment and its proponents' insistence that the insane possess a residual rationality (and residual humanity) that can be called forth and brought into service in efforts to overcome their insanity.[6]

The rise of moral treatment influenced modern techniques for dealing with insanities and addictions in other ways as well. Beyond making it reasonable (hence possible) to enlist sufferers themselves in the effort to subdue their insanities, moral treatment also gave rise to entirely new methods of undertaking this effort. Prior to moral treatment, the management of madness was informed by more or less explicit theories regarding its nature and etiology. Treatments may have been based in humoral or solidist orientations to human biology, or in theological or metaphysical doctrines of one kind or another, but they were in any case justified with reference to explicit formulations of the malady in question. In the early days of moral treatment the reliance of therapy on theory diminished considerably (Dain 1964; Grob 1994; Scull 1989). Philippe Pinel and William Tuke, the founding figures in the history of moral treatment, were both pragmatic in their approaches, focusing much more on outcomes than theoretical justifications. Though a medical doctor by training, Pinel was impatient with theoretical debates and William Tuke, a layman, was opposed to the reduction of his regimes at York to medical, or otherwise expert, explanations of insanity. This relative indifference to the scientific bases of their treatments provided Tuke and Pinel significant freedom in their development of remedial techniques. As a staunch empiricist, Pinel inaugurated the modern practice of individualized treatment by taking extensive case histories of his clients and tailoring his remedial efforts to the particularities of their problems rather than abstract understandings of their underlying causes (Grob 1994). Even more importantly, both Pinel and Tuke looked beyond the natural and supernatural forces to which human bodies and souls had been regarded heir, and began to implement

---

6. That this movement toward "decentering the human subject" by splintering people into a plurality of distinct agents began in the early modern era would seem to contradict those postmodernists who suggest such processes only began to take place in the later half of the twentieth century (see also Hacking 1986, 1995).

explicitly social approaches to the conceptualization and cure of insanity.

One fundamental technique that both men shared was removal of the afflicted from the social circumstances under which their madness had ensued and been sustained. Both of their regimens entailed engaging clients in some form of productive work, acquainting them with a disciplined, methodically scheduled daily routine, and providing them with soothing forms of companionship and recreation. Such remedies were hardly intelligible by the lights of received medical and theological orientations to madness. While it had been common practice to remove the furiously mad from their homes and communities, this had not been in the interest of cure but to more effectively contain the hardships the mentally disturbed brought upon others. Prior to moral treatment, no relation had been drawn between social environment and the onset of madness, let alone between social environment and cure. As moral treatment became more widely and vigorously touted, however, the therapeutic benefits of living in a "well-ordered institution" were accepted not only throughout the medical community but throughout American society at large (Rothman 1990). That a growing number of people believed such a regimen was more effective than received medical techniques placed significant pressures on medical doctors both to attend to the merits of moral treatment and to explain them using their own medical vocabulary (Conrad and Schneider 1992; Scull 1989). By the time moral treatment had traversed the Atlantic, both processes were well under way (Dain 1964; McGovern 1985).

Many of the most vocal defenders of moral treatment in America were medical doctors and, by the early nineteenth century, medical theories had begun to take root which presumed to explain the social environment's influence on mental health. However, the sentiments driving the production of these theories were by no means unique to medical professionals. Rothman (1990) argues that the medical men who advocated moral treatment shared general misgivings with many of their countrymen regarding the emerging industrial society they saw growing up around them. Their suspicions of its adverse effects on personal well-being were driven less by their medical investigations than by their nostalgia for a bygone era.

Medical superintendents were certain that their society lacked all the elements of fixity and cohesion because they judged it by a nostalgic image of the eighteenth century. Frightened by an awareness that the old order was

passing and with little notion of what would replace it, they defined the
realities about them as corrupting, provoking madness. (Rothman 1990,
p. 127)

Their disenchantment with industrialization was widely shared and
gave rise to a proliferation of social movements aimed at either providing remedies for the corruptions inherent in the new social order
or inaugurating separate utopian societies completely removed from
those corruptions (Kanter 1972). The moral treatment of insanity in the
United States partook of both types of movement. In the first instance,
reformers like Dorothea Dix and Samuel Gridley Howe tirelessly campaigned to demonstrate to policy makers and to the general public that
because madness was a result of the new social order it was incumbent
upon members of that order to relieve the sufferings their new society
had caused. Their efforts were reasonably well received insofar as new
conceptions of the state's role in providing for the health, well-being,
and social control of the populace resonated with their pleas. In the
second instance, medical superintendents advocated removing the insane from society and placing them in environments where they would
receive asylum from the chaos that reigned in the wider social world.
Their vision of the ideal curative institution was decidedly utopian and
was touted in terms a good deal more expansive than one might expect
to hear in support of a new type of hospital. As Rothman (1990, p. 133)
writes,

The broad program had an obvious similarity to the goals of the penitentiary, and both ventures resembled in spirit and in outlook the communi-
tarian movements of the period, such as Brook Farm and New Harmony.
There was a utopian flavor to correctional institutions. Medical superintendents and penitentiary designers were almost as eager as Owenites to
evolve and validate general principles of social organization from their
particular experiments.

Amidst the progressive and utopian rhetoric of the Jacksonian period, however, we must not lose sight of the more mundane and self-
interested forces behind the rise of moral treatment. Medicine at this
point in American history was only beginning to emerge from the ranks
of folk healers to assume a distinctively professional status (Starr 1982).
The growing availability of state funding for institutions mandated to
care for the mad was an attractive incentive for medical doctors who
were by no means yet assured of a livelihood in their chosen vocation.
Though moral treatment had been born, and was indeed received by
medical practitioners in Europe, as a serious threat to the legitimacy of

their craft, it became a useful resource for American medical doctors in their efforts to carve out a professional niche for themselves. Their known role as healers placed them in an opportune position to seize upon, and claim for themselves, the ostensive successes of moral treatment. Furthermore, their production of, and then their claim to, a body of theory that *explained* the method's successes lent them a symbolic legitimacy their lay competitors could not effectively contest (Scull 1989). Despite the basic irrelevance of this body of theory to the actual practice of moral treatment, it proved a crucial political advantage for medical doctors both in their efforts to professionalize their discipline and in their efforts to claim an exclusive jurisdiction over the treatment of madness.

The Rise of the Asylum and the Psychiatric Profession

Advocates of moral treatment had originally prescribed relocating the insane to "homes" wherein an intimate, "family-like," environment could be cultivated. However, the professional ambitions of medical superintendents, combined with the interests legislators had in supporting such places, and the interests families and local communities had in resorting to them, insured that this would not long be the manner in which these facilities were in fact organized (Grob 1994; McGovern 1985; Tomes 1984). The evolution of asylums from small private homes designed to cultivate a sense of moral community between client and counselor into massive publicly funded custodial institutions profoundly effected how the insanities (and ultimately, the addictions) of poor Americans came to be regarded during the nineteenth and twentieth centuries. This evolution is intimately tied to the processes through which psychiatry assumed a professional status. Grob (1994, p. 55) writes:

> The . . . identification of the specialty of psychiatry with asylums and state medicine . . . not only helped shape professional and popular perceptions about insanity, but it contributed also to the prevailing consensus that institutional care and treatment for mental disorders represented the appropriate and professional policy choice. Psychiatry and asylums, therefore, enjoyed a symbiotic relationship for more than a century; each reinforced and conferred legitimacy upon the other. Had both not been so closely related, it is conceivable that subsequent developments might have followed a quite different path.

The practice of confining troubled and troublesome paupers in publicly funded institutions was established long before medical doctors became their primary administrators. It emerged as traditional techniques for dispensing welfare and sanctioning deviance became increasingly inadequate to the realities of an ever more densely urban and industrial society (Katz 1986; Rothman 1990; Scull 1984). Quite independently of medical advice, local municipalities erected almshouses, workhouses, and jails to cope with the growing number of dependents, deviants, and transients that came to dwell in their midst. Nonetheless, medical practitioners did become fixtures around many of these institutions very early on. Rothman (1990, p. 45) offers a plausible explanation of the early medical presence at local almshouses:

> Since the most difficult cases and the ones that the community had the least desire to accommodate were often the diseased, the sick made up a sizable proportion of the almshouse population. As the institution became a collection point for illness, doctors became regular and salaried attendants, and soon they were training students there. The structure remained, of course, the least preferred setting for medical treatment, and people with sufficient funds received care at home. But by the end of the colonial period, the almshouse had become a hospital for the poor.

Even as private mad hospitals became more numerous, spurred on by the optimism inspired by moral treatment, the overwhelming majority of impoverished Americans remained beyond the scope of their care. To the extent these Americans were attended at all, they were handled largely by local almshouses and jails where little or no distinction was made between mentally fit and disabled charges. As greater numbers of immigrants arrived from Europe and industrialization accelerated, it became increasingly evident to policy makers that existing public provisions were ill suited to cope with the troubles presented and endured by certain segments of the lower classes. While state and local governments did pressure private hospitals to take in indigent clients, this was insufficient to overcome the greater pressure applied by their affluent paying customers to preserve the hospitals' exclusivity. Beginning in the second quarter of the nineteenth century, one state after another resolved that separate public institutions would have to be built to accommodate the "pauper insane" (Grob 1994).

Exaggerated claims regarding the efficacy of moral treatment were often used to persuade State legislatures to fund such institutions (Grob 1994; Rothman 1990; Scull 1989). Medical superintendents and their lay supporters argued, with inflated enthusiasm, that if insanity was detected and addressed early in its course, it could be effectively and permanently cured through moral treatment. If properly organized and administered by medical professionals, public institutions could effectively relieve the hardships madness had caused for American society and that American society had caused for the mad. Legislators, however, were less concerned with the minutia of therapeutic efficacy, or advancing a medical specialty, than with minimizing the hardships that deviance and poverty had wrought upon the society at large. The production of public asylums and the medicalization of madness was thus a collaborative project undertaken by medical doctors and state officials for only partially shared reasons. Medical men were primarily concerned to establish their authority and proprietary stake in the treatment of madness. State legislators, on the other hand, were interested in inexpensively managing the throngs of vagrants, deviants, and dependents who were crowding the streets of their rapidly growing cities—and doing so in ways that could be justified to constituents. This collaboration was, then, from its inception, an uneasy alliance and ultimately served to quash the original optimism that attended the treatment of insanity in publicly funded total institutions.

Asylum superintendents during the Jacksonian period had clear, if not always sound, ideas about the nature of madness and its sources in American society. Their views were shaped not only by their medical training but also by their socioeconomic backgrounds, which almost uniformly included membership in the middle classes and commitment to traditional Protestant values. The early medical superintendents were committed to the view that insanity has *environmental* antecedents because, like others of their socioeconomic status and religious predilections, they generally distrusted their emerging industrial society and believed it inimical to mental health. Moreover, their faith that madness had a physical basis was also informed by extra-professional intellectual tendencies. They tended toward biological theories not only because they were medically trained but also because the alternatives conflicted with their faith in the immortal soul (McGovern 1985). If the mind itself was vulnerable to disease then it might also be capable of death. This claim came much too close to the claim that the soul itself was mortal. Hence their theories focused on how the environment, and to a lesser extent, heredity, provoked physical pathologies that might manifest in people's behavior and experiences.

While acknowledging the wider scope of their original concerns, we must remain resolutely focused on medical superintendents' professional stake in promoting both asylums and somatic definitions of mental disorder. In 1844, thirteen superintendents met and formed the

Association of Medical Superintendents of American Institutions for the Insane (AMSAII), the very first medical specialty association in the United States. Membership was restricted to superintendents of mental institutions thereby forging the link between asylum care and the psychiatric profession. It was by their becoming professionally organized and pursuing an exclusive jurisdiction over the treatment of the mad that nineteenth-century psychiatrists were to leave a lasting impression on the management of insanities and addictions among the American poor. Early psychiatrists worked hard to establish and preserve a reasonable consensus among themselves regarding the proper understanding and management of insanities, and to garner the exclusive favors of legislators and the general public when it came to dealing with insanity (McGovern 1985). AMSAII members campaigned for new publicly funded asylums, promoted their assistants and protégés as candidate superintendents for the new asylums, made recommendations for the proper construction and administration of these institutions, and, in virtually every respect, successfully claimed exclusive jurisdiction and expertise in the understanding and treatment of the mad.

By the mid-nineteenth century, superintendents had won their victory. It was generally taken for granted among state legislators, and widely accepted among the lay public, that the best method for treating the mad was to place them into asylums overseen by medical doctors with specific training in insanity (Grob 1994; McGovern 1985). Insanity had been effectively medicalized in the United States. But their victory brought unanticipated hardships on psychiatrists as well. They had so successfully sold the merits of their asylums that the numbers of clients that local communities sought to place in their care far outstripped their capacities (Grob 1994; McGovern 1985; Tomes 1984). Early on, AMSAII members had agreed the occupancy of an asylum should be limited to two hundred and fifty to insure that the regimen of moral treatment remained effective (McGovern 1985, p. 152). However, because the demand was so overwhelming, asylums were soon crowded with numbers well beyond those originally envisioned.

Furthermore, by focusing so exclusively on courting government officials and becoming almost completely reliant on their financial support, psychiatrists made themselves extremely vulnerable to the wishes of people with agendas often very different from their own. While they insisted on professional autonomy, they were ultimately beholden to their public sponsors for whatever those sponsors required of them. As urbanization, industrialization, immigration, and the myriad social problems they saw arising from these processes grew, public policy makers became more desperate to contain the dangerous, disruptive, and dependent classes as cheaply and efficiently as possible. They grew less sympathetic to claims regarding therapeutic efficacy and pushed to bring the organization of public asylums into line with what they felt were society's pressing needs. This entailed, first and foremost, enlarging mental asylums to accommodate more inmates. As families and local communities came to use asylums to relieve themselves of a wider variety of inconvenient people, asylums were increasingly populated with patients deemed incurable. The increase of so-called "chronic patients" inhabiting asylums depreciated the perceived efficacy of moral treatment and in turn eroded the legitimacy of its advocates. This made room for neurologists to promote their own hereditarian theories and ally themselves with public officials in opposition to the old guard of medical superintendents. Neurologists lent scientific credibility to the movement away from moral treatment and toward custodial care of the pauper insane (Grob 1994; McGovern 1985).

By the turn of the twentieth century, public asylums had become massive custodial institutions, wherein the treatment regimen that had legitimated their construction was all but a memory. The societal response to madness among poor and marginalized Americans had evolved into one of confinement and neglect. The humanity that moral treatment had conferred upon the mad was largely forgotten. Insanity effectively ceased to be construed as an *other inside* the patient, distinct from the patient's self, and from which the community owed the patient some duty of relief. Instead, once again, the attribution of insanity rendered the transient, impoverished, or minority American beyond moral rights and obligations—wholly *other*. Instead of fostering therapeutic optimism regarding the social deficits observed among certain poor and marginalized Americans, the rise of the public asylum had the exact opposite effect. It eventually served to institutionally enforce a regard for those putative social deficits as products of intrinsic, and largely irremediable, hereditary pathologies that effectively, and often permanently, barred sufferers from civil society. This situation remained largely unchanged until the mid-twentieth century.

Let us recap the relevance of the foregoing descriptions with respect to three essential points. First, the practice of enlisting the afflicted as collaborators in their own recoveries was extinguished by the rise of the asylum, effectively recasting those who ostensibly suffered as wholly and irremediably *other*. As asylums grew and moral treatment gave way to custodial care, efforts to kindle the residual rationality of the afflicted person gave way to efforts to enforce mere docility and compliance. Dialogue and the effort to return patients to their local communities gave way to their coercive and often permanent exclusion from those communities. Therapy ceased to be the plausible excuse for confinement it once was and left asylums vulnerable to the charges of ineffectiveness and inhumanity that began in the late nineteenth century and continued into the mid-twentieth century (Scull 1984). The distrust of mental hospitals propagated by both their humanitarian and their libertarian critics alike was one important catalyst to the reformation of federal mental health policy in the sixties which, in its turn, had profound effects on the shape of services available to the people who came to participate in my research settings. I will return to this subject in Chapter 3.

Second, the consolidation of the psychiatric profession and the decisive medicalization of insanity has had an enormous impact (Conrad and Schneider 1992). That medical doctors became the most authoritative voices in the realm of ostensibly *involuntary* deviance has led to a deep entrenchment of the view that all such deviance is caused by disease (Scheff 1984). Rather than understanding human biology as concomitant to human behavior and experiences, we tend instead to mistakenly regard it as causally prior to behavior and experience (Kramer 1993; Mirowsky and Ross 1989). Psychiatrists remain by far the most powerful dictators of the proper practice of mental health care and have only too recently reasserted their professional power by orchestrating a large-scale return to basic biology in the field of mental health (Kirk and Kutchins 1992). More specifically, psychiatrically authorized techniques were ubiquitous resources in the settings in which I conducted fieldwork. It is unlikely that any of this would have come to pass had American psychiatrists not become professionally organized and forged alliances with powerful political actors during the nineteenth century.

Third, these events introduced the state as a critically important player in American mental health care, particularly as it pertains to poor, minority, and homeless Americans (Grob 1994; Katz 1986). The early medical superintendents and lay reformers lobbied legislators to provide humane care for those whose dependency had resulted from the revolutionary changes that were transforming American society. In the short term, their efforts seemed successful. During the first half of the nineteenth century public policy appeared quite responsive to the recommendations made to legislators by those who had lobbied for their support. However, as asylums became more deeply incorporated into an increasingly centralized system of public welfare and social control, the tables gradually turned. Medical superintendents found themselves and their fledgling science beholden to the demands of legislators and government agencies (Grob 1994; Katz 1986; McGovern 1985; Rothman 1990). The state's profound power to influence how we orient to dependency and deviance has continued into the present day and was evident in both the establishment of the programs in which I conducted fieldwork and in the very ways that insanity, addiction, and recovery from these ostensive disorders were identified and managed in them.

THE INFLUENCE OF THE TEMPERANCE MOVEMENT

The temperance movement was first championed by members of America's social elite. The movement was inaugurated by the politically and intellectually influential physician, Dr. Benjamin Rush, and the earliest temperance societies were founded by physicians, ministers, wealthy businessmen, merchants, and large farmers (Levine 1984). Gusfield (1986) argues that, initially, temperance activities reflected the concerns of well-born, well-educated North-Easterners to promote what they viewed as their own morally superior lifestyle in the face of shrinking political and economic power. Beyond their social status concerns, however, early temperance advocates were also disturbed by what they observed to be the growing disorder endemic in their expanding urban industrial communities (Boyer 1978). For them, habitual drunkenness came to serve as a convenient explanation for many of society's ills (Gusfield 1986; Levine 1984; Rothman 1990). Levine (1984) writes,

> In temperance thought poverty, crime, slums, abandoned wives and children, business failure and personal ruin were caused by alcohol, and not by any major flaws in the organization of the society and economy. Liquor was a scapegoat in the classical sense of the term: something to be sacrificed in order to rid America of its major ills and problems.

Though temperance advocates were concerned with issues of social control from the start, it would be a mistake to view the movement as a primarily repressive one. No doubt economic and political self-interest did motivate many temperance boosters. But very early into its development the temperance movement became allied with several of the progressive and populist movements that swept the United States during the nineteenth century including prison reform, the abolition of slavery, women's rights, and education (Barrows and Room 1991;

Baumohl and Room 1987; Herd 1991; Gusfield 1986). To understand these alliances, and what they reflect about the temperance movement's appeal to nineteenth-century Americans, we must attend not only to the factional interests expressed in temperance activity—those that set old money against new, capitalists against workers, Protestants against Catholics, natives against immigrants, and so on—but also attend to the faith with which early temperance supporters seemed to embrace Enlightenment doctrines that declared the unalienable rights and inherent perfectibility of human beings. As Herd (1991, p. 357) writes,

> The rise of temperance reform was associated with a broad diffusion and acceptance of the Enlightenment in American society. The central principle underlying this philosophy was that human society is constantly evolving toward a state of ultimate perfection. The emancipatory ideals of Enlightenment thought were, however, greatly tempered by a focus on order, restraint, and gradualism. Progressive social change was not anarchical; rather, it proceeded under conditions of enlightened self-examination and reason . . . This philosophy argued that a "free" social order depended on a rigid form of self-government. Persons were charged to rid themselves of violent and irrational impulses.

A good many "benevolent" and "reform" movements, including temperance, undertaken by well-to-do Americans during the early and mid-nineteenth century reflected these dual concerns. On the one hand, they sought to enforce the basic human rights of those who had historically been denied them. On the other hand, they sought to ensure that when it came time to exercise these rights, people were adequately civilized to make mature and responsible use of them (Boyer 1978). No doubt different factions within the temperance movement differentially emphasized these two concerns, but the basic affinity between them must not be overlooked. It is within this ideological framework that the popular appeal of viewing habitual drunkenness as the effect of a disease can best be understood. Many nineteenth-century reformers were convinced that their industrializing society was producing too much human misery and that Christian virtue demanded the plight of its victims be eased (Rothman 1990). However, they faced the following dilemma: How was the criminality, drunkenness, immorality, idleness, and vulgarity they associated with the urban poor to be reconciled with a faith in their intrinsic humanity, worthiness, and redeemability? How were the industrial conditions under which the urban poor were forced to live to be blamed for their problems without implicating the urban poor themselves as moral beings?

The notion of alcohol addiction served this purpose handily. According to Rush's enormously influential formulation, addiction began with a chronic voluntary use of liquor, but over time became habitual and ultimately intractably beyond the sufferer's control. He described alcohol addiction as "a disease of the will" and advised abstinence as the only cure (Levine 1978, p. 152). This image was seized by temperance advocates (and other reformers concerned with the plight of the poor), and by the mid-nineteenth century was securely lodged in the American popular imagination (Levine 1978, 1984; Valverde 1998). The apparent wretchedness of certain segments of the urban poor was to be explained by the vicious temptations to which they were constantly exposed in urban ghettos. These temptations were at first indulged voluntarily, perhaps because of the immaturity of youth, but ultimately became disease-like habits that could not be voluntarily overcome. Temperence advocates widely disseminated the idea that habitual intoxication (and the panoply of problems attributed to it) was the effect of a disease or disease-like phenomenon, an *other inside* those afflicted. They also endeavored to formulate methods for curing habitual drunkards. In doing so, they came to play a major role in shaping scientific beliefs, public policy, and popular sentiments in the United States regarding alcohol use and alcohol-related problems, particularly among the urban poor. These ultimately influenced the American regard for other types of drug use as well.

Initially it was medical doctors, inspired by Enlightenment doctrines and the Second Great Awakening, who played the greatest role in promoting the disease concept of alcohol addiction (Levine 1978, 1984). Beyond introducing this idea and legitimizing its inclusion in a good deal of temperance rhetoric, some leading medical figures called for the establishment of public facilities akin to insane asylums dedicated exclusively to the care of chronic inebriates. Baumohl and Room (1987, p. 136) write,

> The ... movement to provide professional and state-supported treatment for inebriates ... [a]lthough blooming later than the movement to offer public treatment for the mentally ill, ... was at first inspired by the same Enlightenment faith in human malleability (if not perfectibility) through reason and science and, in America, by the democratic benevolence of the Second Great Awakening, which reached its apogee in the 1830's. Benjamin Rush advocated hospital care for drunkards shortly after the turn of the 19th century, and the Connecticut State Medical Society proposed the establishment of an asylum for inebriates in 1830. Samual

> Woodward, the patriarch of institutional psychiatry in North America, and also a temperance orator, published in 1838 the first widely read tract in support of inebriate asylums.

Though medical men played important roles in legitimizing the view that habitual drunkenness is a disease, the medical *profession* was, for a variety of reasons, always somewhat cool to this idea. In the first place there were many who doubted there was a somatic basis for addiction. Though theories were offered, they were not widely embraced by the medical community (Conrad and Schneider 1992; Valverde 1998). Secondly, some feared that granting legitimacy to the view that addiction is a disease would appear to condone what many, both within and outside the medical profession, regarded as the irresponsible and vicious lifestyles of chronic inebriates. Thirdly, those drunkards who had already been admitted into mental asylums were known as a particularly troublesome class of clients. According to Baumohl and Room (1987, p. 144–5),

> Typically, as an alternative to incarceration, drunkards were admitted to an asylum by their families while acutely intoxicated or in the throes of delirium tremens. Within a week, however, they were restored to "perfect consciousness," and at that point they resented the association with madmen and became querulous, rebellious, and liabilities to the institutional routine and harmony necessary to the management of moral treatment.

Lastly, and perhaps most significantly, by the mid-nineteenth century, insane asylums were becoming severely overcrowded with chronic (and other) cases deemed undesirable by medical superintendents. Superintendents were thus extremely concerned to prevent, as far as possible, the widespread admission of vagrant pauper inebriates into their facilities. For these reasons the medical profession remained an ambivalent source of treatment for those deemed to suffer from alcohol addiction. From the earliest years of the temperance movement, the actual work of helping inebriates was undertaken not only by medical practitioners but by lay mutual help groups as well. Thus despite the widespread espousal of the view that alcohol addiction was a disease, what Gusfield (1981) has called the "ownership" of alcohol addiction nonetheless came to be shared by both medical and lay experts (most of whom gleaned their expertise from personal experience with the problem). This accident of history has had profound effects on how Americans orient to the relationship between insanities and addictions and was an important early antecedent to the establishment of the programs in which I did fieldwork.

I have mentioned that the temperance movement began with the efforts of well-to-do Americans to morally improve the lower classes. It was not long, however, before Americans of more modest stations began to embrace the cause. For middle and lower class Americans the temperance movement provided an avenue of social status elevation (Gusfield 1986). It did so by providing them a way to affiliate with people whose social status appeared higher than their own and to distinguish themselves from those of otherwise comparable status. A pervasive egalitarian ethos among its supporters allowed both women and men of traditionally lower stations to assume positions of prominence within the movement. It was thus that reformed drunkards came to speak publicly at temperance gatherings on their own behalf, telling tales of their alcohol-related hardships and persuading others to pledge themselves to abstinence (Baumohl 1986). Thus, while inside the walls of the insane asylum, therapeutic optimism, moral solidarity with the afflicted, and the role of the ostensibly afflicted in fostering their own recoveries were declining, they were observably on the rise outside those walls among people presumed to suffer from alcohol addiction.

Organizations like the Washingtonians were established by reformed (and reforming) drunkards who took an interest in those who remained enslaved to alcohol. And like the early proponents of moral treatment for the mad, their members were convinced of the drunkard's humanity despite his fallen state (Baumohl 1990). These organizations pioneered the use of mutual help groups among people working to remain abstinent from alcohol. They introduced the "experience meeting" (wherein drunkards shared their experiences with each other in efforts to shed their addiction to drink) and inebriate homes (where lodging and sober companionship were provided to those drunkards who needed or wanted them). Insofar as they pioneered the use of concepts and techniques that were later adopted by twelve-step fellowships and other varieties of therapeutic community, these groups played an enormously influential role in shaping modern concepts and techniques for the management of drug problems.

However, even in pioneering mutual help and in introducing a greater number and wider range of Americans to moral treatment, the Washingtonian inspired inebriate homes reached only so far into the ranks of the ethnic and impoverished populations of urban industrial

America. Despite their comparative successes, these institutions were both too few and perhaps still too xenophobic to embrace all who might have benefited from them (Valverde 1998). Their professed interest in accepting only those who demonstrated a sincere desire for treatment worked out in practice to a tacit policy of accepting primarily what Baumohl (1990, p. 1193) has called "fallen members of the broad middling classes." Thus he notes that "although the [inebriate] homes preached universal curability, they selected voluntary, motivated clients who would fit within their genteel melieux" (Baumohl 1990, p. 1193). As poor immigrants continued to arrive and settle in America's cities and the economically unstable years of the late nineteenth century produced unprecedented poverty in America, middle and upper class sympathies for the less fortunate waned. Baumohl and Room (1987, p. 151) write,

> The Panic of 1873 and the subsequent depression of 1873–78 sharply curtailed the revenues of states and yielded extraordinary numbers of homeless men; indeed it brought the noun "tramp" into the American language. Although social critics like Henry George, and the labor press in general, saw "trampism" clearly for what it was—a symptom of economic disorder—most reformers and middle-class citizens held the unemployed wanderer accountable for his plight. Even when recognizing that the tramp was initially a victim of circumstance, many averred that "men thrown outside of social influence, . . . even if at the outset possessing good impulses and habits, . . . become, in a short time, desperate, degraded, or criminal, and perhaps all three." In particular, such degradation virtually became equated with habitual drunkenness.

The philanthropists, and the state and city politicians, who had provided essential support to the Washingtonian and neo-Washingtonian inebriate homes, became increasingly disillusioned with them. Inebriate homes were considered incapable of containing the urban disorder attributed to the intemperate poor (Baumohl 1986, 1990; Baumohl and Room 1987). Within the context of what they perceived as more desperate times, many temperance advocates turned their attentions away from the redemption of the chronic drunkard and toward legal prohibition of alcohol. Some prohibitionists had always been skeptical of the disease theory of addiction and others simply espoused the logic that even if alcohol addiction is a disease, an ounce of prevention was better for all than a pound of cure. For those who remained committed to some form of organized treatment for alcohol addicts, the focus shifted from recovering the residual humanity of the chronic inebriate toward containing the intransigent social problems the indigent drinker posed for society at large.

A group of medical doctors formed the American Association for the Cure of Inebriates (AACI) in 1870, with the hope of garnering for themselves the same clinical, research, and political base for their specialty that members of the AMSAII had achieved for theirs. A major part of this effort was the promotion of state-funded inebriate asylums modeled after state insane asylums. Members of the AACI played on the perceived inadequacies of neo-Washingtonian inebriate homes to suggest the value of establishing larger public facilities under the administrative control of trained medical doctors. Partly because of the pessimism engendered by their hereditarian theories of alcohol addiction, and also because of their recognition of the interests legislators might have in supporting such institutions, inebriate asylum promoters did not speak to the curative capabilities of their proposed asylums. Instead, they touted the importance of coercive or involuntary admissions and retentions of chronic drunkards within their walls (as opposed to the largely voluntary participation demanded by inebriate homes) and to the public benefits of removing chronic drunkards from civil society.

Public inebriate asylums were endorsed by many of those who had become the unwilling custodians of indigent drunkards. Baumohl (1990, p. 1195) writes,

> Jailers were happy to be rid of the rounders; police court, almshouse and general hospital administrators were similarly disposed; in 1875 the AMSAII endorsed the creation of inebriate asylums "on substantially the same footing" as insane asylums, stipulating that the institutional treatment of drunkards should be involuntary and of years' duration if necessary. In addition to whatever good they might do drunkards, specialized asylums would be extremely convenient for other overwhelmed institutions.

But despite these endorsements, inebriate asylum boosters usually proved unable to persuade legislators that their institutions would bring any benefits that were not already available from the jails, prisons, workhouses, almshouses, and insane asylums. Though a handful of inebriate asylums were established toward the end of the nineteenth century, they were always financially embattled and, by 1919, had been eliminated or converted to other uses. Americans concerned to ameliorate alcohol problems turned increasingly to prohibition and other coercive methods for overcoming the putative evils of alcohol in American society. When the Eighteenth Amendment was passed in 1918, the fate of treatment services for indigent drunkards was effectively sealed. Indigent drunkards would be punished and confined for their unseemly behavior and virtually no effort would be made to return them to the community for over a decade. What had once been considered *others inside* the afflicted, from which efforts must be made to free them, now rendered the afflicted themselves wholly *other*.

Thus in a fashion strikingly similar to that by which moral treatment gave way to custodial confinement of the indigent insane, moral treatment and mutual help eventually gave way to custodial confinement and coercive control of indigent drinkers as well. In both cases, Enlightenment faith in the redeemability, and intrinsic humanity, of the afflicted inspired efforts to enlist their involvement as allies in the work of overcoming their diseases. And in both cases, the interest in reclaiming the humanity of the afflicted gave way to a concern to contain the public troubles for which they were personally blamed. These processes were both closely associated with the descending class and status positions of those thought to suffer. As its ranks were presumed to swell with homeless vagrants and impoverished immigrants, the population of alcohol addicts ceased to be seen as afflicted by nefarious disease agents, and thus deserving of public sympathy and support, and became instead a collection of irredeemable *others* who inspired not sympathy but fear, and who by their own willful immorality, viciousness, and irresponsibility posed unconscionable threats to the public order.

THE RISE OF "NARCOTIC" DRUG USE AS AN AMERICAN PUBLIC PROBLEM

The early evolution of American concepts of "narcotic" drug problems also took a course quite similar to the early evolution of American concepts of insanity. As with insanities, narcotic drug addictions first emerged as afflictions that beset the better classes of Americans (cf. Brecher 1972; Conrad and Schneider 1992; Courtwright 2001; Duster 1970; Goode 1993; Lindesmith 1947; H.W. Morgan 1981). Originally, chronic opiate users were thought to suffer from weak wills. Understood as a vice, their apparent drug dependence, and the social failings it was found to induce, generally pushed early American narcotic habitués to the margins of their moral communities. However, it was not long before medical observers began to seek explanations that exonerated well-off narcotics users from moral culpability (cf. Beard 1871). Regarding their drug use as symptomatic of a disease seemed a plausible and forgiving account for the transgressions of otherwise respectable people. It also cast the problems of potentially paying customers in terms that suggested their amenability to professional medical intervention. However, as problematic drug use became more routinely associated with cultural *others* like ethnic minorities, prostitutes, gamblers, youth gang members, and impoverished city dwellers, this explanation lost much of its attraction and intrinsic credibility.

The earliest mentions of problematic drug use in the United States emerged in the mid-nineteenth century and focused on those whose use was initiated in the care of physicians (Courtwright 2001; H.W. Morgan 1981). Prior to 1830, mentions of problems arising from the medical use of opiates focused primarily on overdose. However, after 1830 physicians began to express concern over their patients' apparent habituation to opiates. The rise of temperance thought probably influenced some to consider narcotic drug addiction in the same spirit as alcohol addiction. Temperance may also have contributed to an increase in the use of opiates as a liquor substitute. Courtwright (2001) opines that the increased concern regarding drug addiction may also have resulted from an increase in the number of individuals ostensibly suffering from the problem. Severe epidemics of cholera and dysentery struck the United States during the years between 1830 and 1850. Insofar as these diseases were routinely treated with opiates, it is reasonable to infer that many who had been treated thusly carried on in their use of opiates and thereby increased the visibility of opiate use and the problems associated with it.

However, despite growing medical concern, the use of opiates to treat a vast array of medical complaints continued largely unabated until the 1890s. This has been attributed to several factors. The apparent benefit of using opiates increased with the introduction of the hypodermic needle to American medicine in 1856. After 1870, medical books and journals carried numerous warnings of the ill effects of prolonged opiate use, but many medical practitioners did not routinely consult this literature. The apparent success of opiates in relieving patients' suffering, and fortifying the physician's image as a successful caretaker, likely encouraged their continued use. No doubt the income to be made by providing this popular treatment was also a powerful incentive. Doctors often self-medicated as well, either disregarding the ostensive risks or believing they were immune to them. Those doctors who accepted the wisdom in carefully monitoring their patients' opiate use also encountered setbacks. Physicians who practiced in remote areas found it difficult to visit their patients regularly. This prompted many to leave drug supplies with their patients rather than making repeated trips to a patient's bedside. Furthermore, pharmacists and "patent" medicine peddlers dispensed opiates freely, seriously undermining the efforts of anyone who sought to limit their use.

As a result of these influences, the problem of narcotic drug use spread through the populations who had reasons for, and the means of, seeking medical treatment. Narcotic habitués originally tended to predominate in the upper and middle classes because it was they who could afford medical care. Chronic opiate use became particularly common among women of these classes because their medical complaints tended more often to suggest the use of opiates than did medical complaints common to men. Following the Civil War, though, many veterans also became chronic users after being administered opiates for diseases or injuries they had suffered during wartime. Medical theories began to emerge to explain how upstanding citizens might grow capable of the kinds of failings observed to flow from their need for narcotics. At the same time, the lion's share of the blame fell not upon users but upon the insalubrious physicians, pharmacists, and patent medicine peddlers who had induced users into their narcotic slavery. Medical warnings and proscriptions against opiate treatments grew sharper, eventually spawning campaigns to legally regulate how physicians and pharmacists could dispense them. As newer and seemingly less dangerous drugs became available, medical doctors curtailed their reliance on opiate treatments. After 1890 the number of iatrogenic drug habitués gradually began to fall (Courtwright 2001). While the existence of iatrogenic addicts had been widely known among the general public, they were never regarded a particularly menacing social problem. Middle and upper class narcotic habitués were considered casualties of the careless practice of medicine. They were pitied and perhaps sometimes resented but were not thought to pose any real threat to society.

Beginning in the mid-nineteenth century, though, another class of opiate user, the Chinese opium smoker, came onto the American scene. As a rule, Chinese immigrants had always been badly treated in America. However, when their value as low-wage "coolie" laborers on the railroad and in the gold mines of the west coast waned in the 1870s, racist resentments began to inspire every manner of attack on their livelihoods and lifestyles (Courtwright 2001; H.W. Morgan 1981; Musto 1987; Reinarman 1994). This culminated in the Chinese Exclusion Act of 1882, which suspended Chinese immigration into the United States and inaugurated a racist and otherwise xenophopic immigration policy in

America whose legacy continues to be felt. Prior to federal legislation, cities and states with large Chinese populations introduced ordinances and laws against one salient feature of the menace the Chinese were said to present—opium smoking. Though the Chinese were the primary focus of these measures, concern was not in the first instance expressed regarding their own opiate use. By the mid-1870s, small numbers of whites had begun to smoke opium, provoking fear and disgust among those who felt that the intimate contact between Chinese and whites in the luridly sensual context of opium dens was more unseemly than opiate use itself (Courtwright 2001; H.W. Morgan 1981; Musto 1987). The dissolute habits of Chinese immigrants were viewed as consistent with their backward heritage but their corruption of respectable white Americans could not be tolerated (H.W. Morgan 1974).

The notion that addiction is a disease to which otherwise upstanding citizens succumb had no place in nineteenth-century discussions of opium smoking among the immigrant Chinese. Whereas well-to-do white morphine habitués and opium eaters could be properly regarded as otherwise respectable *victims* of an *other inside* them in the guise of opiate addiction, Chinese opium smokers were understood to indulge in their vice because they were intrinsically immoral and inferior beings. They were themselves *others* who posed a threat to mainstream American society and, as such, partook of vices that reflected the dissolution of their race.[7] Hence their drug use was more properly met with coercive control than with medical treatment. Similar reactions met the white gamblers, prostitutes, and assorted criminals who, by their own lack of respectability, first deigned to associate with Chinese opium smokers and share in their immoral pastimes. When fears grew that opium smoking was spreading to more respectable classes, the

7. Medical theories of drug addiction in the late nineteenth century reflect the double standard that distinguished well-healed drug habitués from those from marginalized minority groups and the lower classes. According to then current theories, "brain workers" and the more evolved nervous systems of Western whites were more vulnerable to inebriety (the disease of addiction) than were members of marginalized minorities and the lower classes. Baumohl (1990, p. 1194) makes this point nicely in his discussion of George M. Beard, the most influential theorist of addiction in the late nineteenth century, "The "vice of intemperance", [Beard] wrote, "is a survival of savagery in civilization . . . It is among the depressed classes, who yet retain the habits, and constitutions of the last century, that intemperance abounds." The disease of inebriety was something else again; it was a "disease of refinement," of "an indoor life, of brain-workers, of civilization."" and again, " "The peasantry of foreign countries, and negroes and Indians, are good materials for drunkards," he wrote, "but do not often become inebriates." (Baumohl 1990, p. 1202)"

potential of opium smoking to enslave and corrupt otherwise innocent citizens began to receive an observably greater emphasis (cf. Kane 1881).

The same xenophobia characterized the rise of public concern over cocaine use. Prior to the turn of the twentieth century, cocaine was a popular and seemingly harmless stimulant enjoyed in a wide variety of forms by a wide variety of people. However, when southern community leaders decided that cocaine use made blacks more threatening to whites, public attitudes changed (H.W. Morgan 1981; Musto 1987; Reinarman 1979). Again, public concern was not focused on helping blacks who had fallen victim to addiction. Instead it focused on claims that cocaine-crazed blacks became violent, and posed threats to the white community. Rather than being cast as a matter deserving of medical attention, cocaine use in the black community was met with fear, legislation, and coercive control. By the 1890s, legislative restrictions on nonmedical uses of opiates and cocaine were being passed throughout the United States spurred on by a xenophobic distrust of the habits of lower class and minority *others* (Musto 1987).

The lobbying efforts of physicians and pharmacists also influenced the passage of legislative controls. Both groups were well aware of their professional stake and were concerned to limit any hardship legislation would bring upon themselves. On the other hand, by the turn of the century, many physicians and pharmacists were convinced of the necessity for reform. Hence, they were not wholly opposed to legislation specifying when and how ostensibly dangerous drugs should be dispensed—particularly if it fortified their professional privilege against lay competitors. Though measures were being passed at the municipal and state level, federal involvement in domestic legislation was inhibited until 1908. Until this time, federal involvement in policing moral matters was thought unconstitutional and was therefore not widely sought. This changed when State Department officials pushed a small piece of legislation through Congress banning the importation of smoking opium. This legislation resulted from a felt need to present evidence of domestic concern at a conference the State Department had organized in Shanghai to discuss opium problems throughout the world. Though its interest in this issue was driven by matters of international trade, the State Department became a major player in federal legislation regarding domestic narcotics control in the early twentieth century.

The State Department eventually achieved passage of the Harrison Narcotic Act in 1914. By drawing upon federal powers of taxation, the Harrison Act made three basic provisions for federal involvement in domestic narcotics control: (1) it demanded that anyone engaged in the production or distribution of drugs controlled under the Act register with the federal government and keep records regarding their transactions with those drugs, (2) it demanded that anyone involved in buying or selling the controlled drugs pay a tax. This gave the Treasury Department power to surveil drug production and distribution and to enforce the provisions of the Act by federal police measures, and (3) it demanded that unregistered persons only purchase drugs upon prescription by a physician, and that prescriptions must be given only for legitimate medical reasons. This last provision sparked violent controversy when it was asked whether maintenance of an addict's supply was a legitimate medical reason (Duster 1970; Musto 1987). The Treasury Department took a hard line, insisting that maintenance was not a legitimate medical reason. But some within the medical profession insisted that it was. The issue was resolved in a series of Supreme Court decisions.

The first came in 1916, on the case *United States v. Jin Fuey Moy*. Here the Court concluded that the federal government could not pronounce judgment on the proper practice of medicine and denied the Treasury Department the right to prosecute doctors for dispensing narcotics to maintain addicts. In 1919 the *Jin Fuey Moy* decision was effectively reversed in the two cases *United States v. Doremus* and *Webb et al. v. United States*. Speaking to the reasons for this drastic change in judicial outlook, Musto (1987, pp. 132–4) writes,

> Between the *Jin Fuey Moy* decision in 1916 and the vigorous attack on addiction in 1919, profound social changes had occurred in the United States. World War I had been fought, the 18th Amendment had been adopted, and the liberalizing movements of LaFollette, Theodore Roosevelt, and Wilson had declined into a fervent and intolerant nationalism ... Since narcotics use even in more peaceful times had evoked the image of a Negro cocainomaniac or a seductive Chinese, it was not that the popular image of the drug user changed but that the minority opinion in favor of maintenance became intolerable ... Maintenance of addiction could no more be defended than maintenance of alcoholism. Both classes of indulgence were to be treated not by maintenance but by a remedy appropriate to social cancers: surgical extirpation.

By outlawing maintenance, the federal government dealt a devastating blow to a medical specialty that was already troubled. The number of iatrogenic addicts was decreasing as doctors curtailed their prescription of opiates (Courtwright 2001). Thus putative narcotics addicts were increasingly concentrated among poor and marginalized minority groups and/or the so-called criminal classes who procured their drugs illegally. While this fact itself repelled many physicians who might have treated more respectable narcotics users, it also influenced the kinds of concepts that achieved currency among those who still deigned to bother with addiction medicine. The medical consensus of the late nineteenth century was that narcotic drug addiction stemmed either from degeneracy or from neurasthenia (Courtwright 2001; Jaffe 1978; Valverde 1998). According to the first approach, degenerates, either by their own actions or by an hereditary predisposition, come to suffer a degradation of their nervous system functions. Thusly, they grow progressively incapable of meeting the moral and intellectual demands of human life and descend into animalistic habits like addictive drug use. While most felt degeneracy could be prevented, few felt it could be reversed.

George Beard's theory of neurasthenia held that people have a limited nervous capacity that is severely taxed by the complex demands of modern life. Those at the vanguard of civilization, "brain-workers" such as professionals, entrepreneurs, and those with highly refined nervous sensibilities, were particularly susceptible. When in the throes of this condition, some people became prone to addictive drug use. Sufferers from neurasthenia, literally "nervous exhaustion," might be cured by first removing them from the taxing environments that had caused their illness, and then providing them with restful recreation and professional guidance in reorganizing their lives. The theories of degeneracy and neurasthenia were convenient resources for members of the AACI, who sought to establish a two-tiered system of care for addicts. Private asylums could benefit paying customers who suffered from neurasthenia, an *other inside* them from which they could be and should be freed, while custodial facilities could be built at taxpayer expense to confine the incurable and otherwise incorrigible lower class degenerate alcoholics and addicts who were themselves irreconcilably other and hence would inevitably remain both dangers to themselves and to the community.

When the concepts of degeneracy and neurasthenia were dismissed by a new generation of scientists, and the question of drug addiction became more highly politicized in the early twentieth century, debate regarding its nature took a more polemical turn. Those who remained committed to the curability of addiction, figures like Charles Terry, Ernest Bishop, and George Pettey, came to insist that addiction did not belie underlying neurological disorders at all but was a normal physiological reaction to which anyone could succumb (Courtwright 2001; Musto 1987). On the other side of the debate were the likes of Lawrence

Kolb who argued that only *psychopaths* were vulnerable to addiction. As a result of the declining number of iatrogenic drug habitués, the publicity given to drug users from marginalized groups or with ostensibly criminal propensities, the failure of clinicians to produce effective recovery statistics, the chilling effect of antimaintenance laws, and Kolb's institutional power base within the United States Public Health Service, the image of drug user as incorrigible psychopath won the day. Originally a resource for inviting sympathy, and the prospect of a return to respectable society for well-born Americans, the newly ascendant concept of narcotic drug addiction now sealed the status of impoverished and minority narcotics users as intrinsically inferior and irretrievable *others* for whom confinement became the only legitimate response.

Despite the fact that Canyon House and Twilights were treatment programs, the specter of criminal prosecution and confinement weighed heavily on people's activities and experiences in them. Some clients participated in these settings because they had been ordered to by the criminal courts. Furthermore, clients' sense of their own and each other's drug problems often implicated the legal problems they perceived drug use to have caused for them. Some knowledge of the relationship between drug criminalization and our concepts of drug addiction is thus invaluable for developing an adequate ethnographic understanding of the practices that comprised my research settings. At a more general level, knowledge of these events helps us grasp more basic patterns in the ways that troubles associated with homelessness, poverty, and cultural marginality are managed in the United States as matters of public policy. The fact that certain concepts of addiction became important resources for the criminalization of troubled and troublesome Americans has had an important bearing on both the events that gave rise to the establishment of my research settings and the specific activities that took place in them.

CONCLUDING REMARKS

In this chapter we have seen how the American mental health, alcohol, and drug addiction fields each began as collective efforts to recover (and empower) the lost humanity of once respectable members of society. We have seen how concepts of insanity and addiction were originally developed as resources in these efforts and served both to mitigate the scorn their actions might otherwise have provoked and to guide efforts aimed at their redemption. However, concepts of insanity and addiction were ultimately turned to purposes that were diametrically opposed to those for which they were originally produced. When these concepts were turned upon the troubles presented and endured by *others* like ethnic minorities, impoverished city dwellers, and migrant workers, they began to evolve in considerably more punitive directions. Instead of informing efforts to achieve their recoveries, concepts of insanity and addiction came to serve in explanations and justifications for the (often permanent) exclusion of putative sufferers from American society. Disease concepts like degeneracy and psychopathy seriously undermined belief in the humanity of the afflicted and portrayed them as quite beyond hope of recovery by any manner of remedial effort. As such, insanities and addictions were much more likely to entitle the afflicted to confinement and neglect than to empathy or therapeutic treatment.

Though they came to share a public mandate for the social control of the dependent, disruptive, and dangerous classes, and were strikingly similar in their ultimate effects, the mental health, alcohol, and drug addiction fields developed uniquely in important respects as well. Psychiatrists were ultimately reduced to administrators of custodial institutions, but they nevertheless retained much of their original link with medicine and were thus able to preserve the legitimacy of a predominantly medical orientation to insanities. As the stereotypical image of narcotic drug addiction transformed from one of genteel fragility to one of impoverished urban depravity, most medical doctors avoided treating addicts even before they were faced with criminal prosecution for doing so. The few physicians who remained in the field after drug criminalization ultimately proffered little more than medical justification for criminal incarceration despite their strident efforts to preserve a medical jurisdiction over the problem. Those physicians who deigned to treat alcohol addicts suffered from the outset because of their marginal status in the larger field of American medicine and were dealt virtually fatal blows with the passage of the Eighteenth Amendment and the nationalistic climate that followed World War I. With the onset of Prohibition, medical doctors, except those who administered insane asylums, were almost completely dissociated from the implementation of public responses to alcohol problems among the indigent. While the disease concept of alcohol addiction was not totally eliminated, it was rendered largely irrelevant to the management of impoverished Americans deemed to overuse alcohol.

3   Addictions and Insanities

Two Fields and Their Phenomena

THIS CHAPTER is divided into four sections. I first discuss the formation and growth of Alcoholics Anonymous (AA) and the so-called Alcoholism Movement in the modern alcoholism treatment industry. Particular attention is given to how these events came to organize how alcohol addictions are conceptualized (and configured) among impoverished Americans. In the second section I discuss the rise of AA-inspired "social model" approaches to illicit drug addiction among poor Americans, and the increasing commingling of drug and alcohol addiction treatment in publicly sponsored programs. In the third section I speak to the rise of community mental health and biopsychiatry. In the last section I discuss the emergence of concern regarding "treatment-resistant" clients among professionals in the fields of mental health and substance abuse, and how those "dually diagnosed" with both mental illnesses and addictions provoked notice largely as a result of that professional concern. I conclude by summarizing how these events conspired to give particular forms to insanities and addictions as distinct, but mutually exacerbating, types of *others inside* certain homeless and/or poor Americans.

ALCOHOLICS ANONYMOUS AND
THE ALCOHOLISM MOVEMENT

By the time the Eighteenth Amendment was repealed in 1933, the alcohol-related problems of the poor had receded from the forefront of the American popular imagination. As Gusfield (1986) notes, the Great Depression cast a starkly economic shadow on the problems of the American poor, and alcohol was no longer the plausible scapegoat for those problems it might once have seemed. By now the country's most visible drunkards lived among those drawn to the cheap accommodations, day labor, and charity available on America's skid rows. When they were regarded worthy of public measures, skid row drinkers were incarcerated in the "drunk tanks" of city and county jails, detoxified in the charity wards of public hospitals, or sent for more extended stints to "dry out" in state mental hospitals. Christian missionaries promised redemption through religion but reached only a very few (cf. Baumohl 1990; Wallace 1965; Wiseman 1970). Though these arrangements were certainly less than illustrious, this did not elicit much popular concern. As a problem confined to a relatively small collection of homeless and derelict old men, alcohol abuse was not considered worthy of much public attention (Roman 1991). By the late thirties, though, this attitude began to change, largely because of the growth of Alcoholics Anonymous and the Alcoholism Movement.

In May 1935, two years after the repeal of Prohibition, two self-described alcoholics met in Akron, Ohio. These men, Bill Wilson and Dr. Bob Smith, were the founders of Alcoholics Anonymous, and this occasion is widely marked as the first AA meeting (Pittman 1988; Trice and Staudenmeier 1989). Both men were white, middle-class, Christian professionals who, but for the many falls from grace they attributed to drinking, embodied the archetypal image of mainstream American citizen. Both had tried many remedies for their alcohol problems, and both had suffered many failures in their efforts to remain sober. Drawing on the nondenominational evangelism, frank confession, and spiritual enthusiasm they had shared as members of the Oxford Group (a popular Christian fellowship of the day), they found in each other something they had failed to find anywhere else. Dr. Smith wrote of Bill Wilson,

> *he was the first living human with whom I had ever talked, who knew what he was talking about in regards to alcoholism from actual experience. In other words, he talked my language.* He knew all the answers, and certainly not because he had picked them up in his reading. (Alcoholics Anonymous 1976, p. 180; original italics)

As this passage attests, the first AA members favored the wisdom of personal experience over that of science or professional training. In stating that Bill Wilson "talked my language," Dr. Smith also makes plain the moral community, or sense of "we," that he and Bill Wilson had achieved, and which AA members continue to consider the heart of their program. Dr. Bob and Bill W., as they became known, soon began recruiting others into their newfound fellowship. Like the Washingtonians of the nineteenth century, the groups organized by Bill Wilson and Bob Smith provided occasion for confession of one's alcohol problems, mutual support, and formulating techniques for staying sober. By 1939, AA had distilled their recovery program into the famous twelve steps.

And they had published the so-called "Big Book," which outlined their views on alcoholism and recounted several personal tales of alcohol addiction and redemption through the AA fellowship. Though still modest in size, AA had established itself, worked out its own views on alcohol addiction, and worked out the fundamental principles of its recovery program, with almost no input from professional health care givers.

Long before Bob Smith and Bill Wilson met, the temperance claim that anyone could succumb to alcohol addiction had lost its credibility (Levine 1984). Most Americans who drank had little difficulty integrating alcohol use into otherwise healthy and satisfying lives. AA members, no less than anyone else, were thus convinced that their own problems must stem from something inside themselves rather than from the intrinsic properties of alcohol. AA endorsed Dr. William Silkworth's view that alcoholics shared an allergy that induced excessive drinking. This endorsement was not based on science, but on the intuitive good sense it made to AA members who were understandably cool to the more disparaging theories in common circulation:

> It did not satisfy us to be told that we could not control our drinking just because we were maladjusted to life, that we were in full flight from reality, or were outright mental defectives. These things were true to some extent, in fact, to a considerable extent with some of us. But we are sure that our bodies were sickened as well. In our belief, any picture of an alcoholic which leaves out this physical factor is incomplete. . . . [Dr. Silkworth's] theory that we have an allergy to alcohol interests us. As laymen, our opinion as to its soundness may, of course, mean little. But as ex-problem drinkers, we can say that his explanation makes good sense. It explains many things for which we cannot otherwise account. (Alcoholics Anonymous 1976, p. xxiv)

AA members liked Silkworth's theory because it construed alcoholism as a physical disease, rather than a moral or psychic flaw. However, much like the medical theories linked to the moral treatment of insanity, Silkworth's theory is largely irrelevant to the actual therapeutic practices undertaken in AA. AA members have never worried about the biological nature of their putative allergy. Instead, they have sought to help one another subdue the specific behavioral patterns they attribute to that allergy. Hence, the allergy theory is relevant to therapeutic practice only insofar as it legitimates the notion that alcoholics drink too much not because they are psychologically or morally defective but because they suffer from a genuine physical disease, an *other inside* them. It thereby allows for the production and sustenance of moral community between AA members themselves (and between them and their nonalcoholic friends and family members), despite the myriad alcohol-related transgressions that might otherwise have alienated them from their fellows. The AA faith in insights drawn from personal experience, as well as their characteristic fusion of a physical definition of disease with strictly social remedies for it, were ubiquitous in both of my research settings. And, of course, so was the work of creating and sustaining moral community with recourse to putative *others inside* program participants.

Though there was marked enthusiasm for these ideas within AA's meager ranks, they were not yet popular among medical professionals, nor among public policy makers in the late thirties. And, as yet, they exercised almost no influence over the management of drunkenness among the poor. Though AA members did sometimes collect new members from skid rows, jails, and hospitals, their impact was still negligible. But two years after the Big Book's publication, in March 1941, the *Saturday Evening Post* ran a cover story on them. The *Post* had a circulation of over three million and this cover story is widely considered the main reason AA membership quadrupled from 2,000 to 8,000 in that year. By the end of World War II, AA was nationally recognized. But the vast majority of its membership continued to consist of native-born white men from middle and upper middle class backgrounds (Robertson 1988).

Just as AA was becoming an important fixture in the fledgling field of alcoholism treatment, scientists were also taking renewed interest in chronic inebriety. After Repeal, most Americans considered the haughty moralism exhibited by the Anti-Saloon League and other Prohibitionists priggish (Burnham 1993). Room (1985, p. 16) writes "[i]n the aftermath of Prohibition and Repeal in the U.S., a whole middle-class generation came to maturity with the conviction that alcohol concerns were reactionary, ungenerous and sectarian." Most seemed to believe that alcohol caused problems only among a small class of homeless men, skid row derelicts who drank very heavily. This restricted image of alcohol problems was promoted by claimsmakers from the liquor industry who promulgated the slogan "The fault is not in the bottle. It's in the man" (Gusfield 1982, p. 13). It was also promoted through the efforts of industrial giants like John D. Rockefeller, Jr., and Pierre DuPont who, for their own financial reasons, supported Repeal and the taxation of liquor sales (Levine 1985). For their part, scientists were only too pleased to solicit the money made available by the liquor industry, private endowments like the Rockefeller and Carnegie Foundations, and from state sources to study very heavy drinkers and to overlook the wider ecology of alcohol use (cf. Jellinek 1942). Studying alcohol problems in terms of disease was an opportune strategy for scientists to construe these problems in personal terms without thereby shedding the scientific cloak of value-neutrality. By adopting the view that alcohol problems stem from a poorly understood disease, scientists sought to recast behavior that had until recently been viewed in strictly moral terms—as evidence of human otherness—in ostensibly value-neutral medical terms—as evidence of nonhuman otherness.

A major landmark in the scientific study of alcohol problems was the founding of the Research Council on Problems of Alcohol (RCPA) in 1937. The Council's main purpose was to seek research funding (Keller 1976). It was first convened as an advisory committee by Dr. Norman Jolliffe of Bellvue Hospital in New York.[1] Jolliffe hoped to secure a half million dollar grant from the Rockefeller Foundation to study the causes of alcoholism. Though multidisciplinary, the committee was dominated by medical doctors and psychiatrists. The Rockefeller grant was ultimately denied, but the committee formally organized as the RCPA and continued to solicit funding. Though its funding success was limited, the RCPA did manage to raise the profile and prestige of alcohol research in academic circles, in particular by affiliating with the American Association for the Advancement of Science. It also prevailed upon the Carnegie Corporation to grant $25,000 to Dr. Jolliffe and his Bellvue colleague Dr. Karl M. Bowman to review the biological literature on the effects of alcohol on human beings. Dr. Jolliffe enlisted E. M. Jellinek as the executive director of the study and the research commenced in 1939.

By 1940, a backlog of reports (which now extended well beyond biology) had accumulated and an appropriate publication outlet was sorely needed (Wiener 1981). Another RCPA member, Dr. Howard W. Haggard, of the Laboratory of Applied Physiology at Yale solved the problem by founding the *Quarterly Journal of Studies on Alcohol* as the RCPA's official publication.[2] Furthermore, when the Carnegie grant was exhausted, Haggard invited Jellinek to join the Yale Laboratory and to

1. Roizen (1994) suggests that the prehistory of the RCPA may be traceable not to Jolliffe and his colleagues in New York but to another research group in Washington, D.C. If his argument is correct then it may be that the RCPA emerged independently of Jolliffe's effort to secure funding from the Rockefeller Foundation. Nevertheless, soon after the RCPA moved to New York in the late thirties, Jolliffe did become one of its leading figures.

2. The *Quarterly Journal of Studies on Alcohol* separated from the RCPA in 1943 and became simply the *Journal of Studies on Alcohol* in 1975 when it began to be published monthly.

begin recruiting a multidisciplinary research team to staff what in 1941 became the Yale Center of Alcohol Studies. The Yale Center (now the Rutgers Center of Alcohol Studies) soon became the hub of what sociologists have dubbed the "Alcoholism Movement" (cf. Gusfield 1982; Levine 1984; Room 1983; Wiener 1981). Through their publications and then, beginning in 1943, their summer school program, affiliates of the Yale Center vigorously promoted the notion that alcohol problems demanded scientific research and treatment rather than reproach or neglect (Schneider 1978). Robert Straus, a sociologist and an early member of the Yale Center research team, notes that though he and his colleagues at the Center had as yet little understanding of whether problem drinking was primarily biogenic, psychogenic, or sociogenic, they nonetheless promoted the notion that alcoholism is a disease,

> as part of a deliberate and calculated strategy . . . to combat stigma and prejudice, to encourage alcoholics and their families to face their problems and seek help, and to modify the prevailing negative attitudes toward alcoholics held by most physicians and members of the other helping professions. (Straus 1976, p. 31)

Perhaps slightly more to the point, his colleague Mark Keller writes,

> We did not know and did not pretend to know the cause or causes of alcoholism . . . We chose to emphasize alcoholism and its treatment because that seemed to be a magic key which, in the new era that was beginning (with the added value of the popularization of Alcoholics Anonymous), would open doors and gain support for our broader conceptions about research and education. But we could only hold forth the hope and belief that, given the chance to study in depth and breadth with the skills of multiple disciplines, we and a growing cadre of scientists and professional colleagues everywhere could solve the fundamental questions. (Keller 1976, p. 23–4)

Though Yale Center scientists were critical of the allergy theory of alcoholism, they were extremely supportive of AA (Conrad and Schneider 1992; Wiener 1981). Given the fact that AA was not a scientific body, and was, indeed, quite cavalier about the relevance of science to their own work, we should ask why Yale Center scientists were so forthcoming with their praise. The answer is simply that, as a political measure, it behooved the Center to celebrate AA. Wiener (1981) notes that a major objective of the Yale Center was to present alcohol problems to the American public in a light that favored funding for scientific research. Two related elements of this effort were particularly crucial. First, those who suffered from drinking problems had to be cast as a sympathetic population deserving of public investment. For Yale Center researchers this meant publicizing the existence of middle-class "hidden alcoholics." This was to counter the common belief that alcoholics were nothing but a few reprehensible *others* who dwelled beyond the pale of respectable society, scavenging among society's flotsam on skid row (Beauchamp 1980; Kurtz and Regier 1975; Roman 1991; Room 1972; Wiener 1981).

Alcoholics Anonymous was a useful showcase of self-confessed alcoholics from good backgrounds who, by their very existence, testified both to the vast number of otherwise hidden alcoholics and to the fact that they were often respectable citizens and hard-working, family types. Their drinking problems were not so easy to attribute to intrinsic moral depravity as were the drinking problems of homeless skid row habitués. Thus, in a spirit reminiscent of the early temperance movement, the Alcoholism Movement proclaimed it an insult to human decency to allow good Americans to remain forsaken. Significantly, however, they did so by explicitly contrasting the middle-class "hidden alcoholics" represented by AA to the otherness and oblivion that were implicitly cast as the suitable station of homeless skid row derelicts. The disease theory of addiction was, then, in the first instance, revived to exculpate middle-class drinkers specifically in contrast to those lower class homeless *others* who dwelt on skid row (Room 1983).

The second, and related, use made of AA by Yale Center researchers was as evidence that alcoholics were not all incurable psychopaths but were sometimes amenable to rehabilitation. As Keller (1976, p. 22) observed, "Alcoholics Anonymous ... helped the Center of Alcohol Studies by reinforcing the teaching that alcoholics were not all skid row bums, that they could be rehabilitated." It is worth highlighting the reemergence here of an elective affinity between middle or upper class status and the prospect of recovery. This affinity was first observed in the Inebriate Homes of the mid-nineteenth century and continues, to this day, as a virtual truism of research on recovery rates among both treated and untreated addicts (cf. Waldorf, Reinarman, and Murphy 1991; Wallace 1990). It was evident in my research settings as well. Counselors often referred to the more promising prognosis of clients who had held jobs and had come from respectable families as opposed to those who had not. The first group, it was said, merely needed to be "*re*habilitated." The second needed to be "habilitated" from scratch.

Yale Center researchers conferred scientific legitimacy on the disease theory of alcoholism, and did much public relations work to promote this theory. But another group also emerged from the Yale Summer

School of Alcohol Studies to become important in both the promotion of the disease concept of addiction and the integration of this concept into state-sponsored responses to those deemed to suffer from alcohol and other drug problems. This group was the National Council on Alcoholism (NCA). Formed in 1944 as the National Committee for Education on Alcoholism, the NCA quickly became the largest and most powerful voluntary action organization concerned with alcohol issues in the country (Wiener 1981). The NCA was organized by Marty Mann, a publicist and one of the first female members of AA, and two colleagues from the summer school. Originally, the NCA was closely affiliated with the Yale Center but in 1950 became independent. The NCA began its efforts by adopting and promoting a four-pronged credo formulated by their first public relations officer, Dwight Anderson. Anderson (1945, p. 367) expressed the credo as follows:

> Here are four postulates: ... first, that the problem drinker is a sick man, exceptionally reactive to alcohol; second, that he can be helped; third, that he is worth helping; fourth, that the problem is therefore the responsibility of the healing profession, as well as the established health authorities, and the public generally.

This credo very clearly insists that problem drinking be viewed as evidence of an *other inside* problem drinkers from which they are capable of being freed and from which it is our duty as fellow citizens to free them. Anderson's credo was first promoted through publications, radio broadcasts, and national speaking tours undertaken by prominent members like Marty Mann. It has since been promoted through the establishment of national, state, and local chapters of the NCA which do everything from lobbying legislators, business leaders, and private individuals to support research, education, and treatment programs to providing referral services for individuals who themselves desire help for alcohol-related problems. Because AA will not lend its name to public campaigns of any kind, the NCA has become the most prominent option for AA members who wish to do public work concerning alcohol-related issues. The organization is full of volunteers who are themselves either AA members or intimately associated with someone who is an AA member. This fact has powerfully influenced the work done under the NCA aegis. Wiener (1981, p. 34) writes,

> Although grateful for the workers who come out of the ranks of AA, NCA is continually faced with distinguishing its separation from the self-help group. To illustrate: NCA prides itself on its counseling-for-referral service, but it has a constant battle getting volunteers to accept the fact that AA is not right for everyone, that alternative modes are available.

Since its inception, the NCA agitated for state financing of alcoholism treatment outside the confines of mental hospitals. Arguing that alcoholism is a disease with its own unique characteristics, the NCA insisted that alcoholics were not properly served in psychiatric settings that did not acknowledge alcoholism as an independent disorder. This, combined with the growing dominance of the AA approach throughout the Alcoholism Movement, animated efforts to garner state support for alcoholism-specific treatment programs that implemented an AA-inspired approach. The NCA won its first victory in this regard when, in the mid-forties, Connecticut established a tax-supported agency to provide treatment for alcoholics and education about alcohol problems (Room 1982; Straus 1991). Slowly, other states developed commissions to coordinate policy on alcohol problems. Small amounts of state funding became available to programs instituted specifically to treat alcohol addiction. In the fifties, halfway houses and community outpatient clinics emerged in a number of states that were sustained in part by state funds (Rubington 1977; Weisner and Room 1984). Though these facilities were staffed by a variety of helping professionals, thinking and practice regarding alcohol addiction were heavily informed by AA's twelve-step philosophy.

Despite these successes, the vast majority of homeless and impoverished inebriates remained beyond the scope of AA-inspired treatment programs. Throughout the fifties, most impoverished drunkards, or "chronic public inebriates" as they were called, still met with multiple arrests and multiple periods of incarceration in city and county jails (Pittman and Gordon 1958; Room 1978). However, amidst the political activism and reform movements of the sixties, civil liberties lawyers took an interest in the criminality of public drunkenness, and took steps to change what they deemed a repressive American tradition. Their arguments were based on the Supreme Court decision *Robinson v. California* (1962). Here, the Court resolved that in the case of opiate addiction, a person could not be punished merely because he or she suffered from an illness. Room (1976, p. 120) notes that there were several strategies that might have been implemented to attack public drunkenness laws. Hence, "[t]he adoption of the disease concept of alcoholism as the preferred strategy of defense was not an inevitable choice, and reflected the alliance of the civil-liberties lawyers with the alcoholism movement."

In two cases, *Driver v. Hinnant* (1966) and *Easter v. District of Columbia* (1966), civil liberties lawyers successfully argued that the disease of alcoholism was a valid defense to the criminal charge of public intoxication. However, two years later, in a narrow 5–4 decision, the United States

Supreme Court upheld the constitutionality of convicting an alcoholic under a state law prohibiting public drunkenness (*Powell v. Texas* 1968). This effectively returned the legal decision to prosecute public drunkenness to the states but it did not preclude the federal government from putting other kinds of pressures on the states and local municipalities to medicalize chronic drunkenness. Beginning with the federal commitment to mental health policy reform that was embodied in President Kennedy's *Community Mental Health Centers Act* (1963), a vast influx of federal funds was made available to both researchers and public service providers to improve programs dealing with mental health problems. The problems of alcoholism were not ignored. In 1966 the National Center for the Control and Prevention of Alcoholism was established as a unit within the National Institute of Mental Health (NIMH).

This federal initiative gathered major impetus when in 1968, Harold Hughes, a self-described recovering alcoholic and a member of AA, was elected to the United States Senate. Shortly following his arrival in the Senate, a Special Subcommittee on Alcoholism and Narcotics was formed in the Committee on Labor and Public Welfare, and Hughes was named its chairman (Beauchamp 1980). Hughes began holding national hearings on alcoholism and, with the backing of the NCA and others in the Alcoholism Movement, shepherded through Congress the *Comprehensive Alcohol Abuse and Alcoholism Prevention, Treatment, and Rehabilitation Act*. Under this legislation the National Institute on Alcohol Abuse and Alcoholism (NIAAA) was created in 1970 as a separate branch of the National Institutes of Health. The NIAAA was originally authorized to

> confer *formula grants* (i.e. based on a population formula) to the states in order to establish programs for treatment and prevention; *project grants* to public and private non-profit agencies to conduct demonstration projects, and provide education and training and services for the treatment of alcoholism; and *contracts* with public and private agencies for the above services. (Wiener 1981, p. 28)

The NIAAA institutionalized the disease concept of alcoholism at the federal level and provided unprecedented momentum to the AA-inspired treatment industry that was emerging throughout the country. At a more general level, the NIAAA was part of a broad escalation of federal interventions into the management of public health and welfare in the sixties and early seventies. This escalation in federal involvement put a great deal of pressure on state and local governments to reform their own programs and policies regarding not only the control of alcohol, but drug and mental health problems as well, so as to maximize their eligibility for federal funding (cf. P. Morgan 1980). In California, and in other states, federal funding reforms produced what P. Morgan (1981, p. 246) calls a "social problems apparatus," a state level bureaucracy which is charged to "manage ... problems too costly to be addressed through the welfare state alone, and too difficult to be legitimized through punitive public order policies." These novel bureaucracies developed on the cusp between the public welfare and criminal justice systems and have often served to blur distinctions between the welfare and social control functions of government.[3]

Americans who for their troubles had once been ignored or incarcerated were increasingly subjected to a wider and more ambiguous array of contacts with state agencies. But the very ambiguity of this array of contacts has served to reinforce the public suspicion, resentment, and fear that has historically fallen on impoverished recipients of the state's attentions (cf. Dear and Wolch 1987; Polsky 1991; Wolch and Dear 1993). Thus, while people who had traditionally been excluded from the political, economic, and cultural mainstream of American life began to fall more often within the scope of government agencies, their resulting status with respect to the society at large has remained liminal at best. By blending recipients of public welfare and recipients of public punishment, the state social problems apparatus served to further stigmatize, and effectively institutionalized, the otherness of many Americans whose primary offense was, and is, their poverty. These bureaucracies have proven eminently capable of adaptation to the shifting winds and tides of national, state, and local political economy.

In keeping with federal guidelines, officers of the state social problems apparatus were, and continue to be, charged to oversee the dispensation of state and federal funds by contracting out alcohol, drug, mental health, and other kinds of health services to the counties or directly to private nonprofit agencies (Weisner and Room 1984). Most counties in turn delegate a good deal of the services they are mandated to provide to private nonprofit agencies as well. Thus the availability of federal funds through formula grants, project grants, contracts, and through

3. Many researchers have shown that a blending of social control and social welfare agendas has always marked the implementation of American public welfare policies (cf. Katz 1986; Patterson 1981; Piven and Cloward 1993; Quadagno 1987). They have also noted that welfare underwent considerable expansion in the thirties and again in the sixties. I am not suggesting here that the blurring that occurred in the sixties and early seventies was somehow different in kind, only that it was significantly elaborated through new alcohol, drug, and mental health programs.

public welfare programs like Medicaid, Social Security Disability Insurance (SSDI), and Supplemental Security Income (SSI) has produced profound changes in the ways private nonprofit organizations operate as well. Two of these changes are particularly relevant to the present discussion. First, the influx of funds from federal agencies has lured what Gusfield (1989) calls "troubled persons professionals" into rather fierce competition for the available monies. A multitude of nonprofit organizations made up of professional researchers and/or service providers have emerged and evolved to effectively compete for government funding. While they have developed coalitions, constituencies, and learned to lobby effectively on their own behalf, these organizations are largely beholden to the agendas set by government funding agencies.

For nonprofit organizations primarily concerned with the provision of treatment services this has entailed carving out distinctive places for themselves within the alcohol addiction treatment system. To the extent they have opposed yielding to established medical or psychiatric criteria for proper therapeutic practice, AA-inspired programs have had to develop their own criteria of accountability to funding and referral agencies (Schmidt and Weisner 1993; Wiener 1981). They have done so largely by diverting attention from medical or psychiatric credentials toward concrete achievements with respect to the outcomes state funding and referral agencies themselves expect and demand from the treatment programs they support. Weisner (1983, pp. 120–1) notes that survival in the new system has also entailed "cultivating relationships with, and in drawing clients from health, mental health, criminal justice and welfare institutions" and goes on to suggest the reasons this has been the case:

> First, the tremendous growth in the treatment system created the perpetual need for a large enough clientele to warrant continued and even increased funding ... Second, the drive for a legitimate place within the social service bureaucracy fostered a desire for an articulate, non-marginal clientele, in contrast to the more problematic public inebriate. Third, the potential for drawing funds from a wide variety of sources often rested on the ability to expand the types of problems within an alcohol definition, and thus within the treatment system. Fourth, as it expanded, the alcohol treatment system continued to strive for respectability, often by cementing relations with other institutions.

Publicly funded alcoholism treatment programs (particularly those that operate outside a strictly medical model) have thus been pressured to serve any number of functions traditionally undertaken by the social welfare and criminal justice systems but to nevertheless do so under the auspices of the disease concept of alcohol addiction. And while they themselves are often inclined to admit a more "articulate, non-marginal clientele," which is easier to handle and presents better prospects for producing the high recovery rates so useful to sustaining funding, service providers are continually pressed to fulfill the service needs their funding agencies earmark as highest priority (P. Morgan 1981; Peyrot 1991; Schmidt and Weisner 1993; Weisner 1983; Wiener 1981). This has meant that treatment programs must be able to recreate themselves in the image of state funding priorities as these change from year to year but to do so without squandering what Bourdieu (1990) might call the symbolic capital they have invested in their identities as alcoholism treatment programs. As it happens, the concept "alcoholism" has proved a remarkably malleable framework under which to subsume a variety of different kinds of social welfare and social control interventions. Thus, the putative *others inside* participants in such programs, which are known and treated as alcohol addictions, have come to be conceptualized as profoundly complex entities that are astonishingly versatile in their abilities to wreak havoc in the lives of those who are said to suffer from them.

In 1981, Congress passed the *Omnibus Budget Reconciliation Act* which eliminated category-specific funding in the fields of alcohol, drugs, and mental health and replaced it with consolidated "block grants" that were to fund all alcohol, drug, and mental health services at the discretion of the individual states. This legislation marked the onset of a period of significant budget reductions at the federal, state, and local levels that lasted into the early nineties. As a result of these reductions, many publicly funded alcohol, drug and mental health programs were denied funding, consolidated, or forced to assume a still wider range of functions (Schmidt and Weisner 1993). Furthermore, securing access to the shrinking funding pool became a good deal more difficult. Success in this regard has become strictly contingent upon persuading funding agencies that a proposed program will effectively manage client groups that are demonstrably underserved within existing systems and who present problems that cannot be ignored by legislators and/or public agency officials. It was in this political context that Canyon House and Twilights emerged and were able to garner public support.

In addition to their direct effects on service provision, the effect that federal funding initiatives have had on *scientific research* has also been profound. The bulk of scientific research in the fields of alcoholism, illicit drugs, and mental health is funded either directly or indirectly by federal agencies and is thus beholden to the value these agencies place on some research questions rather than others. As Wiener (1981, p. 51) notes, even the shape of the agencies and the kinds of researchers who generally study public problems are heavily influenced by the social organization of federal funding:

> Requests for Proposals (RFP's) appear in *Commerce Business Daily*, published by the Department of Commerce. Access to this publication, time limits on the preparation of proposals, and the tremendous cost of preparation, all created obstacles for the smaller contractor. Advantage fell upon large consulting firms, with people one respondent characterized as "good at being experts in anything—who have perfected the art of proposal writing and can include impressive credentials on their *vitae*."

Though some of the specific details have changed since Wiener wrote this passage, her observation remains entirely valid. The Rand Corporation, under whose auspices my own study was funded, is a perfect case in point. Rand was chartered in 1948 as a nonprofit institution "to further and promote scientific, educational, and charitable purposes, all for the public welfare and security of the United States of America" (Stienberg, Lyon, and Vaiana 1992, p. iii). Originally a subsidiary of the Air Force, Rand developed a reputation as a think tank concerned mainly with matters of international policy. However, Rand researchers began to focus as well on domestic policy issues in the mid-sixties as major funding opportunities emerged for this kind of work. As an established research corporation, already well honed to compete for government funding, Rand was an opportune base from which to conduct state-funded domestic policy research. Rand scientists were among the first to secure NIAAA funding in the early seventies and have remained a major force in alcohol, drug, and mental health policy research. My own research was supported by a NIAAA demonstration project grant awarded to Rand researchers in 1990. This study would not have occurred had this funding not been made available by the NIAAA and effectively sought by Rand researchers who had "perfected the art of proposal writing and can include impressive credentials on their *vitae*." I will return to this topic in Chapter 5.

The Ascendance of the Social Model in Publicly Funded Drug Treatment

Following the almost complete eradication of medical maintenance programs in the twenties, arrest and imprisonment became all but the only public response to those who used so-called narcotic drugs. The fact that the vast majority of narcotics users were now members of the underworld or from lower class and minority backgrounds helped to make a policy based solely on punishment and social exclusion seem reasonable to most Americans. However, by the late twenties, over a third of all federal prisoners had been convicted for Harrison Act violations, and prison wardens were complaining that convicted narcotics users were overcrowding their facilities (Courtwright 2001; H.W. Morgan 1981; Musto 1987). In 1928, proposals were heard in Congress for two federal "narcotic farms" to relieve some of this burden. To promote their prospective benefits, advocates highlighted the possibility of medically treating addicts on these farms. However, in Congressional hearings the Surgeon General indicated that the Public Health Service had no interest in the proposed farms, clearly demonstrating the extent to which they reflected correctional, rather than medical, initiatives (Maddux 1978; Musto 1987).

In 1935, the first farm was established in Lexington, Kentucky. The second was established in Fort Worth, Texas, in 1938. Despite their original opposition to them, the farms were placed under the nominal jurisdiction of Public Health Service officers who administered these institutions under the watchful eyes of the Justice Department and the Federal Bureau of Narcotics (FBN). While their subordination to law enforcement agencies deeply disenchanted the physicians in charge of the farms, their placements nevertheless provided them with what proved to be very useful institutional footings from which to promote the medicalization of illicit drug addiction (Musto 1987). The leader of this effort was Dr. Lawrence C. Kolb, the first medical director at Lexington. As noted in Chapter 2, Kolb held that drug addiction is generally symptomatic of psychopathology and should therefore be treated as a medical, rather than a law enforcement, problem (Courtwright 2001; Musto 1987). To his credit, Kolb did oppose the punitive policies of the FBN, and the hysterically xenophobic propaganda unleashed by figures like the Spanish-American War hero Richmond Hobson who argued that drug addiction is a "malignant racial cancer." But Kolb was also properly criticized for the veiled moralism of his own theories. Alfred Lindesmith (1940, p. 920), for example, argued that Kolb's " 'scientific' theories of drug addiction are more adequately understood in terms of the emotional attitudes they express than in terms of the evidence. [His] theories reflect the unfavorable prestige position of addicts in the class hierarchy." Thus even by the lights of Kolb's ostensibly medical perspective, illicit drug addicts were still portrayed as intrinsically inferior *others* with little prospect of inclusion in the American moral community.

After 1936 the narcotic farms were officially called hospitals but they were plainly organized as prison facilities—complete with bared doors, windows, and corridors, strict security regulations, and inmate uniforms. Medical treatment was limited to detoxification, work, and a bit of psychotherapy for the minority of inmates willing and able to transgress the "convict code" that specified noncooperation with institutional authorities (cf. Hughes 1966; Jansen 1966; Maddux 1978). In principle, therapeutic benefits were also held to flow from the mere fact of confinement to a drug-free environment. But hospital staff were quite aware of the dismal relapse statistics on those who did time on the farms. As medical scientists they remained attentive to therapeutic innovations and carried out exploratory clinical research of their own. Nevertheless, medical techniques for coping with illicit drug addiction changed little in the years between 1935 and 1960. Indeed, the climate of medical research and treatment became worse in the early fifties. In the midst of a nationalistic clamor epitomized by McCarthyist witch-hunts for alleged communists (and any other group who might conceivably undermine the nation's moral tone), mandatory minimum sentences were decreed and escalated for drug-related crimes at both the federal and state levels (Musto 1987). The fear and distrust that had pervaded the treatment of drug users throughout the country increased while the number of prisoners sent to the narcotic farms swelled well beyond their capacity.

In order to maximize inmate contact with a limited number of staff clinicians, group therapy was initiated at Fort Worth in 1950 and at Lexington in 1951 (Jansen 1966; Maddux 1978). Though they were implemented first as a pragmatic necessity, group methods slowly evolved into explicitly featured principles of therapeutic practice on the farms. The self-conscious emphasis of group processes and the therapeutic relevance of the milieux at the federal narcotics hospitals reflected a more pervasive influence of social psychiatry throughout the mental health professions in the fifties (cf. Bloor McKeganey, Fonkert 1988; Caudill 1958; Dunham and Weinberg 1960; Jones 1952; Stanton and Schwartz 1954). However, at Fort Worth, a more specific justification for group therapy emerged in the early sixties (Tittle and Tittle 1963). To quote the Deputy Chief of the Addiction Treatment Service at Fort Worth,

> Our treatment staff is indebted to the recent studies of two graduate students in sociology for helping us to understand the origin of resistance to group therapy in our institution. They found a negative attitude toward

psychotherapy to be more often held by those patients who adhered to a prisoner value system or the so-called "prison code." The important result of this study was that our clinical staff, trained to view our treatment problems and goals from an intrapersonal and interpersonal frame of reference, turned toward the literature and concepts of the prison sociologist for possible answers to clinical problems. (Hughes 1966, pp. 91–2)

Hughes (1966) went on to note that the clinical staff's receptivity to making patients themselves "therapeutic agents" was largely responsive to their acknowledgment of the role played by the convict code in scuddling treatment. Hughes' emphasis of the convict code suggests his willingness to let inmates exercise therapeutic authority was driven less by a respect for their insights into the nature and management of addiction, than by a concern to divide the ranks of what he and his colleagues regarded as a hostile and criminal culture (see also Shelly 1966). Given the popularity of the therapeutic community model throughout psychiatry in the fifties and early sixties we should avoid overstating the importance of public officials' sense of the convict code. However, it would be equally foolhardy to interpret their receptivity to social model themes as merely reflecting a renaissance of the democratic spirit in psychiatric thought and practice. Concerns to improve control over inmates were also plainly evident.

The high rates of relapse among former narcotic farm residents impressed upon professionals in the field the need for continuing surveillance of drug offenders once they were returned to the community. Their interest in aftercare dovetailed, in the fifties, with a growing emphasis of community care in mental health and of parole and diversion in corrections (Rothman 1980). Though certainly influenced by intellectual trends in the mental health professions and criminology, these emphases were also driven by government officials impressed by the reduced costs that community care/control seemed to promise (Scull 1984). One embodiment of the confluence of psychiatric and correctional interest in community care/control was the advent of a more intrapersonal focus among parole officers, or what Simon (1993) calls "clinical parole." Another was the rise of civil commitment facilities where narcotics users were detained for the specified purpose of treatment and diverted from routine criminal justice processing (Anglin 1988; McGlothlin 1976). A third was the emergence of halfway houses for various populations who had formerly been incarcerated. By the early sixties, a spirit of innovation and experimentation in community-based programs for various kinds of dangerous, disruptive, and/or dependent populations had spread throughout the country.

According to Sugarman (1974, p. 9), it was in efforts to "initiate some new method of helping drug offenders that would be more effective than the then prevailing routines of incarceration, detoxification, and probation or parole" that New York state probation authorities began exploring innovative models and thereby happened upon Synanon, the self-help program founded in Santa Monica, California, in 1958. With a grant from the NIMH, the Probation Department of New York's Second Judicial District (Brooklyn and Staton Island) founded Daytop Lodge in 1963. Daytop was the first state-funded drug abuse treatment program based explicitly on the Synanon "concept," and its founding marked the introduction of recovering addicts themselves as key contributors to the formulation and management of drug addiction in state-sponsored agencies (cf. Hubbard et al. 1989). This event inaugurated the practice of making former illicit drug addicts paid counselors in state-funded programs. Moreover, for the first time in American history, clients were themselves recognized as potentially possessing valuable insights into the nature of their own and each other's addictions. Though they were a good deal more authoritarian than AA, publicly funded therapeutic communities based on the Synanon concept nevertheless reflected a major departure from the state's traditional criminal justice approach to managing narcotic drug problems.

The Synanon concept was developed by Charles "Chuck" Dederich, and was based on his rather loose adaptation of the insights he had learned in AA to a residential setting catering mainly to homeless, impoverished, and criminally active drug users. Dederich rejected the theory that drug addicts were incurable psychopaths and, in doing so, anticipated, and quite likely encouraged, more optimistic and inclusive methods for dealing with people thought to suffer from drug addictions. But unlike Narcotics Anonymous (which began to apply AA principles directly to the management of drug addictions in 1953), Dederich did not endorse the allergy theory of addiction or in any way try to exonerate addicts from responsibility for their drug problems. Instead of casting their problems as products of an *other inside* them for which they should *not* be held directly responsible, Dederich construed addicts as indeed very much responsible for the problems their drug use had caused. Synanon devotees took the view that drug addicts were simply immature or stupid. They just needed further parenting and education regarding the responsibilities that adult life entails (Yablonsky 1965). Crucially, however, though practicing addicts were still regarded as morally deficient beings, their deficiencies were nonetheless treated as matters they themselves were capable of remedying.

Synanon insisted that addicts behave "responsibly," and conform to the dictates set by their superiors in the program. While often rigidly hierarchical and disciplinarian, Synanon "concept" houses are fundamentally premised on making inductees feel the warmth and community they might expect to feel as members of a family (Frye 1986; Skoll 1992; Sugarman 1974; Yablonsky 1965). In principle, inductees are accepted into the house community so long as they demonstrate their willingness to submit to the quasi-parental authority of ranking residents and counselors. This has traditionally entailed contributing to the maintenance of the house, exhibiting an enthusiastic willingness to partake in the collective life of the house, and striving to overcome one's personal deficits as these are assessed by one's "brothers and sisters" in the house.[4] Those perceived as remiss in any of these areas have historically been subject to confrontations, or "haircuts," wherein they are publicly accused and reprimanded in house meetings called "games." During a game, transgressors are submitted to merciless dressings down, forced to acknowledge the shortcoming[s] for which they are being charged, and sentenced to a penalty that usually involves some sort of public humiliation. Following this ceremony, they are reassured that they are still loved, are not regarded as inherently different from anyone else in the house, and will remain welcome as long as they genuinely strive to toe the line (Sugarman 1974; Weppner 1983; Yablonsky 1965). Many have found the extreme emotions evoked in these encounters to catalyze profound self-revelations and personal bonds. However, others have found them intolerable and "split" from programs where they are forced to participate in such rituals. Programs influenced by Synanon still rely on "games" and other grueling methods for motivating personal change, but many have toned down the feverish pitch that had routinely been reached in earlier days (Institute of Medicine 1990).

4. Synanon eschewed categorical distinctions between counselors and clients, insisting that everyone living in the house should play both of these roles. Therefore, rather than defining the rights and obligations of staff in contrast to those of clients, programs that have followed the Synanon concept have usually tried to invoke authority in terms of a continuous hierarchy that extends from the most recent newcomer to the most senior administrator. In principle, program participants could come to hold any position in the hierarchy. However, as the therapeutic community movement has expanded, diversified, and come to include more professional and para-professional clinicians, this principle has come to be implemented with various degrees of orthodoxy.

State-funded programs that integrated or adapted elements of the Synanon concept began to proliferate in the mid-sixties, thanks primarily to the federal government's stepping up of support for programs that managed narcotics offenders beyond the confines of the traditional criminal justice system. Because of the increased severity of antidrug laws, jails and prisons had become overcrowded with narcotics offenders, encouraging authorities to grow more receptive to alternative approaches (Klien 1983). Furthermore, critiques of the cruelty and ineffectuality of draconian criminal justice policies had been growing louder since the late fifties (Lindesmith 1961; Peyrot 1984). Economic prosperity, increasing middle and upper class liberalism, and growing political activism among marginalized Americans also combined to promote what became a broad increase in federal welfare expenditures during the sixties and early seventies. These factors catalyzed several dramatic innovations in the ways illicit drug users were treated in state-sponsored agencies.

The beginnings of a movement away from punitive criminal justice approaches had been evident at the federal level as early as 1962. In that year the United States Supreme Court determined that merely suffering from the disease of narcotic addiction is not a criminal offense (*Robinson v. California* 1962). Federal support for therapeutic approaches was made more tangibly evident in 1966 when Congress passed the *Narcotic Addict Rehabilitation Act* (NARA). This legislation enabled provision of federal funds for community-based supervision and treatment of narcotics addicts. In keeping with this trend, the *Community Mental Health Centers Act* was amended in 1968 to explicitly provide for the treatment of drug (and alcohol) addicts in federally funded community mental health centers. At about the same time, the Office of Economic Opportunity began to support "multimodal" community-based programs for treating addictions (Institute of Medicine 1990). These programs, together with their counterparts in community mental health centers, inaugurated the practice of systematically individualizing treatment in state-sponsored programs and expanded the range of social and personal issues considered clinically relevant to drug addiction. In doing so, they legitimized the idea that drug addictions stem from a complex patchwork of social structural, interpersonal, and intrapersonal problems, which take unique forms for particular people and are likely to change over time. This idea remains, to this day, a robust feature of the "biopsychosocial model" of clinical care. Thus, much like their counterparts in the field of state-sponsored alcoholism treatment, proponents of the biopsychosocial model in the field of state-sponsored narcotic drug treatment came to conceptualize addictions as remarkably complex entities that are extremely versatile in their abilities to wreak havoc in people's lives. The biopsychosocial model has been extremely influential in programs that are staffed by recovering counselors and emphasize mutual help themes—that is, programs like Canyon House and Twilights.

Federal funding for drug treatment programs continued to increase at a remarkable rate during the late sixties and early seventies, reaching an apogee of $300 million in 1974. After 1974, funding tapered slightly but remained reasonably stable until 1981 (Institute of Medicine 1990). This period saw the growth of a rather massive government infrastructure at the federal, state, and local levels, which in many ways paralleled developments in the field of alcoholism treatment. Federal agencies, most notably the National Institute on Drug Abuse (NIDA), were formed to oversee and administer federal policy regarding research and treatment. Similarly, bureaucracies were formed at the state and local levels to oversee and administer state and local drug policy. Researchers and service providers organized to compete for available funding and those that survived became adept at recreating themselves in the image of changing public funding priorities (Peyrot 1991). When, in 1981, Congress passed the *Omnibus Budget Reconciliation Act*, they effectively eliminated much of the federal funding upon which existing programs had relied. This sent shock waves through each of the affected fields. Widespread closures, consolidations, and reorganizations of both public and private agencies occurred throughout the alcohol, drug, and mental health fields.

Most significantly for this analysis, block grants set in motion a merger of the alcoholism and drug abuse treatment fields into the one field of "substance abuse" or "the addictions" (Schmidt and Weisner 1993; Weisner 1992). In order to save on administrative costs, most states, including California, fused their drug and alcohol bureaucracies. Many counties did the same. In 1986, merger of the drug addiction and alcoholism treatment fields was further encouraged by passage of the *Anti-Drug Abuse Act*, which authorized major increases in federal funding for treatment programs that served illicit drug users. This legislation pushed many treatment programs that had formerly served an exclusively alcoholic population into accepting clients with illicit drug problems in order to qualify for support as "weapons" in the federal "war on drugs." Further federal legislation in 1988 provided still more funding for drug treatment and further inducements for mergers. Whereas in 1982 only 26 percent of the substance abuse treatment programs in the United States served both alcohol and drug clients, in 1990 a full 76 percent of them did so (Schmidt and Weisner 1993, p. 381). In a dramatic symbolic gesture to the magnitude of these developments, the National Council on Alcoholism changed its name to the National Council on Alcohol and Drug Dependency.

These changes were more than merely nominal and organizational. A *conceptual* merger occurred in the discourse of public policy makers, clinicians, researchers, and public advocates as well. In 1987, the diagnostic criteria for drug and alcohol problems became identical for the first time, and were listed under the one heading "psychoactive substance disorder" in the revised version of the *Diagnostic and Statistical Manual, Third Edition* (American Psychiatric Association 1987). Though it seems undeniable that these institutional and conceptual changes were primarily responsive to federal funding mandates, they were also responsive to changes among prospective client populations. Beginning in the early eighties, epidemiological studies showed a consistent pattern of multiple drug use and abuse among those found to suffer alcohol-related problems. The "pure alcoholic" was, in other words, becoming a less common client profile. Independent of funding pressures, this no doubt encouraged clinicians to expand the scope of their therapeutic foci. Weisner (1992) has warned that the merger of the alcohol and drug addiction fields may negatively influence the public image of alcoholics by blurring the distinction between them and illicit drug addicts. By the same token though, we might also expect to see some small improvement in the public image of illicit drug addicts by virtue of their association with the less marginalized personae of alcoholics. My fieldwork suggests this merger may have helped to extend the view that illicit drug addiction, no less than alcohol addiction, is evidence of a bona fide *other inside* those who suffer. This marks an important change from both the criminal justice approach and orthodox concept houses, both of which see drug abuse in terms of intrinsic personality flaws. By attributing drug addicts' troubles to an *other inside* them, program members might now more effectively preserve a sense of addicts' moral and psychological integrity (and thereby strive to facilitate their inclusion in the American moral community) to a greater extent than was possible in earlier eras.

Deinstitutionalization, Community Mental Health, and Biopsychiatry

Until World War II, American institutional psychiatry had been suffering a rather dismal stasis and had, in many respects, been deteriorating outright. The mental hygiene movement and psychoanalysis, with their apparent theoretical vitality and wealthier clienteles, had lured away many of the discipline's best and brightest. These movements had also promoted the growth of new disciplines like social work and clinical psychology that began to exercise their own influences on the American regard for mental health (Grob 1983; Rothman 1980). These developments had little impact, however, among the majority of psychiatrists, who continued to face the daunting task of managing throngs of impoverished Americans with seemingly intractable problems in the dilapidated wards of state mental hospitals. Most asylum inmates were not thought capable of serious improvement given available therapeutic technologies. The vanguard of psychiatric research, moving as it was toward less severe forms of disorder, promised little hope of improvement in this regard.[5] Having long since lost control over the number, types, and circumstances of patients admitted to and released from their facilities (Gronfein 1985a), institutional psychiatrists were reduced to little more than administrators of custodial warehouses wherein the country's most dependent, least understood, and least manageable people were stored.

Widespread disaffection among psychiatrists with their professional niche (and with their conceptual and therapeutic armamentarium) was indisputable when Dr. William C. Menninger and several like-minded colleagues founded the Group for Advancement of Psychiatry (GAP) in 1946. Menninger had been chief of the army's Neuropsychiatry division during the war. Like many of his colleagues who had served, practicing psychiatry in the context of battle convinced Menninger of a causal connection between environmental stress and mental illness. It also persuaded him of the value in early interventions and the viability

5. During the thirties, many institutional psychiatrists found a modicum of hope in the therapeutic prospects of radical somatic treatments like insulin shock, though they bore no relationship to the prevailing scientific wisdom regarding the nature of mental disorder. Even this small hope was chastened though when news of the horrible lengths to which Nazi psychiatrists had taken somatic interventions, and the spirit in which they had done so, finally reached across the Atlantic (Grob 1994).

of treatment without institutionalization. After the war, he began promoting these ideas among his civilian colleagues (Menninger 1948). In the years just after World War II, the GAP succeeded in thoroughly shaking up their discipline. Their work catalyzed a revitalization of the American Psychiatric Association, publication of the first edition of the Diagnostic and Statistical Manual of Mental Disorders (DSM I), and the assumption of control over virtually every university department of psychiatry in the country by psychiatrists with psychodynamic and psychoanalytic sympathies (Grob 1991a; Kirk and Kutchins 1992). Most importantly, they succeeded in moving many of their colleagues to shed the largely ineffective, indeterminate, and hitherto fairly unwarranted faith in somaticism that had dominated professional psychiatry since before the turn of the century.

Lending popular support to this intraprofessional loss of faith in institutional psychiatry, several lay exposés of mental hospitals achieved notoriety during the forties as well (Rochefort 1993). Journalist Albert Deutsch, though sympathetic to asylum psychiatrists themselves, was by no means gentle in his condemnations of state hospitals (cf. Deutsch 1948). Albert Maisel's photographs in *Life* magazine of VA mental wards (Maisel 1946), the accounts of journalist/activist Mike Gorman, and Mary Jane Ward's novel *The Snake Pit* (and the acclaimed film based on it) each contributed to a pervasive sense of serious misgiving regarding the state of America's provisions for the mentally ill. Interestingly enough, however, these works tended not to hold psychiatrists themselves culpable. Their criticisms were focused instead on the stinginess of state governments and the indifference of the American people (Grob 1994; Isaac and Armat 1990). The sad plight of asylum inmates, then, was not cast as a technical failure of psychiatric medicine but as the reactionary withdrawal, that is, the moral failure, of better-off Americans from the duties of citizenship.

At the same time, the apparent successes of the New Deal and the American experience in World War II had fostered a popular faith in the value of federal leadership on social problems, like the plight of the mentally ill, that were seen as national in scope. This growing popular regard for federalism was astutely recognized and turned to advantage by psychiatrists affiliated with the Division of Mental Hygiene (DMH) in the United States Public Health Service. The DMH had existed since 1930 but its mandate was confined to the field of narcotic drug addiction. Toward the close of World War II, though, officials within the DMH sensed the time had become propitious for organizing efforts to expand the scope of their authority. In the early forties, soon after he succeeded Lawrence C. Kolb as head of the DMH, Robert H. Felix embarked on an ardent campaign to expand the federal role in dictating policy regarding the nation's mental health. Both politically savvy and connected, Felix was well suited for the job. His first major success was the *National Mental Health Act* in 1946. This legislation provided federal funds for mental health research and training and made modest provisions as well for the funding of clinics and treatment centers. It also helped to get state and local officials more interested in the new ideas that were attracting attention in Washington. Most significantly, it provided for the founding of the National Institute of Mental Health (NIMH), which formally opened its doors in 1949 with Felix as its director. The NIMH became a rallying point for a new generation of leaders in American psychiatry bent on moving their profession beyond the confines of the asylum and beyond the narrow somaticism of their predecessors (Grob 1991b).

Beyond the personal predelictions of its leadership, the very fact that the NIMH was organized primarily to oversee the funding of research proved influential in moving psychiatry in new directions as well. NIMH officials had to develop scientific criteria for evaluating the merits of the research proposals they received. This attention to scientific method and research design proved advantageous to scholars in the social sciences quite independently of the fact that their agendas happened to resonate with those of the NIMH leadership. Categories of psychiatric disorder in the fifties amounted to little more than vague descriptions of behavioral symptoms and, as such, were not easily brought to heel before biological research agendas (Grob 1994). Unlike their medically trained colleagues, social scientists did not face the conceptually thorny task of relating behavioral abnormalities to physical pathologies. Specifically trained, as they were, in methods of rigorous research design, and armed with operational theories regarding the social causes of deviant behavior, social scientists were well equipped to effectively solicit research funding from the NIMH. Among the earliest projects funded by the NIMH were several ethnographic studies of mental hospital life which, at least in academic circles, proved immensely influential (cf. Goffman 1961; Stanton and Schwartz 1954). Ethnographies that richly described patterns of daily life on the wards of mental hospitals and detailed the specific ways in which these routines served to *dehumanize* hospital inmates gave powerful scientific support to the view that the social environment could and should be a central focus for those concerned to understand and remedy insanity.

Before they were touted by those intent only to close mental hospitals, these insights informed efforts to revitalize mental hospitals and to *rehumanize* hospital inmates by returning to them the dignity, self-reliance, and sense of moral community that had been denied to them under earlier regimes. The principles of moral treatment reemerged in the fifties under the guise of the therapeutic community movement in psychiatric care (cf. Belknap 1956; Caudill 1958; Dunham and Weinberg 1960; Greenblatt, York, and Brown 1955; Jones 1952; Stanton and Schwartz 1954). Staff/client ratios improved in many hospitals, allowing for more interpersonal contact and more personalized methods of therapy. Furthermore, significant increases in per capita expenditures also served to improve the quality of institutional care in many facilities (Grob 1994). But despite tangible improvements in many state hospitals, institutional care remained in extremely poor favor among those associated with the burgeoning community mental health movement. To those convinced they were on the brink of a new age in mental health care, fostering only a "sense of community" within the walls of state hospitals seemed a terribly inadequate substitute for a genuine return to "the community" that they piously believed linked those who lived beyond the hospitals' walls.

Thanks to their connections within the federal government, prominent psychiatrists like Felix and Menninger did much to push their profession into the political limelight and garner federal support for major psychiatric reforms. Their interests in environmental antecedents and remedies and their emphases of the public health, more than strictly clinical, dimensions of psychiatry gave shape to reform proposals that were heard at this time. Nevertheless, the history of modern American psychiatry cannot be properly understood as a history shaped only by "great men." As noted earlier, these men undertook their work in a context of widespread dissatisfaction within the psychiatric profession as a whole, lay critiques of institutional psychiatry had lent public salience to the problem, and the two decades following World War II were unusually favorable to the inauguration of federal programs. In addition to these factors, we must add at least three others that were key catalysts to the transformation of psychiatric care in the fifties and sixties. These were: (1) the invention of new chemotherapies, (2) the efforts of civil liberties lawyers to limit involuntary commitment of the mentally ill, and, most importantly, (3) the individual state's interests in delegating the financial burden of caring for the mentally ill to the federal government.

In 1954 the Food and Drug Administration approved a request from the pharmaceutical company Smith, Kline and French to begin marketing the drug chlorpromazine under the trade name Thorazine (Gronfein 1985b). The company immediately undertook a massive effort to introduce the drug to institutional psychiatry. In Scull's words,

> both state legislators and state hospital staffs were bombarded with a hail of sophisticated propaganda designed to convince them of the virtues and advantages of the drug as a cheap, effective form of treatment suitable for administration on a mass basis to mental hospital patients. (Scull 1984, p. 81)

This campaign paid off handsomely for Smith, Kline and French, increasing their total annual earnings in two years by more than three hundred percent (Gronfein 1985b). Thorazine's appeal among institutional psychiatrists was its apparent capacity to placate the most disturbed and dangerous patients. Prior to Thorazine, the most disturbed patients were essentially left to aggregate on the back wards, isolated in their own reveries. After Thorazine, such patients could be found interacting both with staff and other patients. Many patients whose unintelligibility and/or social withdrawal had rendered them wholly *other* to their captors, seemed now, thanks to Thorazine, capable of modest reentries into civil communion (Swazey 1974). Of course, their ostensible successes were generally quite modest, but given the desperation of earlier times, they were often hailed as glorious triumphs. It was thanks, in part, to the enthusiasm sparked by Thorazine and similar drugs that the prospect of a revitalized asylum reemerged in the fifties as a potentially realizable goal (Grob 1994; Gronfein 1985b; Swazey 1974).

But beyond lending momentum to the therapeutic community movement among institutional psychiatrists, the new drugs were also of rhetorical value to Robert Felix and his allies in the movement to replace state hospitals with community mental health facilities. Though originally cautious in their reception to the new drugs, psychoanalysts and social psychiatrists eventually embraced them as rhetorical resources in their push toward deinstitutionalization (Grob 1994; Isaac and Armat 1990). If tranquilizing drugs could render the most violently disturbed fit for civil interaction within state hospitals, why could they not also do so without the hospitals? Thusly, with only the slightest scientific justification, did claims of revolutionary advances in psychopharmacology become a staple feature of the campaign for a nationally orchestrated community mental health network (Gronfein 1985b). These claims very likely served to quell the concerns of many who might have otherwise opposed the deinstitutionalization of hospitalized mental patients.

Beyond their influence on public policy, these events profoundly affected modern clinical practice as well. Pharmacological therapies became integral to what President Kennedy called the "bold new approach" in American mental health care. During the late fifties and sixties many psychiatrists involved with the community mental health movement began to routinely combine "talk" and pharmacological therapies, and to supplement them with a wider range of community support services. This therapeutic eclecticism has since become standard practice. The important point to keep in mind here is that this eclecticism in psychiatric care was not driven, in the first instance, by scientific insights regarding the nature of insanity. Instead it was spawned by the eminently pragmatic concerns of mental hospital staffs to suppress *social* disorder on their wards and the concerns of psychiatric reformers to persuade public policy makers that community care was a tenable goal for even the most violently disturbed patients. As will be shown, they also implicated the concerns of fiscal conservatives to reduce the public costs of caring for the impoverished mentally ill. The production of theoretical models of insanity designed to scientifically account for the efficacy of contemporary psychiatric techniques is thus, at best, post hoc and, at worst, an obfuscation of the actual processes through which these therapeutic techniques became alloyed.

While the rolls of state mental hospitals had been slowly shrinking since the mid-fifties, and prototypical community clinics were already sprouting up throughout the country, the event that marked the turning of this trend into a veritable revolution in American psychiatry was President Kennedy's signing of the *Community Mental Health Centers Act* into law in 1963 (Mechanic and Rochefort 1990; Segal and Aviram 1978). It was with this event that deinstitutionalization and community psychiatry were transformed from popular agendas within the mental health professions into explicitly codified national policy. The *Act* mandated construction of community mental health centers (CMHCs), which were envisioned to replace the traditional state hospitals as the locus of mental health care in America (Isaac and Armat 1990; Torrey 1988). It also introduced an unprecedented federal commitment of time and money to the management of the nation's mental health. State and local mental health bureaucracies were modified in accordance with federal guidelines (and to administer federal funds) and the mental health professions were mobilized to fulfill the new national agenda.

Embodying, as they did, the pervasive emphases placed on prevention and early intervention, the mental health professionals who came to oversee and to staff CMHCs gave broad scope to the kinds of problems that properly fell within their clinical jurisdiction. In doing so they effectively blurred the line between putatively severe forms of psychiatric disorder and less severe "problems in living" (Dunham 1976). They nevertheless remained committed to the view that mental illnesses were properly understood as genuine diseases (Conrad and Schneider 1992). Thus, in a manner that paralleled concurrent developments in the substance abuse treatment industry, insanities came to be conceptualized in CMHCs as *others inside* people that were extremely versatile in their abilities to wreak havoc in people's lives. No matter what their specific forms, however, mental disorders were understood to develop progressively, primarily in response to environmental stressors. This sense of the phenomena warranted a clinical emphasis on minimizing environmental stressors, early detection, and early intervention. It also diverted professional attention away from those whose problems had already become serious and chronic features of their lives (Kirk and Therrien 1975; Morrisey 1982; Torrey 1988).

CMHCs were originally intended to replace state hospitals, but as they were transformed from blueprints into realities it soon became clear that they were not going to do so. Not only were they improperly organized to deal with the types of problems that afflicted released or prospective state hospital patients, but CMHC staffers soon proved largely uninterested in working with the very disturbed (Grob 1994; Gronfein 1985b; Kirk and Therrien 1975; Torrey 1988). Official notice of the problem was evident as early as 1967 (Isaac and Armat 1990), but responses were slow in coming. The flight of psychiatrists from CMHCs served to further exacerbate things. When funding waned, and it became clear that responsibility for the most severely disturbed clients would be theirs, most psychiatrists fled for more rewarding, lucrative, and tranquil pastures. Those psychiatrists who remained soon found themselves doing primarily administrative work and writing prescriptions (Isaac and Armat 1990; Torrey 1988). The failure of CMHCs to forge adequate links with state hospitals and their unwillingness (and incapacity) to serve the needs of those who became known as "chronic patients" resulted in the production of an entirely new federal program to fill the gap. In 1977 the NIMH launched the Community Support Program, which began distributing funds to help the states facilitate the adjustment of those deemed chronically mentally ill to life outside the hospital (cf. Grusky et al. 1985). This program met with a modicum of success and has made important contributions to the American public mental health system—primarily by promoting and refining the technique of case management. The case management approach was clearly evident in both of my programs, particularly in Twilights, the nonresidential program.

Though spokespeople for the community mental health movement took much credit for reducing the rolls of state hospitals, the sources of these reductions were, in fact, elsewhere. The primary source appears to have been the passage of amendments to the Social Security Act in 1965 which, among other things, authorized two programs—Medicare and Medicaid—to fund medical care for the aged and the poor (Grob 1994; Gronfein 1985a). Regulations on the use of Medicare and Medicaid encouraged states to send mental hospital patients to nursing homes, board and care facilities, and so-called welfare hotels. The availability of Medicare, Medicaid, and eventually SSI, and SSDI also provided incentives to prospective operators of such facilities to begin speculating in what Scull (1981) has called a "new trade in lunacy."[6] Almost immediately following the implementation of Medicaid and Medicare, release of mental patients from the state hospitals began to accelerate at an unprecedented rate. Nursing homes, board and care facilities, welfare hotels, and the like began to spring up throughout the United States to take advantage of the newly favorable market that had emerged for their services (Emerson, Rochford, and Shaw 1981; Gronfein 1985a; Scull 1981; Segal and Aviram 1978).

In order to maximize profits, proprietors have tended to offer only the bare minimum in accommodations and services. However, as competition has grown fiercer some have sought to court the favors of their

---

6. This highlights the complexity of issues pertaining to the membership of those deemed mentally ill in the American moral community. On the one hand, one might reasonably suggest that providing people with entitlements and/or disability insurance is clear evidence of efforts to confer citizenship rights upon them and to facilitate their adjustment and inclusion into the American moral community. On the other hand, these provisions have spawned resistance from local communities to entitlement recipients settling in their midst, and have clearly stimulated a dehumanizing impulse in the form of what some have called the "comodification" of the mentally ill (Emerson, Rochford, and Shaw 1981; Scull 1981; Segal and Aviram 1978). If we are to fully grasp the extent to which, and the manner in which, putatively mentally ill Americans are socially included and excluded, we must appreciate the multiple levels at which their inclusion and exclusion, and indeed their humanization and dehumanization, are realized (Segal and Baumohl 1980; Segal, Baumohl, and Johnson 1977; van Steenbergen 1994).

clients, their referral sources, and public funding agencies by catering to their respective wants and needs (Emerson, Rochford, and Shaw 1981). Such efforts have sometimes resulted in improvements but, because they are tempered by the availability of government funding, improvements are generally modest. The spread of these facilities has created a process of "transinstitutionalization" (as opposed to deinstitutionalization), wherein individuals once isolated inside huge, state-operated custodial institutions are now isolated in smaller custodial institutions whose operation is nominally private but essentially reliant on government funding (cf. Dear and Wolch 1987; Scull 1981; Torrey 1988; Warren 1981). Even more ominously, because of inadequate services and follow-up, many prospective clients either cannot or will not use these facilities and are thus left to fend for themselves (Hopper, Baxter, and Cox 1982). Lacking adequate incomes, social skills, and/or support networks, these people often fall through the cracks of extant private and public support systems (Segal, Baumohl, and Johnson 1977), only to take their place among the nation's homeless and most destitute.

Beginning in the mid-sixties civil liberties lawyers undertook to limit the involuntary commitment of the mentally ill. This also significantly shaped how poor Americans deemed mentally ill are currently understood and managed. In California, the fruits of these efforts are embodied primarily in the *Lanterman-Petris-Short Act* (LPS) which was passed in 1967, put into effect in 1969, and modified in 1974. Segal and Aviram (1978, p. 46) suggest that this law "was supported by what has been called an unholy alliance of liberals and conservatives. The liberals saw in the law an opportunity to guarantee patients' civil liberties and to improve treatment. The conservatives thought it would lead to a reduction of state expenditures in areas that should be the responsibility of local communities."

Stated briefly, the LPS was designed to ensure that prospective mental patients' legal and civil rights were safeguarded, and to shift the responsibility for treatment from the state to local communities (Morrissey 1982; Segal and Aviram 1978). By making involuntary commitment more difficult, it was intended to limit the role played by state hospitals. The LPS also prompted passage of the *Community Mental Health Services Act* in 1968 which provided funding for county-based mental health services, brought the state hospitals and local community mental health facilities together into one overall service system, and authorized county mental health directors to decide which agencies would assume which responsibilities (Morrissey 1982). By so funding and politically empowering counties, this legislation eliminated many of the fiscal and political incentives that local communities once had for "dumping" difficult patients onto the rosters of state hospitals and legally enforced a community-based system of managing the impoverished and mentally ill.

Pertaining to the conceptualization of insanity, these developments have forced publicly funded mental health care agencies to emphasize issues broadly related to the tenability of their clients' lives in the community over narrowly construed psychiatric symptomologies (Emerson 1989; Estroff 1981; Holstein 1987, 1993). Indeed, decisions as to whether these agencies continue to receive public funding are usually predicated on their demonstrable successes with respect to clients' vocational involvement, housing status, arrest history, involuntary hospitalizations, physical health, or other like measures of the tenability of clients' community living arrangements. Hence, there are powerful pressures to deal with clients' putative mental health problems primarily by fostering and preserving the tenability (as defined by their funding sources) of clients' adjustments to community living and only secondarily in terms of the kinds of diagnostic issues that preoccupy academic psychiatrists (Brown 1987; Kirk and Kutchins 1992; Pepper and Ryglewicz 1984; Rhodes 1991). At Canyon House and Twilights this meant that the insanities and addictions of program participants were construed primarily in terms of their having threatened, or potential to threaten, the tenability of clients' unique community living arrangements. Though psychiatric symptoms of the traditional sort were by no means irrelevant to such determinations, they were considered less important and were, in any event, rarely distinguished from broader determinations of tenability. The specific details of how such determinations were made at Canyon House and Twilights will be addressed in Part II.

A final matter that has powerfully influenced how insanities were construed in my research settings is the return of biopsychiatry in the seventies. Kirk and Kutchins (1992, p. 10) suggest this return was responsive to two problems that plagued psychiatry during the community mental health era. The first problem stemmed from the profusion of mental health professions that came to compete with psychiatry in the market for outpatient psychotherapy. During the community mental health era, psychiatrists partially abandoned their claim to a special expertise rooted in medicine, and nonmedical mental health professions like psychology and social work ceased to look very different from psychiatry. Clinical psychologists and social workers took their place alongside psychiatrists in the CMHCs and competed with psychiatrists for clients in private practice as well. In addition to competition from non-medical mental health professionals, psychiatrists were also plagued by their marginal status in medicine itself. Psychodynamic and psychoanalytic approaches to psychiatry failed to live up to the image of science and rational clinical judgment favored among psychiatry's sister disciplines in American medical schools (Kirk and Kutchins 1992; Mirowsky and Ross 1989). A return to biological concepts of insanity was regarded good medicine for both of these problems.

Additional factors also promoted a return to biopsychiatry. Well-publicized attacks on the scientific legitimacy of psychiatry by antipsychiatrists like Thomas Szasz had their effect. The seeming failures of psychodynamic and psychoanalytic models to cope with the problems suffered by chronic patients disillusioned many mental health professionals (Grob 1994). Bader (1989) suggests that biological explanations provide psychosocial therapists with invaluable accounts for their inability to help certain clients. They also provide solace to the families of people who ostensibly suffer from mental disorders. Psychodynamic theories profoundly implicate mothers and fathers in the etiology of their children's problems. Biological theories do not. Unsurprisingly, biological models are heavily favored by groups like the National Alliance for the Mentally Ill (NAMI) that are comprised predominantly of patients' family members. These groups have become powerful players in the politics of American mental health (Mechanic 1989). And lastly, while psychodynamic theories were losing their appeal among those providing care to the seemingly most disturbed, greater publicity was being heaped upon the clinical powers of chemotherapies.

Lithium, in particular, was widely touted as effective with patients diagnosed with bipolar disorders (then called manic-depression). Furthermore, the observation that lithium did little to help with schizophrenia lent credence to the view that mental illnesses are discrete biological entities that behave, and respond to treatments, in distinctive ways (Kramer 1993). In a short time, neuroleptics came to be associated with the treatment of psychosis, tricyclics and MAO inhibitors with depression, and lithium with mania (Klerman 1989). As seemingly disease-specific medications sparked new interest in psychiatric classification, DSM II came in for a variety of criticisms. In the mid-seventies the American Psychiatric Association began in earnest to revise DSM II to produce a more "scientific," and above all, statistically reliable, system of diagnostic classification (Kirk and Kutchins 1992). Though the DSM III was heavily criticized for neglecting issues of validity (Mirowsky and Ross 1989), and was found of questionable use in actual clinical practice

(Brown 1987; Kirk and Kutchins 1992; Rhodes 1991), it was nonetheless received with resounding support by mental health professionals. As an administrative resource, the DSM III (and its newer versions) is handy for justifying third-party payments and, more generally, for developing post hoc rationalizations for the provision or nonprovision of services. Most importantly the DSM stands as a powerful icon, symbolizing both the currency, and scientific legitimacy, of psychiatric diagnoses.

The return of biopsychiatry influenced practice in my programs in at least two important ways. First, particularly among impoverished Americans, psychotherapy has been largely overshadowed by pharmacological therapies as the *sine qua non* of specifically psychiatric mental health care. Though very serious disorders have been medicated for decades, the rise of biopsychiatry has fostered an even greater emphasis on chemotherapies than was evident in the past. Clients in my programs were seen by psychiatrists very briefly and almost exclusively to discuss their medications. Second, the new emphasis on classification was evident insofar as admission to the programs required a diagnosis of some specific Axis I mental disorder as defined by DSM IIIr.[7] While these diagnoses were only rarely actually invoked during the course of therapeutic practice, they were still known features of clients' biographical profiles and did inform some of the interventions taken with them. Perhaps more importantly, though, the emphasis on classification fostered a general sense that clients' troubles were symptoms of specific diseases, biological *others inside* them, which it was the work of treatment to control.

CHRONICITY AND THE RISE OF DUAL DIAGNOSIS AS A PUBLIC PROBLEM

As was mentioned earlier, by the late sixties the management of severe mental illness was already noticed as the Achilles heel of community mental health. Nevertheless, well into the seventies, advocates were in-

---

7. Beginning with DSM III, officially recognized psychiatric diagnoses have been made according to a multiaxial assessment procedure (see American Psychiatric Association 1980; Spitzer and Williams 1982). Major psychiatric disorders like schizophrenia and bipolar disorder are diagnosed as Axis I disorders; personality disorders and specific developmental disorders are diagnosed as Axis II disorders; relevant physical diagnoses are noted as Axis III disorders; psychosocial stressors are noted and rated on a scale of severity as Axis IV diagnoses; and on Axis V the highest level of adaptive functioning the patient was able to sustain for at least a few months during the past year is registered. This procedure is intended to yield a comprehensive biopsychosocial evaluation of a patient's condition and to inform appropriate interventions.

clined toward blanket defenses of CMHCs and allegations that their critics harbored nefariously partisan political motives (Torrey 1988). Finally, in 1977, the U.S. General Accounting Office (GAO) reported officially to Congress what those in the know had already long understood. CMHCs were nowhere near providing adequately for those whose disabilities appeared most severe (GAO 1977). That same year, largely because of GAO criticisms, the NIMH launched the Community Support Program (CSP) to focus more direct attention on mental patients whose adjustments to community living were judged the poorest. The CSP supplied seed funds to help several states develop community support systems for the chronically mentally ill (Love 1984). Though they were allowed some discretion over how they designed and implemented their systems (Grusky et al. 1985), CSP directives specifically insisted that local communities more thoroughly assess and more comprehensively attend to the needs of those who were, in the now well-known words of Segal, Baumohl, and Johnson (1977), "falling through the cracks" of the existing community mental health system.

The public policy mandate first embodied by the CSP received powerful support when, beginning in the early eighties, NAMI began to grow and more effectively lobby on behalf of their mentally ill friends and family members. During the Reagan presidency, efforts were also made to restrict public funding to only those agencies that could demonstrate that their clients were *severely* disabled (Torrey 1988). This, combined with Republican funding reductions, also helped spawn what became a veritable explosion of clinical and scientific interest in "young adult chronic patients" (Pepper and Ryglewicz 1982). Pepper and Ryglewicz (1984, p. 6) write,

> Both this broad definition [young adult chronic patients] of an otherwise heterogeneous patient group and our research itself came in response to reports from within our own system and from a variety of other settings of new and taxing problems in service delivery presented by chronically disturbed and dysfunctional young adults. Some of these clients had made themselves personae non gratea even to mental health agencies by their disruptive and incorrigible behavior. Some presented problems of recurrent serious violence in their parents' home or in locked wards of psychiatric hospitals. Many defied diagnosis by presenting a psychiatric disorder complicated by drug abuse—or was it a toxic psychosis mimicking schizophrenia? Finally, many either overtly rejected treatment or simply wandered away from the most carefully planned path of aftercare.

It was perhaps the recurrency and intractability of these similar clinical caretaking problems that first warranted proliferation of the category "young adult chronic patient" in place of more diagnostically precise (but clinically irrelevant) patient categories. But it was (1) the widespread recognition that community mental health had failed to live up to its basic promise to be a more humane and inclusive approach to managing madness, and (2) the mandate introduced in the CSP, effectively promoted by NAMI, and then given teeth by Republican funding policies, that pressed most mental health professionals to stop ignoring young adult chronic patients on the grounds that they were "treatment-resistant" or beyond the scope of their professional responsibility. Prominent figures in the mental health professions began to insist that the problem was more than just a bunch of disagreeable patients who refused psychiatric services or failed to comply with doctors' prescriptions. The problem, they now argued, was intrinsically relational. That is, it was not only a product of the severity of patients' disorders, or their intransigence as individuals, but of the "interactive fit" between patients (as well as those who had never become patients), the professional skills and interests of service providers, and the design of (and linkages between) relevant public service systems (cf. Bachrach 1982; GAP 1987; Meyerson 1987; Segal, Baumohl, and Johnson 1977; Talbott 1980).

In the late seventies and early eighties public agency officials at the federal, state, and local levels, in concert with psychiatric researchers, mental health care providers, and advocates, began to convene conferences and special task forces to address what specific reforms would be needed to more effectively deal with young adult chronic patients in government-funded service systems (GAP 1978, 1987; Menninger and Hannah 1987; Pepper and Ryglewicz 1982, 1984; Talbott 1978, 1984). Among the first, and most heavily emphasized, features of the problem was the widespread use of illicit drugs and alcohol by members of the target population (Bachrach 1987). Researchers, service providers, community advocates, and administrators were nearly unanimous in concluding the importance of attending to the drug habits of young adult chronic patients. More specifically, it was noted that many of the contacts service providers had with young adult chronics were precipitated by drug-related problems and that drug involvements also tended to complicate diagnosis and interfere with treatment planning and follow-through. Community advocates, among others, criticized the widespread tendency among mental health programs to exclude patients with drug or alcohol problems and a similarly pervasive tendency of substance abuse treatment programs to proscribe the use of even prescribed psychoactive medications (Cohen and Levy 1992; Schmidt 1991).

While the genuinely clinical problems client drug use presented for service providers cannot be overlooked, there was also a more encompassing, social structural, appeal to highlighting the drug habits of young adult chronics. The historical context that provided first for the more or less independent development of national systems in mental health, alcoholism, and illicit drug control, and then the subsequent push for their integration with the block grant approach to federal funding (and the war on drugs), effectively prodded professionals working in these hitherto distinct fields to consider one another—and the overlaps, conflicts, and possibilities for cooperation that existed between them. Were it not for this ever so historically contingent arrangement in the provision of public services, the invocation of addictions by mental health professionals (and the similar invocation of insanities by substance abuse treatment professionals) would not have been necessary, nor available, as a serviceable account for either system's past failures with young adult chronics. In the end, it was only due to across-the-board funding cuts, and political pressures to allocate the remaining funds only to programs that managed severely disabled clients, that treatment professionals in both fields were compelled to acknowledge those past failures at all. And it is only thanks to the foreordained horizon of category-specific services that they found themselves handily armed with the option of deferring to one another's separate body of professional expertise to justify their respective past failures and coalesce in their efforts to overcome them. One important example will illustrate the point.

In 1982, officials affiliated with the Alcohol, Drug Abuse, and Mental Health Administration (ADAMHA), the parent organization of NIMH, NIAAA, and NIDA, convened a small conference to discuss the multiple needs of young adult chronic patients (Glass 1982). Because the conference was organized to address the contributions that might be made, *by each of the three institutes respectively,* to the improvement of services for young adult chronic patients, there were strong structural encouragements for conference participants to highlight the problems of chronic mental patients with alcohol and illicit drugs, and to note the barriers to their proper care that had emerged from the myopias and political ranglings attendant to categorically distinct service systems. As a result of this and similar efforts throughout the country, the problems that substance use among young adult chronic patients presented for service delivery were soon widely acknowledged. And more importantly, they were acknowledged as in large part a failure of the mental health, alcohol, and illicit drug fields to have formed adequate linkages and cooperative relationships in the past. By the time Leona Bachrach (1987, pp. 37–8) made the following comments, many powerful figures throughout the mental health and substance abuse treatment professions had already come to share her views:

> I personally feel that administratively separating the three institutes that make up the federal Alcohol, Drug Abuse, and Mental Health Administration (ADAMHA)—a policy that has been emulated by many states—has had a very adverse effect upon the care of chronic mental patients who have problems with substance abuse. Instead of seeking ways to integrate treatment for people who have multiple disabilities, these arbitrary service divisions make it extremely difficult to plan and deliver services that can make some sense of their diverse treatment needs...It seems that neither the mental health service establishment nor the substance abuse service establishment has had either the incentive or the ingenuity to plan services that exceed its own categorical boundaries. Chronic mental patients with substance abuse problems often appear to be caught up in this bureaucratic web.

What has not been as widely acknowledged, however, is that the historical emergence and maintenance of categorical boundaries between what Bachrach calls the mental health and substance abuse service establishments have done more than impede the efficiency with which public agencies address the needs of those with "multiple disabilities." They have also given specific forms to the "multiplicity" of people's disabilities in the first place! That addictions and insanities are currently conceptualized as autonomous but mutually exacerbating diseases is the product of a specific historical nexus wherein two fields (and the respective *others inside* that these fields have crafted as their particular worldly nemeses) have converged. It is the story of the independent emergence and convergence of these fields and their phenomena I have hitherto been concerned to tell. Once again, this is by no means to argue that insanities and addictions are somehow less than real, or that it is never appropriate to regard these phenomena in biological or psychological terms. It is rather to insist that these phenomena are also eminently amenable to sociohistorical analysis and that indispensable insights into the relationships that inhere between insanities, addictions, and human affairs are only available by analyzing them in this way.

CONCLUDING REMARKS

In this chapter we have followed the evolution of the publicly funded mental health, alcohol, and drug addiction fields through the twentieth century. We have seen how these fields grew into more or less discrete nationally organized systems, each of which is focally concerned with the understanding and management of human troubles that periodically have been and are now, in various ways, construed as the products of nonhuman *others inside* people. Though historically separate in many respects, these fields have developed parallel to one another, often competing for government funding, for clients, and for the authority to name, explain, and manage the *others inside* to which they consensually, and with widespread popular support, insist human beings are heir. Indeed, in recent years we have witnessed a partial fusion of the alcohol and drug addiction fields such that in many instances alcohol and drug addiction are construed in all but identical conceptual fashion. This type of fusion was evident in my own ethnographic research settings.

Over the course of the last three decades or so, practitioners within each of these fields also began to routinely invoke the curious claim that insanities and addictions are distinct but mutually exacerbating types of *others inside*. This practice was undertaken first by treatment professionals in the interest of defining some of their most troublesome clients out of their own areas of professed expertise and professional responsibility, and then later in the interest of establishing linkages between the fields of mental health and substance abuse services. The effort to improve services for those who had in the past been system misfits or rejects was driven by the increased pressures that community advocates and then public policy makers placed on service providers to more effectively manage those whose adjustments to community living were judged the poorest. In response to this mandate, leading researchers and clinicians began to conceive of the problem not only in terms of individual personal deficits and disorders but in terms of the "interactive fit" between clients, clinicians, and extant service systems. The "dual diagnosis" of both insanities and addictions has emerged as a prominent resource in this effort. With recourse to dual diagnoses, the putative historic deficits of both the mental health and substance abuse treatment fields may be honorably admitted and renewed efforts to overcome those deficits may be engendered which are responsive to the calls from higher echelons of government for systems integration and linkage.

We have seen how the legitimation and growth of the mental health, alcohol, and drug addiction fields were deeply influenced by resurgences of regard for the membership of putative sufferers within their national, state, and local moral communities. To the extent they have been construed as legitimate members of our moral communities, attributions of troubles to nonhuman *others inside* people (rather than intrinsic personal flaws) have been accepted as that much more plausible as have calls that sufferers themselves be enlisted as active collaborators in the design and implementation of their recoveries. Perceptions of undeserved suffering among those with whom we have assumed a sense of community solidarity have tended to catalyze the production and growth of collective efforts to relieve their suffering. The perceived likelihood of sufferers achieving some level of recovery from their respective disorders has also retained its inverse relation to their cultural and economic marginality. Though some attribute this to the cost of effective care, or to the greater vulnerability of marginalized and impoverished populations to forces that cause, sustain, and/or exacerbate disorder, there is a good deal more to it than that.

The *others inside* people that the mental health, alcohol, and drug addiction fields claim as their respective raisons d'être have, in the last half of the twentieth century, come to be regarded ever more emphatically in terms of the myriad adverse effects they exert on the tenability of clients' community living arrangements. In contemporary publicly funded treatment systems, the *others inside* people understood and managed as insanities and addictions are uniformly construed as profoundly mysterious nonhuman agents that exert their influences in a staggering variety of ways but always so as to strain the tenability of sufferers' membership within their respective local, state, and national communities. Conversely, recovery from these putative disorders has come to be more emphatically construed and cultivated in terms of returning sufferers to the fold of their respective communities in ways that are satisfying to members of those communities and can be effectively sustained by them. It is with due regard for these facts that we must construe contemporary empirical relationships between insanities, addictions, people, and social life. More than merely rendering homeless, or otherwise marginalized and impoverished, Americans more vulnerable to insanities and addictions, or less capable of securing adequate treatments, social, economic, and cultural deficits increasingly figure in the very constitution of these disorders as the practical nemeses with which sufferers, treatment professionals, and American society actually grapples. Let us now move into Part II of the study where my argument will be further elaborated ethnographically.

II A Tale of Two Programs

4   Canyon House

THOUGH CANYON HOUSE was certainly a product of the histories outlined in Part I, it was also the site of distinctive patterns of practice that were by no means inevitable effects of those histories. History was, instead, mediated through embodied strategies, artfully articulated by specific people who, for different reasons, found Canyon House a compelling resource. In this chapter I discuss the organization and operation of Canyon House, linking these to the broader events discussed in Part I. More specifically, I describe the program's local history, its administrative structures, the distinctive logic of therapeutic practice, and finally, when and how putative *others inside* people were made to figure as embodied causal agents within the local social context that was Canyon House.

THE ORIGINS OF CANYON HOUSE

In 1985, Brad Peterson had been an active member of Alcoholics Anonymous (AA) for five years.[1] He was also a consultant with the California Association of Alcoholic Recovery Homes (CAARH). In this capacity he advised state, county, and city officials, and helped private citizens negotiate the maze of licensing, funding, and other administrative exigencies of operating recovery homes for alcoholics in California. CAARH was the preeminent organization in California representing alcoholism treatment professionals who did not abide by strictly medical or psychiatric models of care. Though much of CAARH's support came from AA members, its agenda consisted less in promoting AA itself, than insuring the political viability of what they called "social model" recovery programs in the increasingly competitive alcoholism treatment industry described in Chapter 3. Toward this end, CAARH established and promoted standards of practice for their member recovery homes, lobbied county and state bureaucrats on the virtues of social model programs,

---

1. This section is based primarily on an extensive interview with the founder and director of Canyon House and CEO of Social Model Treatment Group, Inc. (the nonprofit parent corporation of Canyon House).

and educated others in the field regarding the distinctive merits of social model recovery approaches (Wiener 1981).

While with CAARH, Peterson was contacted by Doug Mailer, a wealthy southern California businessman and a committed member of AA. Mailer had recently purchased a 32-bed, single-room occupancy (SRO) hotel and sought to convert it into a social model recovery home. He told Peterson he did not want to run the home himself but hoped to bring in the county and/or one of the local nonprofit corporations already involved in alcoholism treatment to do so. Peterson phoned Norman Benson, director of the Los Angeles county Office of Alcohol Programs (OAP), and told him of Mailer's plan. Benson told Peterson that county seed money was available but that he must persuade the local county supervisor of the wisdom in taking advantage of Mailer's generosity. Peterson did just that, $50,000 was released from the county coffers, and Mailer's SRO hotel was converted into a recovery home just as he had hoped. Following this success, Mailer told Peterson that if he ever needed capital for a like venture, he should not hesitate to call.

Peterson had already been considering founding and running his own program and Mailer's offer further kindled his thoughts. To get a preliminary sense of his options, Peterson did a needs assessment survey of Los Angeles county. Following the *Omnibus Budget Reconciliation Act*, what he found were rather fallow grounds. The only new programs that promised much hope for support were those designed to serve a handful of "special populations" who were demonstratively underserved within the existing systems. The special populations then attracting most concern were pregnant women, women with young children, and juveniles, but Peterson felt he had little experience with these populations. He felt better equipped to confront the needs of another special population that had been attracting increasing attention in Los Angeles county—the mentally ill.[2] The Los Angeles chapter of the National Alliance for the Mentally Ill (NAMI) had been growing in both size and political clout throughout the early eighties. Reflecting the national trends discussed in Chapter 3, NAMI's Los Angeles chapter persistently complained to county officials that mentally ill substance

2. Before consulting for CAARH, Peterson had been a counselor in a recovery home for alcoholics and drug addicts. While there, he became convinced that people whose mental problems were not confined to addiction were very poorly served in such programs. He had, in fact, attributed a close friend's mental breakdown to the program's inability to recognize and address his friend's schizophrenia. Doug Mailer also had a personal investment in this issue because his daughter was diagnosed mentally ill.

abusers were "falling through the cracks" of the existing service delivery system—prevented from taking psychoactive drugs in social model drug and alcohol programs and denied admission into mental health programs because of their substance abuse.

In 1985, the Los Angeles county Board of Supervisors responded to growing pressure from NAMI and their political allies by ordering the OAP, the Drug Abuse Program Office (DAPO), and the county Department of Mental Health to pool their efforts to produce a program for the dually diagnosed. Concerned about the ramifications of this collaboration with the Department of Mental Health, Norman Benson (the OAP director) sought advice from Peterson as to how they might resist consigning OAP funds to a program that taught controlled drinking.[3] Peterson told Benson he thought the county would eventually have to deliver some sort of program for the dually diagnosed. Therefore, it was in its best interest for the OAP to take the lead on the project, and insist that their own commitments regarding addiction treatment be honored. Benson agreed. First and foremost, the OAP insisted the new program teach abstinence. And second, it insisted the program emphasize the social model themes of client empowerment and peer involvement. Their proactive strategy paid off. County mental health officials agreed to OAP's terms and, for their part, insisted only that the new program somehow address clients' psychiatric problems. Following these preliminary agreements, the OAP also led the work of composing an official Request for Proposals (RFP).

Brad Peterson suggested to Doug Mailer that they seriously consider submitting a proposal for this incipient program. He told Mailer that, first of all, this was to be a relatively large county grant ($500,000). Secondly, it was the first time in years that the county had offered to so generously fund an entirely new type of facility. Because it was widely perceived to be filling a newly recognized need for services, this program appeared to promise a level of funding security, and perhaps even growth potential, in the local public services market that was not likely to be matched again soon. Finally, it was an opportunity to work with

---

3. This concern reflected a more extensive battle that raged in the alcoholism treatment industry throughout the eighties (cf. Fingarette 1989). Advocates of AA and the social model approach were committed to abstinence as the only realistic treatment goal. They controlled most public agencies in the alcoholism treatment field including the Los Angeles OAP. Clinical psychologists and social workers sympathetic to behavioral modification approaches (and the possibility of controlled drinking) occupied positions of power in county mental health bureaucracies.

a population for which they both felt a personal concern. On the down-side, the competition promised to be severe. All the major nonprofits in both substance abuse and mental health could be expected to sub-mit proposals. Mailer agreed to give it a try. The two men formed their own nonprofit corporation and began preparations. They called them-selves the Social Model Treatment Group in a deliberate effort to put grant review panelists committed to the social model approach on no-tice regarding their own similar commitments. Peterson resigned from CAARH and Mailer loaned the corporation some money to pay Peterson for full-time research and development on the project. This proved to be the one major advantage they had over the competition. Whereas the established nonprofits were preoccupied with the day-to-day work of running their existing programs, Peterson was free to concentrate all his attentions on this one project. The big nonprofits would wait for publi-cation of the county's official RFP before they began writing their own proposals, so Peterson had what became a valuable five-month jump on the field.

Peterson traversed the country looking for program models, only to find nothing remotely comparable to what he had in mind. First, there simply were no programs specifically organized to treat dually diag-nosed clients. And though there were certainly social model programs treating alcohol and drug addictions, in the mid-eighties, Peterson found nothing that was comparable in mental health. He liked the "psychosocial" rehabilitation model, which entailed training commu-nity living skills and assertiveness with psychiatrists regarding medi-cations issues. But this model did not include the peer-support compo-nent that Peterson hoped to incorporate into his own program. Peterson then read of a facility in France that appeared to embody the principles he had in mind. This program, called L'Arche, was administered by a Catholic priest and staffed by both clergy and Jesuit volunteers. It served clients diagnosed with developmental disabilities and mental illnesses in a shared residential setting. Like social model drug and al-cohol programs, it emphasized peer support, client empowerment, and a blurring of distinctions between staff and clients. Peterson resolved to model his own approach to psychiatric care on the L'Arche design. Now he had only to formulate the characteristics of the L'Arche approach "in language that could survive the L.A. county RFP process."

The broad outlines of what became Canyon House began to take shape in Peterson's mind. The program would be fundamentally based on the close-knit, residential community arrangement he had taken from AA, CAARH, and L'Arche. It would emphasize peer support and peer insight, client empowerment, and, perhaps most importantly, the treatment focus would be on "wellness" rather than "illness." That is, treatment would seek to foster healthy and satisfying lives rather than merely subduing clients' putative diseases. From the Synanon style "concept houses," Peterson took the importance of longer term interventions, and graduated phases of treatment (i.e., incrementally conferring more independence and responsibility on clients as they demonstrate their ability to handle it). Peterson accepted that medications were essential, but Canyon House residents would be trained to take an active role in managing their medications. They would be taught to educate themselves regarding their diagnoses and collaborate with their doctors in devising medications regimens appropriate for them.

When the official RFP was finally released, its language was auspiciously subdued as to both OAP's leadership and their interest in a peer-oriented and abstinence-based program. The RFP was flexible as to the program's design (there simply were no models for combining psychiatric and substance abuse treatment to which the county might demand adherence). It also indicated that proposals would need to include detailed descriptions of the prospective program's site. In 1985, NIMBY (Not In My Back Yard) sentiments ran high in Los Angeles. County supervisors had no desire to alienate constituents by installing mental health and drug programs in their neighborhoods. Peterson and Mailer had, in fact, already found an unusually suitable property in the Los Angeles foothills. It was remotely located and could be acquired cheaply. Because only about one hundred people lived anywhere near the site, it was fairly safe politically. Even if local residents did protest, one hundred remotely located voters were not a major thorn in a supervisor's side. In clinical terms, the site's isolation provided a natural barrier to impulsive departures and thereby minimized the likelihood of clients' spontaneously relapsing while in residence. The sylvan surroundings also provided a calming therapeutic contrast to the stressful street life from which most clients were expected to hail.

The Social Model Treatment Group won the grant and was scheduled to open Canyon House in Spring 1986.[4] Some county money was released to cover start-up costs but the grant was made officially contingent upon Canyon House being fully operational and populated to

4. Peterson later learned from grant review panelists that the Social Model Treatment Group was awarded the grant for two main reasons. First, theirs was the only proposal that was responsive to the OAP's "hidden agenda" to promote the social model approach to addiction treatment. Second, theirs was the only proposal that claimed to have a suitable site already lined up.

capacity by the appointed date in Spring. Peterson began the arrangements, hired staff, and all appeared to be going well until it came time to
license the facility. The historic division between state drug and alcohol
and mental health bureaucracies meant that no state agency was authorized to license a program for people with *both* psychiatric and substance
use disorders. Peterson told the state licensing agencies of the situation
but was met with little cooperation until he called the Governor's office
and threatened to go public with the story. Chastened at the prospect
of another government waste/incompetence story, the Governor's office intervened. Old licenses were dredged up and appropriate waivers
were found. Canyon House received its operating license just one day
before the county deadline to fill their beds.

THE ADMINISTRATIVE STRUCTURE OF CANYON HOUSE

Canyon House was established expressly to recuperate a population,
"young adult chronic patients," that had been falling through the cracks
of the existing system of public services. As noted in Chapter 3, members of this population were related less by their specific diagnoses, than
by their "resistance" to the panoply of treatment options hitherto available to them (Cohen and Levy 1992). Brad Peterson had no illusions
about this and was not surprised when programs throughout the Los
Angeles area began referring their most troublesome cases to Canyon
House. Officially, clients needed a major (Axis I) mental illness and a
drug or alcohol addiction to be admitted. But, according to Peterson,
referring agencies often treated this as a formality. They didn't think of
Canyon House as a place for docile clients with dual disorders. Canyon
House was somewhere one sent "troublemakers," clients who posed
management difficulties within one's own program. If a troublemaker
did not already have an Axis I diagnosis, a provisional one was found.
Furthermore, if someone had an Axis I diagnosis, almost any level of
substance use could be cast as problematic and a referral to Canyon
House could be justified. Anxious to establish their indispensability
within the county system, Canyon House began by admitting these re-
ferrals with few questions asked. As the demand for their program grew
more certain, however, Canyon House could, and did, begin to exercise
more discretion.[5]

5. During my fieldwork, Canyon House generally tried to avoid clients (1) with histories of serious violence, (2) too gravely disabled to meaningfully contribute to their own
recoveries, and (3) who were not committed to recovery.

Canyon House could accommodate a maximum of forty clients at once. During my fieldwork, twenty-seven of these slots were funded by the county, ten by the Rand study of which I was a part, and the remaining three were available to privately sponsored clients. Because Canyon House was specifically mandated to take "difficult cases," it was expected that many admissions would be both destitute and without public support. Therefore the county provided complete coverage for 70 percent of those who filled county beds. The remaining 30 percent had to be receiving Supplemental Security Income (SSI) so that "draw downs" from their medical insurance could be used to supplement county support.[6] The beds funded by the Rand study were filled by homeless people from the west side of Los Angeles county. Thanks to the combined effects of fairly generous county funding, their reputation as a "dumping ground" among referral agencies, and Rand's involvement as a referral source, a formidable number of clients admitted during my fieldwork either came directly from living homeless or had suffered periodic homelessness prior to their admission.[7]

Living homeless, and the fear of doing so, obviously made Canyon House attractive to prospective clients merely for the subsistence needs it promised to alleviate. But even more, their homelessness was often high on the list of reasons clients gave for having concluded that, in fact, they suffered from an insanity and/or addiction. It was not simply that clients felt that the stresses of homelessness exacerbated their ostensive disorders. Rather, they viewed their homelessness as the most serious *symptom* of their disorders and the benefits of "treatment" largely in terms of its promise to alleviate this most troubling symptom. When

6. Since I left the field, county money has grown more scarce. County-funded beds have been reduced to twenty-two, and, of these, 85% must be filled by SSI recipients so that medical "draw downs" can be made. This has the effect of limiting the number of beds available to clients without outside funding resources (those who tend to be most in need of their services) to about three.

7. Most people who experience homelessness do not stay homeless very long but are prone to repeated episodes of homelessness (Burt 1992; Jencks 1994; Rossi 1989; Wright 1989). It is therefore unwise to draw fine distinctions between clients who arrived directly from a homeless living situation and those who had histories of chronic homelessness but were housed just before their arrival. This said, no less than 38 of the 118 people admitted during my fieldwork could be confirmed to have come directly from a homeless living situation. A great many others spoke of their own chronic homelessness, but the vicissitudes of fieldwork precluded my establishing a specific number reliably. Virtually everyone admitted into the program hailed from severely impoverished and marginalized social circumstances.

asked why she sought treatment, Lonni answered typically,

> "Life on the street was just becomin' more and more crazy and danger-
> ous. Most of the homeless people I used to hang around with would get
> high...a certain amount of people that would hang together and watch
> out for each other. All those people started to go against each other...This
> one girl got pissed off 'cause she couldn't get high with this guy. And so
> she started arguin' with me...and then, when I turned around, she had a
> knife...and was talking a lot of shit..." Lonni said this incident "made
> me wake up and see that living on the streets is not a good idea. I thought
> 'I've been homeless for almost seven months...'. I didn't even want to
> deal with that shit. I got tired of that shit. I said it's time for me to get my
> shit together, at least attempt to do it.

Canyon House was small enough so that residents who cared to could
become friendly with the administrative staff. On the whole, though,
staff in regular contact with clients included only the program director, associate program director, housing coordinator, kitchen manager,
vocational rehabilitation coordinator, recovery specialists, night counselors, and case aides. Brad Peterson told me he hired these staff with
the following criteria in mind:

> I concentrate on hiring people I intuitively feel have the heart, or whatever
> you want to call it, to be present to other people who are in distress,
> who are hurting, who are suffering...with a real sense of compassion,
> love, respect, that kind of stuff...Once I have what I consider a pool of
> people who have the heart capacity then I go to people's experience and
> qualifications.

Peterson was committed to see therapeutic practice at Canyon House
rely as little as possible on status distinctions between staff and clients.
Except the program director, every staff member in regular contact with
residents was also in recovery from an addiction and active in AA or
NA (Narcotics Anonymous). The staff drew much of their own sense
of professional legitimacy and therapeutic expertise from their experiences as AA and NA members. They routinely imparted the twelve-step
mutual help ethic to Canyon House residents and often sought to distance themselves from their professional status at Canyon House by
self-identifying as addicts. Beyond staff instruction, participation in AA
and NA was integral to the treatment process. Twelve-step phrases,
terminology, and literature were pervasive. The twelve-step approach
informed therapy for both substance problems and psychiatric problems.

Though there was no mistaking the centrality of twelve-step culture, there were other elements to the recovery regimen at Canyon House. To follow is a brief outline of that regimen:

1. Eight hours of *community meeting* per week. Each weekday morning at 9:00 A.M. residents and recovery staff convened to discuss the day's activities and any issues anyone felt related to the overall efficacy of the program. At this time acknowledgments, conflicts, and concerns were aired and discussed as a community.

2. One hour per week in each of the following didactic groups:
   - Either the *thought disorder group* or the *mood disorder group* and either the *alcohol dependency group* or the *drug dependency group* respectively. In these groups, residents learned what was known about their disorders from various clinical points of view and discussed the resonance of these general ideas with their own experiences.
   - *Women's group* or *men's group*, in which issues pertaining specifically to gender were discussed.
   - *Stress and coping group*, in which managing stress and concrete stressful events was discussed.
   - *Feeling good group*, in which relaxation techniques were taught and practiced.
   - *Family systems group*, in which residents learned and discussed how their families may have contributed to the development of their ostensibly dysfunctional habits and coping styles.

3. Supervised attendance at a minimum of *three outside twelve-step meetings*. Residents were required to attend at least one "cultural meeting" (an AA or NA meeting that is geared toward a specific ethnic group or sexual orientation) every two weeks. Meetings included regular AA and NA meetings and "double trudger" meetings, which are specifically convened to address the unique needs of the dually diagnosed. Program residents were entitled to vote to change the meetings they attended but were not entitled to forego "cultural meetings" altogether.[8]

4. Approximately one hour of *meditation or inspirational reading* per week. Every weekday morning at 7:30 A.M., residents were required to spend ten or fifteen minutes meditating or quietly reading inspirational literature of their own choosing.

8. This raised much ire among many residents who claimed they did not feel comfortable attending, and did not feel it was therapeutic for them to attend, "cultural meetings."

5. At least one hour per week of *individual counseling* between residents and their assigned recovery specialist and at least one visit per month with an assigned psychiatrist. *Psychiatric visits* usually lasted about fifteen minutes and primarily concerned medications issues.

6. Four hours of *outdoor recreational activity* per week. Outdoor activity did not have to be physically strenuous, but if it was not, it had to be interactional. That is, playing cards with someone sufficed but solitaire did not.

7. At least one hour per week in *resident council*, in which residents met without staff to discuss the assignment of chores and meal crew duties, general issues and concerns, and vote on community initiatives (e.g., creating a fund for residents temporarily without spending money).

8. *Chores and meal crew duties*. Chores included tasks like maintaining the grounds, the restrooms, or the common rooms and were done between morning meditation and community meeting. Meal crew duties included assisting in meal preparation and cleanup. Residents worked on meal crew about two hours a day.

Through these activities residents were expected to develop recovery skills that were progressively recognized by movement through three treatment phases. Ideally, this process culminated with graduation after six months. To follow is an outline of the treatment phases as they were published in the "Resident Guide" given to residents upon admission:

Phase I:
Interruption of negative lifestyle, stabilization, exposure to recovery concepts, adjustment to sober environment.

Day 1	Establish an initial treatment plan with assigned recovery specialist
2 weeks	Establish a master treatment plan and review progress to date
4 weeks	Case review
8 weeks	Case review and Advance to Phase II, OR deny advancement OR discharge from Canyon House

Requirements for Advancement to Phase II:
1. Obtain an AA or NA sponsor
2. Complete workbooks on Steps 1, 2, and 3 of AA or NA
3. Comply with medications prescriptions
4. Adequate participation in all assigned groups
5. Adequate completion of all chores and work activities

6. Participation in one hour minimum individual session with primary counselor weekly
7. Meet minimum of 60% of personal goals and objectives as defined in treatment plan

Phase II:

Identifying and working on personal issues, cultivating support systems, sponsor passes, involvement with AA/NA fellowship, day passes, increased responsibility within Canyon House community, increased ability to take personal responsibility for own actions.

9 weeks	Update master treatment plan
12 weeks	Case review
16 weeks	Case review
20 weeks	Advance to Phase III OR deny advancement OR discharge from Canyon House

Requirements for Advancement to Phase III:
1. Minimum of two sponsor passes per month
2. Participation in outside AA/NA meetings
3. Complete workbooks on Steps 4 and 5 of AA or NA
4. Minimum of 3 ten-hour day passes
5. Initiate minimum one hour weekly individual session with primary counselor
6. Continued participation in all aspects of Canyon House community life
7. Ability to accept consequences that may result from personal actions
8. Meet minimum of 80% of personal goals and objectives as defined in treatment plan

Phase III:

Realistic discharge planning, overnight passes, further development of involvement in outside AA/NA fellowship and other support systems, further increased involvement in Canyon House community.

21 weeks	Update master treatment plan
24 weeks	Case review
28 weeks	Case review

Requirements for Graduation:
1. Complete workbooks on Steps 6 and 7 of AA or NA
2. Continued participation in all aspects of Canyon House community life
3. Minimum of two sponsor passes per month

4. Meet personal goals and objectives as defined in treatment plan
5. Continued day passes
6. Continued participation in AA/NA fellowship
7. Meet minimum of 90% of personal goals and objectives as defined in treatment plan

Extensions:

Requires approval from Los Angeles County Department of Mental Health with clinical justification for those residents who would benefit from extended treatment by being able to move to a lower level of care at time of discharge—subject to review every 30 days.

29 weeks	Complete program—graduation OR extend in program and update treatment plan and review every 30 days
32 weeks	Case review—extend, discharge or GRADUATE

If a resident requires psychiatric hospitalization during the course of treatment, then the resident will not necessarily be discharged from the program providing reasonable stabilization can be attained in no longer than 10 days. Upon return to the program, the resident's place in the phases will be evaluated with the primary counselor.

About 15 percent of those admitted graduated from Canyon House. Though a few residents left voluntarily, the vast majority who did not graduate were involuntarily discharged for failures to meet program requirements.[9] Most residents did not want to leave Canyon House. Such was the meagerness of their prospects outside the program, that staff could, and often did, invoke them in efforts to motivate change in clients who were approaching involuntary discharge. Indeed, the prospect of

---

9. In addition to those above, explicit house rules included the following:

1. Complete abstinence from all nonprescribed medications, illegal drugs, and alcohol both on and off the property.
2. Complete abstinence from physical violence or threats of physical violence against oneself or others.
3. Complete abstinence from destruction of property.
4. Absolutely no possession of firearms, knives, or other weapons.
5. All medications and over-the-counter drugs will be locked in a central storage area in the staff office.
6. The lending of money or personal property between residents and between residents and staff is prohibited.
7. Intimate relationships are detrimental to the treatment setting; therefore intimate relationships between residents are prohibited. Intimate relationships with residents or staff of other recovery homes are also prohibited.

living somewhere less desirable (e.g., jail, a board and care facility, the streets) vitiated many residents' desire to leave even after they had graduated. Both voluntarily and involuntarily discharged residents were strongly encouraged to continue their recovery work, and to seek out whatever formal and informal resources they felt that work required. Efforts were made to place all those who wished it into other treatment facilities appropriate to their needs and abilities, and integration into the AA and NA fellowships was a major treatment goal in and of itself.

THE DYNAMICS OF THERAPEUTIC PRACTICE

Promoting Recovery Through Right Living

When Brad Peterson designed the therapeutic regimen at Canyon House he was not only concerned to subdue the putative diseases presumed to afflict residents, but also concerned to foster people's wellness in the broadest sense. Therapeutic practice at Canyon House was not simply a matter of technical diagnosis and medical ministration. It instead consisted in sustaining a therapeutic community conducive to residents' mental health, sobriety, and overall personal growth. In this section I address the moral expectations members of the Canyon House therapeutic community placed upon themselves and one another specifically as collaborators in that community's work. As will be shown later, assessments of an agent's humanity at Canyon House were integrally related to assessments of that agent's performance as a morally accountable collaborator in the work the community shared. This work consisted in several components that bear telling in the present context. I refer to the sum of these components as *right living* at Canyon House.

Admission into the program required that prospective residents persuade staff that they were genuinely dedicated to recovery and able

---

8. Quiet hours are observed between 10:00 P.M. and 7:00 A.M.
9. Smoking is permitted only in the designated areas.
10. A pay telephone is provided for use by residents.
11. Upon return to the program from a pass, residents are required to submit to a drug test including urinalysis and/or breathalyzer.
12. There is a thirty-day restriction from any contact with persons, other than graduates, discharged from this program.
13. Residents violating rules may be subject to disciplinary action up to and including discharge from the program.

Rule violations were usually handled on an individualized basis. However, drug use and violence were uniformly met with immediate discharge.

to do the work through which recovery was sought at Canyon House. As they were integrated into the program community they were called upon to persuade their peers of this as well. In the beginning this might be accomplished through little more than verbal avowals of commitment. In the case of newcomers, failures to adequately participate in the program's work might be chalked up to honest ignorance as in the following passage from a community meeting. Edgar, the resident in charge of chores said,

> "There were cigarette butts on the ground outside the rec room. Who was that?"
> David nodded his head and said, "It was me but..."
> Edgar interrupted, "Okay, I don't know your name. What's your name?"
> David said his name and Edgar continued, "I don't know you so I guess you're new... Anyway, I don't know how much people have told you about what needs doing but you probably should take it upon yourself to find out what needs to be done, okay?"

As residents gathered days in the program, however, simple ignorance became an increasingly less plausible account for lapses from adequate participation, and mere verbal avowals to the effect became less sufficient as marks of commitment to recovery. In the language often heard in such programs, residents were progressively required not only to "talk the talk," but to "walk the walk" that indicated conformity to the locally approved methods for pursuing recovery from insanities and addictions (Bloor, McKaganey, and Fonkert 1988; Denzin 1993; Skoll 1992; Sugarman 1974; Yablonsky 1989). This demand was made explicit in the following excerpt from a community meeting. Despite congratulating Matt for his valuable contributions to group *discussions*, Doug, a counselor, nonetheless dresses him down for failures to *behave* properly. The exchange began when Matt complained that he did not deserve the 6:15's[10] he had received because he had been doing "the best [he] could." Doug said,

> That's a big one for you Matt. Maybe you got outta havin' to apply yourself other places with that "I'm doin' the best I can" stuff but it ain't gonna work around here 'cause we know you can do a lot better. AA teaches us not to listen just to what people are sayin' but also to watch what they're doin' and Matt, brother, you are not doin' the best you can. Everyone can see that man, in your actions, not in your words. You do real good in

---

10. "6:15's" were a form of punishment wherein the resident was required to awaken at 6:15 A.M. the morning following a transgression and write/reflect on a topic deemed relevant to his or her recovery.

the words department brother and I think you've made some important contributions in the groups, made some real good insights. But it doesn't stop there man. You gotta apply those insights in everything you do. I'll tell you something man. I think you're a real good person and . . . I think you could be a real strong part of this community but you gotta get out there and apply yourself. You gotta push yourself. And I'll tell ya somethin' else. I think you've made a lot of progress since you got here. But it ain't enough. You're just gonna have to do a little better than you been doin'.

But if it was not just a matter of growing fluent in a locally approved therapeutic discourse, of what did "apply[ing]" oneself actually consist? The answer is *right living*. To begin to grasp the substance of right living, one must recognize, first of all, that it was quite thoroughly negotiated. Determining on any actual occasion whether someone was engaged in right living required discretion, and there was no scarcity of dispute. People debated whether reading slasher novels, watching pornographic movies, making racist and sexist comments, drinking coffee, smoking cigarettes, and a multitude of other arguably disrespectable practices were or were not consistent with recovery. Beyond debate regarding activities considered morally marginal in the society at large, there was debate over the moral requirements specific to life at Canyon House. The following excerpt from a community meeting illustrates a typical dispute over the substance of right living and how such disputes were generally resolved. Norris said he felt a lot of people were not carrying their own weight, then focused in on Nick,

"I like you man and I don't like to come down on anybody, but hey. Like yesterday, Sherry was workin' hard and doin' her work and then I look over and you're just hangin' out smokin'. I mean that's what got to me more than anything else. Here's Sherry, you know, a chick, and she's bustin' her ass and you aren't doin' nothin'. Don't even lift a hand to help her out."

Nick looked up with a smirk and said, "What? I did my job."

Norris said, "Actually you didn't. You left a big pile of dirt right next to my area and I had to clean it up 'cause I was afraid it was gonna blow into my area and fuck my area up. So I cleaned it. And that's not even the point. I don't mind doin' the cleanin' you know. But you just aren't carrying your weight buddy."

Nick shrugged and said, "Well I think I am. I do my job. Looks like we just disagree. As far as I'm concerned I'm allowed to kick back when I'm done with my job."

Norris shrugged and said, "Well I'm sorry you feel that way man. I guess it's off of me now. I've said what I got to say."

Eve, a recovery specialist, asked the group if they thought Norris was right. The consensus seemed to be that while Nick had been having problems in this department, he was getting better. Eve said, "Maybe you should see if you can't kick a little more in than you have been Nick. Sounds like you're getting better but you're not quite all the way there yet. How does that sound to you?"

Nick nodded and said, "I'll try."

Here a dispute over whether Nick was "carrying [his] own weight" was resolved not with respect to any explicit program rule, but through an extemporaneous referendum conducted among his peers. Neither were these negotiations simply matters of fine-tuning explicit rules. The following two fieldnote excerpts indicate that exactly opposite rulings could in fact proceed from the *in vivo* negotiation of proper program practice. In the first case, Harvey, the chores monitor, had found several problems with the performance of the grounds cleanup team. He raised these problems with each of the people whom he thought had come up short. He then asked the staff if Bob was not also culpable as grounds captain for having poorly supervised the people working under him. Bob objected and Paula, a recovery specialist, exonerated him as follows:

> No Harvey, we don't usually give the grounds captain a 6:15 for being in charge of others who don't do what they need to do. There's only so much a grounds captain can do without doing the chores himself. It wouldn't be fair to hold him responsible for the whole grounds being done.

However, when the same issue was raised another day under different circumstances, the verdict went the other way:

> The biggest chores problems this morning were lapses on grounds maintenance. Patrick, who was the grounds captain, was sleeping in the community meeting and was singled out by Paula and Edgar [the resident chores monitor] for a particularly stringent scolding. After learning that Patrick was the grounds captain, Edgar said, "What happened Patrick? You're supposed to be the captain here and make sure everybody's getting up and doin' what they need to do and instead you're sleepin' yourself. I don't think that's setting too good an example. What happened?"
>
> Patrick remained supine with eyes closed on the couch. With defiant indifference he answered, "Just give me the 6:15."
>
> Paula shook her head and Edgar said, "Yeah, great. Great. You'll take the 6:15." With a resigned and ironic tone, Edgar said, "Okay."

Any effort to reduce the substance of right living at Canyon House to a fixed code of conduct would be futile. Assessments of right living simply were not made in accordance with any such fixed code. However, as long as we remember their intrinsically negotiated character, I do believe that some of the more stable features of right living at Canyon House can be usefully described. Above all else, right living entailed remaining

abstinent from illicit drugs and alcohol. On this score, there was a strict
"one-strike-and-you're-out" policy.[11] To a slightly lesser extent, violence
and threats of violence were met with a zero-tolerance policy as well.
Though small skirmishes were considered inevitable, any "serious" violence was answered with termination. Eve, a recovery specialist, put it
this way in a community meeting following a skirmish that came very
close to escalating into something "serious."

> You've got to know though...and this goes for the whole community,
> not just for Julio, that violence is one thing we just cannot tolerate. It's one
> thing we just can't put up with around here. It's just too costly in terms of
> the community and keeping this a safe therapeutic environment. Violence
> and threats of violence are the big no-no...Newcomers come up here with
> a lot of raw nerves and they go off on people. We've seen it a million times
> but it is not excusable. You gotta know that that is dischargeable behavior.
> We will discharge you for violence and we will discharge you for threats
> of violence...We take this very seriously here.

After abstinence and nonviolence, "honesty" was the most valued
component of right living at Canyon House. Residents were asked to
honestly evaluate their putative personal deficits and "issues." If, for
example, they had received a particular diagnosis, residents were not
expected to meakly defer to professional authority, but they were expected to seriously consider why they had been diagnosed and whether
the diagnosis resonated with what they knew about themselves. They
were expected to honestly acknowledge, and take seriously, the troubles drug and/or alcohol use seemed to have created in their lives. And
they were expected to honestly acknowledge and share their current
troubles. This can be seen in the following excerpt from a community
meeting. Sally, the program director, asked if anyone had anything they
wanted to talk about. Lee Ann, who was slouching on the couch, said,

> "I'm depressed."
> Sally said, "You are? How long have you been depressed, Lee Ann?"
> Lee Ann answered, "Just the last couple of days or so I guess. Some-
> times I'll feel like I'm okay but then I'll fall back into it and know I'm not
> okay...like now" (*ironic laugh*).

---

11. During my fieldwork I observed one exception to this rule that serves nicely to
support my thesis regarding the essentially negotiated character of right living. In this
particular case a former heroin addict had been hospitalized with a kidney stone and was
put on a morphine drip to ease his pain. Though the news of his morphine drip was met
with some concern among both clients and counselors, it did not for a moment threaten
this resident's status in the program and nor was it counted against his days of having
remained clean and sober. By Canyon House lights, this manner of morphine use clearly
fell within the bounds of right living.

Lenny, another resident and a close friend of Lee Ann, asked, "How do you mean you feel depressed?" She began to answer before Lenny could finish his question but after hesitating briefly he continued, "D-d-do you mean you feel . . . l-like s-suicidal?"

Lee Ann said, "No, not suicidal . . . "

Lenny asked, "Would you tell us if you did feel suicidal?" (*nervous laugh*)

Lee Ann said, "Yeah, I would. I don't feel suicidal, I just feel blah, like I'm going nowhere in my life, like a failure."

Bob, a resident, said, "We, she and I, spoke about this earlier and I think Lee Ann is handling it really well. When you're depressed there's the denial—'I'm not really depressed,'—and the embarrassment—'I don't want to admit I'm depressed in the meeting or to the community.' But Lee Ann is talking about it and she's doing the best she can do which is to say 'Hey, I really am depressed, it's not the end of the world or anything but I'm depressed.'"

Lucy said, "Why don't you let Lee Ann talk for herself, Bob?"

Bob replied, "She has spoken for herself. Am I not lettin' you speak for yourself Lee Ann? 'Cause if I'm not I'll shut up."

Lee Ann said, "No Bob's right. I agree with what he's saying. I don't feel like he's not letting me talk. I'm depressed. And I know I won't be depressed forever, but now I am. 'This too shall pass,' right?"

Lyle, a recovery specialist, said, "I want to acknowledge Lee Ann for doing exactly what she should do and that's talk about it when she's feeling bad. I think that shows a lot of strength and just plain good sense on her part and I just want to let her know that we're with her and that she can always talk to any one of us if she feels like talking to someone. We're with you Lee Ann!"

The group applauded and Julie, a resident who was sitting on the couch across from Lee Ann, smiled at her and said, "I'm with ya, Lee Ann."

Honesty was valued not just as an end in itself, but as a means to facilitate recovery. Therapeutic practice at Canyon House was predicated on the presumption that within every resident there lurked at least two discrete *others inside*. These *others inside* were presumed capable of striking in a virtually infinite number of new and surprising ways. Obviously, this included striking through residents' private thoughts and feelings as well as through their overt behavior. But unlike overt behavior, which was usually amenable to surveillance, private thoughts and feelings required deliberate reportage if they were to be communally assessed and governed effectively (Foucault 1978). This type of reportage and communal assessment is further illustrated in the following excerpt from a drug dependency group. Martin said,

I was thinkin' I'd give some of my old connections a call just to see how they were doin' . . . " (*loud laughter from the group*) " . . . yeah, I know. But that's what I was thinkin' and I know that wasn't what I needed to be doin' right now at all, but it made me think I still wasn't admitting I was powerless because I thought I could talk to those people and not be threatening my recovery.

Similarly, Dennis confesses in his thought disorder group to having recently been upset by "weird thoughts" and is congratulated by a recovery specialist for doing so:

> "I also have been having weird, really weird thoughts. Like ever since I got caught stealing down at the mini-market I've been trippin' on looking suspicious and sometimes it really freaks me out!" (*laughs*)
> Eve asked, "What do you mean? What are some examples of those weird thoughts?" Dennis said, "Well like I went into the grocery store the other day to get a soda and some cigarettes and I was looking at the sodas and then I started to feel really stupid because I didn't get the cigarettes in the mini-market, and then I thought about that and said 'Why should I feel stupid about that?' and that made me feel even stupider! (*laughs*) Stuff like that though, getting upset about totally ridiculous little stuff like that. I feel like I'm going crazy!" (*laughs*)
> Many in the group identified with Dennis' having weird thoughts and Eve said, "Well I think it's a good sign that you're bringing it up and that you were thinking about it when you were in the store, keeping yourself in check. I remember there was a time when you wouldn't have said a word about having bizarre thoughts but would have just kept it to yourself and isolated. It shows you've made some progress that you're talking about it these days."
> Dennis said "Yeah. I used to just keep it to myself."

Right living also entailed doing one's assigned chores and punctual attendance of the various mandatory community functions. Obviously, a variety of accounts were proffered for failures to do so which reconciled them with right living. In the main, though, doing one's chores and punctual attendance of program functions was a major component of right living. Failures in this respect were the primary offenses punished by 6:15's. The following excerpt from a community meeting indicates both how seriously such matters were taken and the reprieves that could be granted if staff remained convinced of a client's commitment to recovery. It also provides a succinct rationale for such reprieves:

> Ray, a fairly new resident, is leading the community in 6:15's with well over ten. Paula asked him about them and he said he had "worked it out with Bruno [the kitchen manager] to wash the vans to work 'em off."
> Paula said, "That's good Ray. I'm glad you're working them off but I'd like to know what you're doing to keep yourself from getting them in the first place." Ray said he was asking people for help more if he didn't know what to do and asking people to wake him up in the morning and make sure he doesn't fall back asleep after wake up call. Tracy said, "It's true,

he asked me a question this morning about how to do his chore. I think he's improving. I think that's a good sign that he's improving."

Paula said, "I think that is a good sign too, but Ray? Why do people need to wake you up in the morning? Don't you have an alarm clock?"

Ray laughed sheepishly and said, "Yeah, but it doesn't work."

Paula laughed and said, "Well can't you get another one?! What do those things cost, like two or three bucks or something?! Come on Ray!"

Ray and many others in the group laughed about his reticence to take responsibility for getting himself out of bed.

Celia then remarked, "I gotta question, it ain't an issue, it's more just a question. It's okay to wash the vans to work off your 6:15's?"

Paula said, "Only if you got so many that you'd be here for five years before you could work 'em all off. We realize that some people have a little more trouble than others and we try to work with them because we don't think it's very helpful for someone whose trying to get recovery to be all demoralized all the time about all the 6:15's they have to work off. We'll work with people to get 'em worked off if we see that the person wants to be here and is making a genuine effort and it would take them forever to work 'em off if they did it the way they should. But if you don't have a ridiculous number of them then it doesn't really apply."

By way of contrast, the following excerpt shows what could happen if the staff lost faith in a resident's commitment to recovery. The group was discussing the recent discharge of a popular resident in community meeting. Paula, a recovery specialist, said,

"Yeah, I guess I can understand how people might feel that way. Willy seemed real easy to get along with and he never really caused any trouble so why did he get kicked out right?" People nodded. Paula explained, "Willy got discharged because we decided he wasn't making any progress here and we thought maybe Canyon House really wasn't the best place he could be right now. Willy got many many warnings and he just kept on making the same mistakes—not doing his chores, not waking up for his 6:15's. Finally he was taken in and told 'Okay Willy it's time to get serious and really get committed to what you're doin' up here. It's time to start makin' some real changes if you wanna be up here' and he said he would but then just kept doin' things the same way he always had been doin' 'em so we had to discharge him."

In addition to proper self-management, it was also expected that residents dedicate themselves to fostering right living among their peers. If one was held to have failed to do so, this too could be viewed as a departure from right living. On the other hand, becoming too invested in one's peers' recoveries was regarded dangerous if those peers themselves had not exhibited a similar dedication. The following two fieldnote excerpts demonstrate both sides of this issue. The first exchange took place in community meeting shortly after Clint had declared his unwillingness to get involved with people he felt were insufficiently dedicated to recovery. Paula, a recovery specialist, asked Clint,

"And do you think that's gonna work for you? I don't. If I thought that attitude was gonna keep you sober I'd say 'Go for it.' but I don't think it will. You've taken that attitude out there before and look what happened. Here you are again. You relapsed. I don't think the 'mind my own business' thing is gonna keep you clean. This is a fellowship and that means people lookin' out for each other's recovery. If everyone had the 'I'm not gonna get involved' approach there wouldn't be a fellowship would there?"

Clint said "No. But I can't worry about everybody else's business or it's gonna put me off track in my own recovery. There's just too much shit goin' on for me to try and fix it. It's as simple as that. I've got my own issues to think about. That's hard enough . . . " Paula interrupted and said "Yeah, but one of your issues is that you back off and don't get involved . . . "

Lee Ann, a resident with some seniority in the program, interrupted Paula and said, "I don't put a lot of time into people I don't think are taking the program seriously. It's beating your head against the wall. It's not worth it. I give everybody that comes up here a chance but if they show me they're not working on their recovery themselves why should I break my back working on their recovery? You can't make somebody want it. Clint's right about that. It doesn't make any sense to put more effort into somebody's recovery than they put themselves . . . It's up to them. If they want it, I'm here. If not that's their decision."

Paula said, "But how do you know if somebody wants it if you don't try with 'em? I think there are a lot of people in this room right now that had some real mixed feelings about being in the program when they first got here and if people didn't put themselves out for 'em they wouldn't be here right now. I think everybody deserves that."

Lee Ann said, "That's true. I mean I consider that. I don't just say 'Fuck off' the first time somebody fucks up. I have to see a pattern of fucking up before I give up . . . and I don't really ever 'give up.' I just don't try as much. I don't put myself out for them. If they want me they can always seek me out. But I'm not gonna keep banging my head against the wall trying to get 'em to see what they're doing."

Clint said "Yeah, that's what I'm saying. I don't give up on people a hundred percent. I just let them show me they want it if they do. I don't assume they do anymore."

The following excerpt is from another community meeting several months earlier. Here, Paula herself advises the very same approach espoused by Lee Ann and Clint above. Referring to another resident, Silvy said,

"I talk to her 'til I'm blue in the face even though I'm Black and she just ain't listenin'. I've had it man, it's time for me to give up on that shit."

Paula said, "That's right. It's one thing for us to try to help each other out. That's what the fellowship is all about, but my sponsor told me once you gotta say goodbye to somebody who just ain't tryin' themselves. What you gotta try and realize is that you're more dedicated to that person's recovery than they are and if that's true then you gotta give up and go on with your own recovery. 'Cause there ain't nothin' you can do if that person don't want it themselves."

As these excerpts show, whether, when, and how people fostered the right living of their peers was intimately connected to their assessments of their peers' commitment to their own recoveries. They were also deeply related to assessments they made of their peers' specific personalities, their abilities to participate in different activities, and their respective therapeutic needs. In other words, the substance of right living was tailored to both the expectations people had of one another's unique personal temperaments and their specific "issues." If, for example, someone consistently refused to share in groups, this might be attributed to an "issue" with trust, distinguished from that resident's locally permissible self, and made an object of compulsory therapeutic work. Alternatively, though, it might also be attributed to a nonpathological shyness, in which case therapeutic attention was unnecessary. Hence, in the following excerpt from a mood disorder group, the value of fostering talk about one's feelings in groups is qualified based on an assumption of personal differences between program members. Paula said,

"Okay, Dan doesn't think people talk enough about feelings in the groups. What do other people think about that? Do other people feel that way?" There were a variety of answers to this question. Sheila felt that people don't always know what they're feeling and that sometimes they need time to think things out on their own rather than bringing it into the groups right away. She agreed with Dan, however, that the groups would be better if people spoke more about their feelings. Paula commented, "That's true. We have to remember that everyone in here is different. Some people do better talking in group, others might do better writing their thoughts out in their journals, or sharing with people in situations more private than the groups. I don't think it would necessarily be a good thing for some people if they were forced to speak up more and talk about themselves in the groups. That really scares some people and I don't think we need to put them through that."

This excerpt depicts efforts to legitimate reticence, but assessments of right living were tailored to a variety of other features of people's personal temperaments as well. People's actions and experiences were legitimated with respect to their personal styles of speech, dress, and bodily comportment; perceptions of putatively "normal" variations in their emotional and physical conditions; perceptions of their natural human fallibility; and many others. Sometimes, though, assessments of right living were tailored to expectations regarding people's particular "issues" as well. General presumptions regarding the substance of right living might be slighted if a particular resident's conformity with them was found problematic. This can be seen in the following excerpt in which Calvin was himself chastised after pointing out that Juan had been sleeping during an alcohol dependency group. Though one might assume this gesture must embody right living insofar as it was undertaken to enforce Juan's right living, it was not in fact handled so plainly:

> Facing Juan, Calvin said, "Don't we give 6:15's for sleeping during group?"
>
> Tracy asked Calvin, "Why is it that you always are trying to get people in trouble?" Calvin hesitated before replying, "I don't want to get people in trouble. It was just a joke."
>
> Tracy said, "No it wasn't. You could have nudged him or something like that but instead you yelled out so the whole group could hear. It wasn't just for Juan, it was for the whole group and it was to get Juan a 6:15!"
>
> Calvin said, "That's bullshit. I don't really care if he gets a 6:15 or not. It doesn't matter to me."
>
> Tracy said, "Calvin, you are always the first one to do something like this and I think you need to look at how well you're running your own program before you become a watchdog for everybody else . . . "
>
> Paula, a recovery specialist, said, "Okay, okay, let's wait a second. The fact of the matter is Juan should not be sleeping during group and Calvin was right to call him on it. The second issue is whether Calvin was a little overzealous to make sure Juan got a 6:15. What do people think? Is that the kind of person Calvin is?" Most in the group said they thought Calvin was just joking.

So to recap, residents were asked to apply themselves to their own recoveries. This entailed not only becoming fluent in locally approved therapeutic discourse, or "talking the talk," but also right living, or "walking the walk," that indicated to staff and to their peers that they were both committed to recovery and capable of engaging in the locally approved methods for pursuing recovery. The substance of this work was negotiated but basically entailed abstinence, nonviolence, honesty, chores and meal crew, participation in community functions, and investment in the recovery of one's peers. The specific substance of right living was also tailored to the expectations people had of one another—their level of commitment, their unique personal temperaments, and their specific "issues." Through the exhibition and enforcement of right living, residents and staff strove to include themselves and one another in the Canyon House moral community. Beyond fostering a sense of collective identity, the exhibition and enforcement of right living was clearly also what I would like to call a *humanizing endeavor*. It was a humanizing endeavor insofar as it was precisely through this work that people sought to empower one another, specifically as human selves, against the nonhuman disease agents they held to have periodically governed their behavior and experiences in the past.

Self-Empowerment Through Retrospection

All of the program's various activities shared the fundamental objective of providing residents with "tools" for working on their recoveries. Equally, participation in the program was intended to incite residents as the primary caretakers of their own recoveries. Of course, the tools provided were largely inherited from the legacies discussed in Part I. And, undoubtedly, staff exercised more control than did residents in both identifying these tools and designating their proper use. But the fact remained that *empowerment*, or the cultivation of people's self-control, was both the explicitly sought outcome of treatment *and* an explicitly avowed resource for treatment. Some of the tools in circulation at Canyon House did not directly implicate residents' putative disorders as such but were nonetheless held to facilitate recovery from those disorders. Examples included generic techniques for stress management, relaxation, dispute resolution, and a smidgen of money management and basic jobs skills training. However, most of these tools were designed to help residents better understand and cope with their putative insanities and addictions. In this section I discuss these more common types of tools, highlighting the basically retrospective character of their use.

As noted above, Canyon House was very strongly influenced by the twelve-step legacy. Because ethnographers have already analyzed myriad aspects of the AA recovery program (cf. Cain 1991; Denzin 1991, 1993; Pollner and Stein 1996; Rudy 1986), and because I myself have attended too few actual AA meetings to write knowledgably about them, I do not intend to discuss AA as such. Instead, I want to focus on how the AA legacy was distinctively inhabited and employed at Canyon House. Despite its ubiquity, the AA legacy did not dictate or define therapeutic practice. Indeed, despite their widespread and vigorous proscription among AA groups (cf. Conrad and Schneider 1992, p. 89), the use of psychoactive medications figured as a core component of therapeutic practice at Canyon House. Thus the AA legacy did not assume the guise of a fixed (or nonnegotiable) code of conduct, a unified and consistent weltanschauung, or even an obdurate Durkheimian social fact. Rather, it was one source of what I am calling *generic conceptual templates* that Canyon House members artfully employed in their efforts to understand and manage their various troubles. These generic conceptual templates took the form of categorical generalizations about such things as people, people-like-us, addicts, addicted thinking, addiction, mental illness, medications, the streets, relapse, commitment, and recovery. They hailed from a variety of sources and circulated abundantly among members of the Canyon House community. The AA legacy was one very prominent source from which they were drawn.

Twelve-step templates were multifold and were often employed in contradictory kinds of ways. Nonetheless, their invocations clearly signaled reliance upon the AA legacy, and could serve to encourage residents to consider the likeness of their problems with those of others. These templates were sometimes drawn from written materials published by AA World Services, Inc., or related publishers like Hazelden. As in this excerpt, residents often cited passages from twelve-step literature with which they claimed to identify,

> Clint read something from *As Bill Sees It* suggesting the program was a 24 hour program and said, "That means that you do it all day long seven days a week but all the time you're doin' it you're doin' it just for today. For me that means no more long term resolutions. I've made a million of 'em 'never goin' back to jail, prison, booze.' The problem is I broke every one of 'em. I just got to work on makin' it through today."

More often, though, twelve-step templates were drawn from the rich AA and/or NA oral traditions. People picked up slogans, expressions, and parables at twelve-step events that seemed to capture important features of their own experiences. In the following excerpt from a community meeting, Doug tells of an important lesson he took from an old AA parable:

> "For a long time I thought this thing was a three step program. And I thought I had it down and was doing real good. I thought it was a three step program." Doug began to well up with tears and his voice broke. He paused, then continued, "But the one who taught me that there was more to it than that was a former resident here who was actually very seriously mentally ill. He was schizophrenic and had some real serious symptoms but he shared one day and told the story of the three frogs. I've heard it again a few times since then but he was the first I heard it from and I think it had a more serious impact on me because it was him I heard it from. It shows that you can learn from anyone in the fellowship even if they're as seriously mentally ill as he was and a newcomer. I don't think

he made more than a couple months. Anyway the story goes (*pause, voice breaking*) if there are three frogs sitting on a log and two of 'em make a decision to jump off, how many are left?" Some in the group answered to themselves before Doug answered his own question, "The answer is three (*laughs*) 'cause makin' a decision to jump is not jumping! But that hit me real hard 'cause that was me sitting up on that log! (*laughs*) I'd made the DECISION to change my life a long time ago but I was still up on that log doing things the same old way! I hadn't really changed my life. And that's where that eleventh step comes in 'We sought through prayer and meditation to IMPROVE our conscious contact with God . . .'. That's where the WORK of doing the steps comes in. IMPROVING your relationship with God as you understand Him and improving yourself. Ya can't just kick back and say, 'Yeah I got me a great relationship with God.' If you take that approach it ain't gonna happen. It's a constant process."

What I am calling twelve-step templates were not necessarily conse-crated features of a widely disseminated lore. In the following excerpt from a community meeting, a resident shares some advice his AA spon-sor gave him and offers no indication that this advice was anything other than a poignant generalization his sponsor had himself cooked up:

> "My sponsor told me a real good way to get through those times when you're obsessed with using. He said a lot of times addicts have a tendency to think back on the times they were using and to glamorize it, you know thinkin' how much money they had from dealin' or how good that last rush felt, and he said that the reason they get to thinkin' that way is that they ain't playin' that tape all the way through. What you oughta do when you start thinkin' that way is play that tape all the way through to when you weren't feelin' so good about it, to the next day, or to when you'd spent up everything you had to get that hit, or to whatever it was that got you in here. And then you won't feel so much like glamorizing the drug 'cause when you really think about it, get beyond that denial, and stop kidding yourself, using really ain't that glamorous." There was scattered agreement among the group.

Though both staff and residents often promoted twelve-step tem-plates, this was done suggestively rather than coercively. In the follow-ing excerpt Raymond had been sharing about the verbal abuse he used to take from his uncle when a recovery specialist, Norm, said,

> "If I've learned one thing in all my years of being an addict and knowing other addicts it's that addicts always have one thing in common. If nothing else, there's one thing that we all have and that's Low Self Esteem. Am I right? Has anyone ever met an addict who thought they were okay? You might see people who walk around struttin' their stuff as if they had high self-esteem but if ya get to know that person, ninety-nine times out of a hundred, you're gonna find out that down deep they ain't too happy

with themselves. And that's what the usin' or drinkin' is really all about is dulling that pain of low self-esteem. Am I right Ray? Is that what happened with you or am I off base on that one?" Raymond said, "No. That's right. That's my problem. I've always had low self-esteem." Norm said, "Well hopefully we can change some of that here. Once you start gettin' clean and sober, the next step is exploring and developing who Raymond is and learning about some of the positive things Raymond has to offer and building that self-esteem back up without the drugs."

In the main, twelve-step templates were suggested and residents were left to decide for themselves whether they were useful or not. People valued twelve-step templates not because they captured an invariant essence of addiction and recovery, but because they embodied an accumulated wisdom that has proved useful to many self-confessed addicts over the years. Residents were not expected to identify with every template offered to them (but it was considered cause for concern if they didn't identify with any). Twelve-step templates, then, were simply viewed as tools through which residents might be empowered. Their value consisted only in the extent to which they seemed to capture elements of people's past troubles and thereby made it easier to understand, anticipate, and cope with analogous troubles now and later.

Twelve-step templates were sometimes used to conceptualize insanities as well as addictions. People spoke of "being powerless" over their mental illnesses, the importance of "fellowshipping" with others presumed to suffer mental illnesses, the importance of "being ready" to embrace recovery from one's mental illness, and in a variety of other ways invoked twelve-step templates as resources in their recoveries from insanities. But templates were also drawn from sources other than the twelve-step legacy. Unsurprisingly, psychiatric diagnoses were also often used as generic conceptual templates. In the next excerpt, for example, Tracy had been sharing in community meeting about difficulties accepting her mental illness. She said she was diagnosed as bipolar but sometimes thought she heard voices and was afraid she might also be schizophrenic. Discussion ensued as to the consistency of hearing voices with different psychiatric diagnoses and of the empowering potential of diagnoses as such. Jonathan told Tracy he always heard voices and continued,

All I can do is try to ignore them and focus on other things but I'll tell you it was a great relief for me just to know that they weren't real—to know that I have a disease and the voices are nothing more than a chemical imbalance in my brain. It made it so much easier for me because now my only job is to try and keep the voices from interfering with my life. If they aren't real I don't have to pay attention to what they say. I always have to remind myself of that but it's a comforting thought, it really is.

Jonathan spoke of his "great relief" to discover that his experiences reflected a chemical imbalance in his brain. This discovery was quite obviously informed by the current scientific wisdom regarding the generic nature of schizophrenia rather than a specific datum regarding Jonathan's unique biochemistry. This type of recourse to existing bodies of generic professional expertise was common at Canyon House. Indeed, standardized worksheets were distributed in many of the didactic groups that relied on various psychiatric, psychological, and biomedical authorities. But rather than focusing on full-fledged diagnoses, these worksheets usually focused on more specific types of troublesome behavior and experience. In the following excerpt from a feeling good group, residents had been given a worksheet that listed ten forms of "twisted thinking" that often produce anxiety. After giving people time to peruse the worksheet, Ron, a recovery specialist, asked for a volunteer to begin. Lenny said,

"I feel anxious a lot when I speak in front of big groups like here and at AA meetings." Ron said, "Okay and what kinds of twisted thinking were you using that made you feel anxious, that made you feel that fear?"

Lenny looked over the worksheet and said, "Well let's see. 'Four. Discounting the positive'—I would think that I didn't have anything important to say and that nobody would want to hear it. 'Five. Jumping to conclusions'—I didn't think about the possibility that some people WOULD want to hear what I had to say. 'Magnification. Six.'—I would exaggerate the importance of the moment and think that if I made a fool out of myself it would be the worst thing in the world when really it wouldn't be that bad. It would be bad, but not the worst thing in the world. 'Seven. Emotional reasoning.'—I assumed my negative emotions reflected the way things really were. And 'Nine. Labeling.'—I thought I WAS a fool and so it was unavoidable that I would make a fool out of myself."

Ron said, "Okay that's real good. Looks like you spotted a lot of twisted thinking in the way you were approaching those situations. What do you think you could do to SOLVE some of these problems, these sources of fear . . . you know, Feeling Good, this is a problem solving group . . ."

Many laughed, suggesting this description of the group was getting a bit tired. Ron's tone of voice suggested he anticipated this reaction. Lenny responded to Ron's question, "Well I think I'm improving on this one. One of the things I do is just to raise my hand and get it over with, not dwell on it too long. That's what I just did for this assignment. I also try to think about myself as having important things to say."

We can clearly see in this passage the retrospective quality of the exercise, its promotion in the interest of Lenny's self-empowerment, and the freedom Lenny was allowed in using the worksheet as he chose. Lenny was not asked to think up instances of his having engaged in all ten types of twisted thinking, but to select from the list only those types he himself felt he had actually practiced. As with templates drawn from the twelve-step legacy, residents were granted considerable latitude in assessing the descriptive adequacy and practical relevance of templates drawn from *professionally authorized (or expert)* sources as well.

Despite the variety of sources from which generic conceptual templates were drawn, though, and the considerable discretion residents exercised over how they were used, these templates were sometimes found inadequate to the work of retrospective self-empowerment. This can be seen in the following excerpt from a drug dependency group. Here Warren complains of his tendency to overintellectualize with recourse to the twelve-step idiom. Eve, a recovery specialist, concedes the problem and tells how she tries to avoid it. Warren said,

"My thing right now is that sometimes I feel like I know this program so well that I can explain everything with the steps. It's like second nature to me now and that worries me."

Eve asked, "Why does that worry you Warren?"

Warren answered, "Well it's just that I know the slogans so well that sometimes I think I use it as a crutch you know (*laughs*) and intellectualize things with the AA slogans instead of focusing in on my feelings. I'm a good intellectualizer and I know that but that can get you in trouble if you're letting it keep you from seeing your feelings."

Eve said, "That's true. One thing you always need to watch out for is too much talk and not enough action. I try and get my groups to talk about feelings and leave the slogans behind as much as possible. They can be helpful but they aren't everything. I look for feeling talk and if I hear too much intellectualizing I know something's not working the way it should. You gotta stay close to feelings and not worry so much about the talk."

This excerpt begins to suggest a domain of therapeutic practice at Canyon House that transcended the use of generic conceptual templates to confer meaning and order on people's pasts. Without doubt people relied heavily on generic templates drawn from twelve-step, psychiatric, psychological, and other stocks of knowledge. Furthermore, attention to "feelings" rather than "talk" or "slogans" was by no means impervious to the use of templates regarding the generic nature of "emotions." But still, it is critically important to recognize that residents did not consider the knowledge available at Canyon House solely in terms of generic conceptual templates. Much of this knowledge was not, and could not have been, based on any body of general theory (be it "lay" or scientific) at all.

The therapeutic value people conferred on community involvement is multifaceted and complex. Part of that value was discussed earlier in terms of the exhibition and enforcement of right living. Part of that value was certainly also found in the community's provision of a vast pool of generic conceptual templates that could be used to give sense to one's troubled past. But involvement in the Canyon House community empowered residents in another way as well. It equipped them to learn the details of one another's personal temperaments and "issues" to an extent that could not possibly have been matched by mere reliance on generic templates. People often discussed themselves, their problems, and their recoveries at a level of detail that was quite simply beyond the scope of any brand of template concerning the generic characteristics of "people," "insanities," "addictions," "twisted thinking," "emotional disturbances," "problems in living," or whatever else. In the course of their interactions, people acquired quite particular understandings of themselves, one another, and the *others inside* that ostensibly afflicted them. These formulations drew less upon generic templates and more upon what people knew of their own and each other's specific biographies. This can be seen in the following discussion of a resident, Nancy, in a staff meeting. Paula said,

> "She's doing so much better than when she first got here and I try and tell her that she's got all these blessings coming her way and she's got to look at that and take advantage of it. She's so afraid of those rages that she gets into and what she might do when she's in one but man, I have seen some bad rages and hers aren't really even that bad" (*laughs*). Jane, the assistant program director, agreed, "They really aren't."
>
> Paula laughed, "I mean I've seen rages much worse than hers...I've HAD rages much worse than the ones I've seen her get into! (*laughs*)...I tell her it's perfectly natural to get angry but look how you're handling it NOW as compared to how you used to. You're not drinkin' behind it, you're not cutting on yourself, you're not doing any of those destructive things you used to do behind those rages. Give yourself a little credit!"

In this excerpt Paula does not address the generic character of "rage" and its relationship to Nancy's case so much as she recounts the specific details of Nancy's particular rages and her efforts to empower Nancy with respect to those particular rages. Promoting self-empowerment through retrospection involved developing detailed sensibilities regarding people's personal temperaments and "issues" and applying these sensibilities in the cultivation of both one's own and one's peers' recoveries. This primarily entailed promoting residents' detailed understandings of their own personal aptitudes and deficits and their acquisition of "tools" with which to foster the former and suppress the latter. This personalized dimension of recovery can also be seen in the following excerpt from a staff meeting. Despite the putative severity of his schizophrenia, Martin was on the verge of graduating and was regarded as a Canyon House success story when the following discussion took place. The enthusiasm expressed regarding Martin's awareness of his specific patterns and the steps he is said to be taking to manage them richly indicate how the work of recovery was very much a matter of fostering residents' empowerment with respect to the *specific features of their own particular putative disorders*. Norm said,

"I read in the log this morning he was thinking about killing himself last night? Is that right?!"

Doug, the vocational rehabilitation coordinator, said, "Martin was?!"

Ted, Martin's recovery specialist, said, "No, no. He's talked to me about this too. He said he's hearing voices lately that are telling him to kill himself and he says he knows they're voices and he thinks it's just the pressure of graduating..."

Norm said, "I'm just goin' off what's written in the log..."

Ted said, "I think it mentions the voices in the log doesn't it?"

Norm said he wasn't sure and added, "We got a chance to talk a bit when we were going up to Hemet [to an NA conference] and he said he usually has had his serious down swings in the winter months, that he's recognized that as his cycle and he was real worried that it might happen to him now and push him into a relapse. With graduating now and all that there's a lot of pressure...

"Ted said, "Yeah, we've talked some about that too and I think it's a real good sign that he's aware of that possibility and is acting accordingly. He mentioned in Men's Group that he had grabbed some people after his meeting the other night to have coffee with him because it was being held real near his old connection's house and he was afraid he might go by there if he was alone. That sounds to me like real heads up behavior. I think he's very aware of his patterns and is thinkin' about what he needs to be doing to prevent a relapse. I think he really wants recovery bad and he's watching himself." Norm nodded.

Doug asked, "Well what does all this mean for voc.? I don't want him comin' into voc. if he ain't ready yet. I've had enough Trents and Betsys [two graduates who were said to have suffered dramatic psychotic breaks while in voc.] for awhile!"

Ted said, "He's ready. I think he's ready."

Doug said, "I agree with you that you can interpret what he's doing as heads up but it's real obvious he's got some big problems he's dealin' with here. I just don't want to put him in voc. before he's ready."

Ted said, "Hey graduation is a stressful time but it's never not gonna be a stressful time whether it's winter or not. He's gonna have the same pressures out there and I think he's as ready for voc. as he's ever gonna be. Martin has a mental illness that he's got to watch. That's all there is to it. I think he's doin' a pretty good job, all things considered." The others nodded.

Like promoting recovery through right living, promoting self-empowerment through retrospection was a humanizing endeavor. It was a humanizing endeavor in the sense that it presumed, called upon, and cultivated residents' uniquely human aptitudes to disown, effectively interpret, and overcome recalcitrant and chronically dehumanizing features of their personal being. This entailed examining the past for the patterns taken by one's own and one's peers' troublesome personal behavior and experience and finding tools with which to manage those patterns. By engaging in this collaborative work, people both fostered and fortified a sense of moral community, and indeed common humanity, between themselves. And also like the promotion of right living, promoting self-empowerment heavily emphasized cultivating residents' individual responsibility for accomplishing their own recoveries. This emphasis was manifest in the discretion residents were entitled to exercise in judging both the descriptive adequacy and the practical relevance of the generic conceptual templates to which they were exposed. It was manifest as well in the tailoring of self-empowerment exercises to the specific details of who they were and the specific problems from which they were perceived to suffer.

The Social Reality of Others Inside

Throughout this book I have explicitly opposed the view that the true nature of insanities and addictions can be found only by investigating some unchanging ontological domain beyond the reach of social history and socially situated human activity. In place of this view I have argued that the empirical forms taken by insanities and addictions are always thoroughly affected by social history and socially situated human activity. At the same time, though, I have sought to remain respectful of the regard my ethnographic research subjects had for these phenomena. Given pervasive evidence that people treated their own and each other's insanities and addictions as causally influential things-in-the-world, I have not felt entitled to trade on sociological theories that systematically debunk such notions by reducing insanities and addictions to myths, discursive categories, narrative accounts, or social roles (cf. Davies 1997; Fingarette 1988; Peele 1989; Scheff 1984; Stephens 1991; Szasz 1961). Though the putative *others inside* residents were certainly social artifacts, people did, nonetheless, produce them as discrete and truly consequential things-in-the-world. In what follows, I specify how *others inside* members of the Canyon House community were made to figure as consequential contributors to the ongoing achievement of Canyon House affairs.

First, a warning. The forms that were given to *others inside* at Canyon House often bore little relationship to generically codified nosologies like those provided in the American Psychiatric Association's successive Diagnostic and Statistical Manuals. Therapeutic practice at Canyon House was much more concerned with finding and subduing the specific patterns taken by particular people's problems than with the relationship between those problems and generic, or formal, diagnoses (see also Brown 1987; Kirk and Kutchins 1992; Rhodes 1991). Rather than insisting on the omnirelevance of formal disease classifications, then, it is more ethnographically appropriate to investigate the forms taken by *others inside* by specifying the actual types of events *others inside* could be legitimately held to have caused at Canyon House.

By now it may go without saying that *others inside* were held to have caused a vast spectrum of troubled, troublesome, unusual, and unintelligible behaviors and experiences at Canyon House. It may also go without saying that what was and was not properly viewed as the effect of an *other inside* someone was always a socially negotiated outcome. For example, depending on a variety of factors, residents were often found to both feign and conceal their putative disorders. Given the ever-present possibility that people were dissembling, prima facie evidence of pathology and mental health was never taken entirely for granted. This can be seen in the following excerpt from a staff meeting wherein the authenticity of Ruby's recent seizures is discussed. Jane asked,

> "What are we gonna do with Ruby?" There were a lot of frowns and shaking heads following this question. Eve replied, "I don't know. What *can* we do is the question."
> Jane asked, "Are we gonna have to let her go?"

Eve answered, "I think we might have to. This program is just not equipped to deal with someone with her kinds of problems. Apparently she had another seizure last night..."

John asked, "What about those seizures? What do you think those are about?" There was more shaking of heads then John followed up on his own question, "I mean do we know for sure if they're even real?"

Jane said, "Yeah, some of the residents said they thought she was faking them..."

Eve said, "Really? Why would she do that?"

John said, "Who knows? It could be anything..."

Eve asked, "Why did the residents think she was faking?"

Jane answered, "I think you can more or less tell with seizures if they're real or not. Tracy said her eyes rolled back in her head and she started to shake slowly and then it got worse. But she, like, got down on her side and started shaking around and then got up looking all disoriented." Jane gave a look suggesting she thought it could be an act. John said, "I think they might be fake. I mean she's had like two or three since she got here. That's a bit much I think."

Here the possibility that Ruby was feigning disorder is debated. In the following excerpt from a community meeting, the converse possibility that Dennis was trying to conceal a flare-up of his schizophrenia is raised and discussed. Eve asked Dennis,

"How are you doin', Dennis? I've been gettin' the impression that you've been havin' some problems. This is just one more thing. Gettin' picked up by the cops isn't something I would have expected from the old Dennis but the way you've been lately, I'm not surprised. It seems like the trouble started when you went off your med.'s. What do you think?"

Dennis said, "Yeah, I guess it could be it..."

Paula said, "Remember when you first told us you were having hallucinations again you told us that you didn't want to tell anyone about them because you thought they'd go away and you didn't want to go back on the med.'s?"

Dennis said, "Yeah."

Paula asked, "Is that still how you feel, like if you tell people about what's happenin' with you they might tell you to get back on your med.'s?"

Dennis said, "Well I started taking my med.'s again last night so I don't really feel that way now. I really am committed to my recovery and that's the main thing. I feel like I'll do whatever is necessary to stay in the program and stay in recovery. I don't feel bad about talking about my hallucinations I just don't want my hallucinations to get in the way of my recovery."

These excerpts indicate just how ambiguous the work of distinguishing human from nonhuman agency could be. They also suggest that when findings of human and nonhuman agency were made, they were inevitably provisional and subject to reformulation based on new evidence. What, then, governed whether given segments of personal behavior and experience were attributed to human agency or the non-human agency of an insanity or addiction? To begin to answer this question it must first be recalled that therapeutic practice consisted fundamentally in efforts to exhibit and enforce right living among program residents. When residents were perceived to embody right living they were regarded as succeeding in their recoveries. In such cases, insanities and addictions were never invoked to account for residents' present behavior but were regarded as having been manifest in past behavior and experience and as sources of *potential* problems that called for residents' constant vigilance to prevent relapse. Hence, as we have seen, therapeutic practice also entailed fostering more incisive understanding of the patterns residents' disorders had taken in the past.

However, when clients were found to have lapsed from right living, decisions had to be made as to why they had done so and how best to remedy the problem. Though one might suspect that immediate recourse to the idioms of insanity and/or addiction were made in such cases, things were not quite so straightforward. Instead, these lapses were usually viewed as evidence for what I will call *wrong living*. In cases of wrong living, people were punished in keeping with the belief that they would respond by curtailing their offensive behavior.[12] Depending on its perceived severity, a single instance of wrong living could be met with sanctions running the gamut from a mild rebuke to termination from the program. A chronic pattern of wrong living was

---

12. Ironically enough, people institutionalized for a putative *inability* to adequately control themselves are, nonetheless, usually held responsible to comply with institutional protocol. This is not only true of programs, like Canyon House, that strive to empower their clients as agents of their own recoveries, but is true of more plainly custodial settings as well. Though he has often been simplistically invoked as the foremost theorist of trained helplessness in mental institutions, Goffman (1961, pp. 86–7) wrote,

> Although there is a psychiatric view of mental disorder and an environmental view of crime and counter-revolutionary activity, both freeing the offender from moral responsibility for his offense, total institutions can little afford this particular kind of determinism. Inmates must be caused to *self-direct* themselves in a manageable way, and, for this to be promoted, both desired and undesired conduct must be defined as springing from the personal will and character of the inmate himself, and defined as something he can do something about. [original italics]

This passage intimates much of the oft forgotten nuance in Goffman's analyses of mental hospital life. I dispute only Goffman's overly schematic insistence that "conduct must be defined as springing from the personal will and character of the inmate" in order for it to be "defined as something he can do something about." In my own view, the latter does not require the former. I thank Bob Emerson for bringing this passage to my attention.

certainly grounds for discharge (cf. The Paula-on-Willy excerpt mentioned earlier). Because events held to embody wrong living were events
for which residents were held morally accountable, they therefore implicated the humanity of the agent held to have caused them.[13] Hence,
whatever relationships wrong living bore to findings of insanity and addiction were necessarily indirect ones. Wrong living consisted in events
caused by *human* others, agents properly viewed as subjects of praise
and blame, but transgressive of the community's moral boundaries. Of
course, findings of wrong living were also discretionary and subject to
negotiation as can be seen in the next excerpt from a community meeting. Tracy said,

> "I wasn't gonna bring this up in here. I was just gonna talk to my counselor
> about it after the group but it really frustrates me and I need to bring it up,
> and it does concern the whole community. I wanna know why people get
> excused from coming to group when they're over tired but when they're
> sick they're not excused. That doesn't seem fair to me. I don't think that's
> right. I mean some people really are sick and they need to rest and the
> only reason for being over tired is staying up too late. I think you can't
> help being sick but staying up too late is you're own decision. I don't know
> why one gets off and the other doesn't."
>
> Eve said, "You're talking about Sherry this morning getting excused
> from group 'cause she said she was tired?" and Tracy said, "Yeah." Eve
> nodded and said, "Well this is a tough question. It's not that one gets
> off and the other doesn't. That's not it. When people ask to be excused
> from community activities we have to deal with it on a case by case basis.
> We can't just climb into people's psyches and really know whose got a
> legitimate excuse and who doesn't. We can't do that. All we can do is
> make the best judgment we can at that moment. . . . If someone who never
> misses groups and is usually a pretty motivated person says they're really
> exhausted or their head is in a weird place and asks to be excused I'll look
> at who they are and how they've been doing and usually I'll say 'yeah
> you're excused. Do whatever you think you need to do.' but if someone is
> always saying they're sick, or they have med. problems, or headaches, or
> migraines, or whatever I'll say 'You gotta come to group' 'cause that starts
> sounding like a responsibility problem."

The crux of wrong living, then, was that it was regarded a "responsibility problem." Insofar as therapeutic practice at Canyon House was so
emphatically focused on empowering residents as agents of their own

13. I do not mean to suggest that only human beings are ever held morally accountable, only that program participants never once interpreted their own or a peer's behavior
as that of a nonhuman *moral* being, a pet for example. Program participants did, however, routinely release each other from moral accountability on the grounds that someone was presently disabled by nonhuman *amoral* beings in the guise of insanities and
addictions.

recoveries, there was a decided preference for making residents themselves responsible for the work of formulating and managing their own personal problems. This preference could be exercised in different kinds of ways though. In the previous passage Eve claims to allow residents who have demonstrated a genuine investment in their recoveries a good deal of autonomy in dictating the details of their own recovery work. However, if people were found chronically intransigent or habitually in need of the community's forbearance, then the work of promoting their personal responsibility for their recoveries came to focus less on fostering their *personal autonomy* in dictating the details of their recovery and more on enforcing their *personal accountability* to the Canyon House community. Generally speaking, efforts to establish a particular resident's therapeutic needs, abilities, and obligations in such cases were made collectively—either in staff meetings or in the community as a whole. Collective assessments were particularly likely to arise when residents invoked their own mental disorders to account for their own lapses from right living. Below, Ricky tries to excuse himself for having made some sexually explicit and insulting comments to another resident by invoking his mental illness. Given that everyone in the community meeting knew the hot water he was in, they immediately saw this account as a ploy. Ricky said,

> "I shouldn't have said what I said. I know that. But I'm up here [at Canyon House] 'cause I got me a mental problem that I'm tryin' to get some help with..."
>
> The whole group erupted in a concerted moan and some began to laugh. Doug, a counselor, laughingly said, "Naw, naw, naw!! That don't work. That ain't gonna work Ricky. There ain't gonna be any excuses. We all got mental problems we're up here tryin' to get some help with but *you're* the only person who made a totally inappropriate comment about Tracy's clothes."

Here, Ricky's effort to invoke his putative mental problem is soundly rejected and responsibility for his transgression is placed squarely on his *self* as a morally accountable human agent.[14] In this instance, Ricky's peers found the motives for his actions starkly apparent. But even when human designs were not so obvious, Canyon House members

---

14. In using the expression *morally accountable human agent*, I am drawing on the distinctively ethnomethodological understanding of moral accountability that refers not only to the demands we make upon ourselves and one another to behave virtuously, but also the moral demands we make upon ourselves and one another to behave *intelligibly* (Coulter 1973, 1979; Garfinkel 1963, 1984; Heritage 1984; Ingleby 1982; Pollner 1987; Wieder 1988).

nonetheless exhibited a clear preference for finding human agency in one another's behavior (Weinberg 1997a). *Despite the abstract expectation that residents would occasionally manifest symptoms of their putative insanities and addictions, in practice, there remained a strong disinclination to treat residents' behavior as symptomatic.* The following excerpt is exemplary. David was diagnosed with schizophrenia, and was known as uncommonly vulnerable to episodes of florid psychosis. He had been speaking at length in a community meeting, primarily regarding his anger with residents who exhibited little concern for their peers' well-being. He oscillated between dramatic emotional outbursts and resigned and cynical mumbling. His discussion touched upon many themes, including God's role in creating the problems of which he spoke and his desire to become a priest. After David had spoken for about three or four minutes, Sally, the program director, interrupted him as follows:

> "O.K., thanks David. Does anybody have any feedback for David on any of the things he was saying?"
>
> Lucy, an older client with a serious speech impediment, replied, "I think what David was sayin' is *right* on!"
>
> Bruce, another client, said, "I agree mostly with what you're saying David but I also think you're rambling a little."
>
> David replied, "I know I'm rambling but that's because I got a lot to say..." He went on to speak about the trials he had endured through his life and then returned to Bruce's point, "...but I know I'm rambling too much. It's my hallucinations and I got a lot of anxiety about my life but I'm also just pissed about people not putting anything into this program..." Again, David became extremely agitated. Sally interrupted, "David? David? It's starting to get a bit heavy. I hear a lot of judgmental stuff and a lot of anger. I think it's time to let someone else have the floor."

Though David was called on his rambling, and was asked to tone down his angry outbursts, no one, except David himself, even raised the possibility that his conduct might be symptomatic. David was treated as a morally accountable human agent capable of controlling his actions and emotions throughout this entire exchange. The preference for finding human agency during interactions with people presumed to suffer from insanities and addictions was a pervasive and unremarkable feature of social life at Canyon House. As will be recalled from Chapter 2, the inclination to *humanize* clients was the quintessence of moral treatment as inaugurated by Tuke and Pinel. The previous excerpt provides a glimpse of how this principle was realized in practice at Canyon House. Clients were humanized when they were held morally accountable either for having caused their personal behavior and experiences or for properly exercising control over future personal behavior and experiences.[15]

At Canyon House, insanities and addictions were invoked only when people found it simply too difficult to interpret behavior as the effect of a morally and cognitively competent human agent. Under such circumstances, troubles were held to have issued from sources within a resident's *person*, but not from their *self*.[16] In the following excerpt, two residents, Bob and Silvy, defend another resident, Robert, in a community meeting by invoking the empirical observability of his mental illness. Robert had received four 6:15's for various failures to fulfill his assigned responsibilities. Eric, a resident, began the exchange by treating Robert as a competent interactant, capable of accounting for his failures. However, Robert's peers did not interpret the response Eric received from Robert's *person* as issuing from Robert's *self*, as a morally accountable human agent. Indeed this response provoked another resident, Bob, to invoke the "obvious[ness]" of Robert's mental illness for everyone in the group. Bob was then joined by Silvy in defense of Robert's good faith efforts to participate in the program and the moral groundlessness of punishing him with 6:15's. Eric, the resident in charge of chores asked,

"Robert, you wanna tell us what all those 6:15's are about?"
   Robert's reply was decidedly difficult to follow due to dramatic modulations in volume, his speaking in somewhat cryptic sentence fragments, and a failure to remain on topic.

   15. It may be that the propensity to humanize personal behavior and experience is a good deal more pervasive than my reference to moral treatment would suggest. Garfinkel (1963, 1984) found in his famous "breaching" experiments that research subjects displayed a default orientation to human social interaction that presumed the intentionality and interactional competence of their cointeractants' conduct and began looking for alternative accounts only when that default expectation was somehow shaken. Indeed, Garfinkel found that his subjects often went to great lengths to preserve the sense that their cointeractants were indeed acting deliberately, even if they were forced to acknowledge that they could not as yet fathom those deliberations (cf. Garfinkel 1984, p. 60). These experiments were conducted under a wide variety of practical circumstances using many different research subjects.
   16. This formulation draws upon Harre's distinction (Harre 1987, p. 42) between the *person* (understood as the "human being as a social individual embodied and publicly identifiable") and the *self* (understood as "that inner unity to which all personal experience [and I would add, conduct] belongs as attributes of a subject"). While some social scientists have suggested the value of understanding insanities and addictions as disorders of the self (cf. Denzin 1993; Estroff 1989; Karp 1996), I am suggesting here that in very important respects this conception was not shared by those with whom I conducted fieldwork. Insanities and addictions took worldly form for participants in these treatment settings as entities that existed as *of* the person, but separate from the self, of the afflicted person (though, of course, they were often perceived to powerfully *influence* the selves of afflicted people).

Bob, another resident, interrupted Robert to say, "Robert's been having some trouble with his medications . . . I mean, I don't think I need to
explain to anyone how Robert's been. It's obvious. It's amazing he's only
got four . . . I don't think it's fair to give him the 6:15's when he's doin' the
best he can."

Silvy said, "I agree with Bob . . . Robert is really mentally ill and his
medications don't seem like they're doin' a thing for him at all . . . I don't
think it's fair to give him the 6:15's when he's as sick as he is."

Paula, a recovery specialist, said, "O.K., we'll look into this med. problem and maybe we can work something out for Robert."

This particular segment of Robert's behavior was taken as evidence
of mental illness by many participants in the meeting and served as empirical grounds for their efforts to exonerate Robert from punishment
for his lapses from right living. However, it would be wrong to isolate
this assessment of Robert's behavior from the specific practical activities in and for which it was made. The qualities of Robert's conduct
that induced his peers to invoke mental illness must be understood as
necessarily and intrinsically qualities-in-context. It was by no means
inevitable that behavior striking Canyon House members as troubled,
troublesome, unusual, or unintelligible be treated as evidence of mental
disorder (see also Yarrow et al. 1955). Indeed, as was seen in David's case,
people usually struggled to preserve the sense that residents' behavior
was caused by human agents and that it specifically did not exhibit the
effects of nonhuman *others inside* one another.

Thus, the ostensive causal force of Robert's mental illness on the
course of this exchange was inextricably tied to the "gestalt contexture"
(Gurwitch 1964, p. 105) provided by the locally meaningful organization of program affairs and participants' expectations regarding Robert
as a fellow human agent and a collaborator in those affairs. More specifically, Eric's effort to obtain an account from Robert for his accumulation
of 6:15's was met with a response that arose from Robert's person, but
proved too difficult to interpret as humanly responsive to, or evasive of,
Eric's question. Thus Robert's mental illness emerged specifically as a
surrogate cause of behavior that people—*qua* participants-in-program-
activities—found too difficult to regard as caused by Robert himself. In
light of this formulation, it is more appropriate to view their inclination
to regard Robert's behavior as symptomatic as couched in, and responsive to, interactional and/or organizational contingencies than to adopt
the view of Laing (1969) and other antipsychiatrists that it stems from
an all-pervasive lack of empathy or imagination. No doubt, the fact that
this interactional exchange occurred in a setting specifically organized to

treat insanities and addictions was a catalyst for the discovery of mental disorder in this exchange (Rosenhan 1973). However, it is crucial that this not be overstated. Because even within this treatment context, it was only because Robert's behavior *resisted* interpretation as meaningful human action that it provided evidence of his putative mental disorder's nonhuman agency.

I use the expression *moral derangement*[17] to indicate all human involvement in the world that is not regarded as having been caused by a human agent. At Canyon House, examples of moral derangement could include both fleeting episodes, as when residents were perceived to express deluded thoughts, and more enduring incapacities to adequately participate in the program. In cases like these, residents' putative disorders were held to have overtaken them to such an extent that they themselves, as morally accountable human agents, could not be effectively enlisted as collaborators in the community's work. It is important to acknowledge that it was not that these residents were regarded as having completely lost their humanity (see also Bogdan and Taylor 1989; Goode 1994; Gubrium 1986; Pollner and McDonald-Wikler 1985), but that whatever humanity they were observed to embody was considered disabled by their disorders to an extent precluding right living. As human agents they were judged as mere passengers in persons being driven by amoral *others inside* them. Despite the fact that they were always situated social accomplishments, there were some familiar patterns evident in the ways particular behaviors and experiences were attributed to *others inside* people at Canyon House. The rest of this section will be concerned with specifying these patterns.

The activities through which Canyon House members gave form to the putative *others inside* them often involved the use of conceptual templates regarding generic aspects of addictions and insanities. Not only were such templates used to construe past events, they were also used to attribute segments of present behavior and experience to *others inside* residents. However, I found nothing approaching a determinate algorithm for sorting specific kinds of events with specific kinds of disorder. Of course, people had abstract ideas about the kinds of symptoms that are normally associated with specific varieties of disorder. But in actual

17. The expression *moral derangement* is used to describe behaviors that by their apparent senselessness as moves within the local moral order place the agents held to have caused them beyond the boundaries of that moral order. This displacement is more than simply a matter of condemnation and banishment. It entails being found to have caused something that cannot have been caused by a member of the local moral order.

practice, these sortings were governed by myriad concerns specific to the activities at hand. Putative paranoias, hallucinations, depressions, and the like were sometimes understood as induced by psychiatric disorders but they were sometimes also understood as addiction-induced. Likewise, professed drug cravings were held to exhibit bona fide addictions but were held to exhibit compulsions to self-medicate psychiatric disorders as well. Sometimes, findings of hallucinations, paranoias, depressions, and other such candidate "symptoms" were attributed to the effects of particular medications, to exhaustion, and to other causes that did not directly implicate the agency of insanities or addictions at all.

Assessments of the presence or absence of a particular disorder's nonhuman agency necessarily were based on more than abstract considerations of the generic characteristics of formally recognized diagnoses. These assessments were also based on people's subjective perceptions of how to properly undertake recovery, assessments of people's present practical circumstances (recall the Ricky excerpt mentioned earlier), and assessments of people's unique personal characteristics (including both their nonpathological needs and capacities and their particular problem profiles). Expectations in each of these areas could profoundly affect people's assessments of whether a segment of behavior was properly viewed as symptomatic or not.

The following excerpt from a family systems group will serve to demonstrate how deeply embedded such assessments were in the particular organizational, interactional, and biographical details of the program's work. In this excerpt, Norm, a recovery specialist, assessed a segment of Clint's talk as symptomatic of alcohol addiction. Norm's assessment was obviously predicated on a conceptual template concerning one generic category of "alcoholic thinking" and his sense that Clint was presently exhibiting that category of thinking. Norm said,

> "Addicts are notoriously untrustworthy people. For them their addiction comes first, second and third and whatever they got room for after that they'll see about it. I know that from experience. That's the way I was. If you're not around addicts all the time you might find yourself in a little better position to start trusting both yourself and others."
>
> Clint replied, "I understand what yer sayin' Norm, but I've been burned so many times I sort of feel like I'm spent up, ya know? Like why should I trust anymore..."
>
> Norm scoffed and said, "I'm sorry Clint, but I'm gonna say something and I hope you don't take any offense, 'cause we really are all friends

in here, and it's all about recovery, but: That is such an alcoholic thing to say!! It's all or nothing, 'either I trust or I don't trust.' Don't be all or nothing."

Because treatment in organizations like Canyon House is so fundamentally reliant on participants' willingness to share regarding difficult issues, fostering trust among residents was a central component of treatment. Hence, endeavoring to build trusting relationships with at least a few people in the program was an explicit requirement of right living. Conversely, a steadfast refusal to trust anyone could be construed as wrong living. The issue was somewhat complicated, however, by a widespread expectation that "addicts are notoriously untrustworthy people." Simply put, some people admitted into the program would certainly prove unworthy of trust. This putative fact required that residents be taught to trust discriminatingly. Thus, residents were expected to develop techniques for distinguishing those worthy of greater and lesser levels of trust and to manage their recoveries accordingly. In light of this expectation, program participants widely viewed what Norm called "all or nothing thinking" in this regard as a rather simple, and common, technique to set oneself up for a disappointment that could then be used to rationalize a return to drug use. This generic understanding of addiction and addicted thinking provided a conceptual template for understanding the conduct of particular residents.

In this particular interactional context, Norm took Clint's remarks as an indication that he was no longer willing to trust anyone anymore, a posture that was patently inconsistent with right living at Canyon House. But given the fact that Clint was apparently in the midst of sharing his feelings in good faith (and was thusly exhibiting a willingness to participate properly in the group), Norm judged Clint's momentary departure from right living as a manifestation of "all or nothing thinking," a locally accredited generic template regarding alcoholics. By construing Clint's remarks this way, Norm was able to assume a therapeutic (rather than punitive) posture with him. Though he was sanctioned, Clint's accountability was *therapeutically* cast as a responsibility to henceforth more effectively monitor the *other inside* him that urged a self-destructive "all or nothing" orientation to trust, rather than *punitively* cast as a responsibility for having engaged in wrong living to begin with. Taken out of their specific context, Clint's remarks are arguably interpretable as evidence of paranoia, depression, delusion, and many other candidate symptoms of a variety of disorders other than addiction. It was only the specific details of Norm's knowledge of Clint's biography, Clint's issues, and the practical details of their exchange that compelled Norm to read Clint's remarks as he did.[18]

Findings of the causal effects of *others inside* program members also often drew upon people's more specific understandings of their own and each other's personal temperaments and "issues." Thus, various forms of trouble that bore no prima facie relationship to generic conceptual templates regarding addiction or any psychiatric diagnoses were also sometimes understood as the effects of *others inside* residents. The following discussion took place shortly after Bob made a slightly irreverent remark about the group's proceedings. Though Bob's overall commitment to recovery and to the program wasn't questioned, many took exception to Bob's lighthearted attitude. His tendency to joke about things was promptly attributed not to a generic symptom of some specific disorder but to a putatively dysfunctional "defense" by which Bob tended to unwittingly repress his emotions.[19] Edgar said,

> "Bob I think you should be listening to this. I think a lot of this might be stuff you could find useful if you were taking it seriously. I think this is a real defense that you use. If you always make a joke out of something then that way you can keep things real superficial and not have to consider what you're feeling."

18. A methodological note. Clearly Norm's response to Clint's behavior is integral to our ability to analytically detect the emergence of Clint's alcohol addiction as a causal agent in the above exchange. *But Norm's response did not create the agency of Clint's alcohol addiction.* Norm's response to Clint's behavior is integral to the analysis only in the sense that Norm is our endogenous *witness* (and respondent) to the causal agency of Clint's addiction. This witnessing was grounded in, and informed by, Norm's participation with Clint in the Canyon House moral community and the sense making practices that community availed him. Within the practical context of the group, Clint's questioning why he should trust anymore resisted being construed as right living. But Clint had neither a history of disregarding program requirements nor was he presently exhibiting any deliberate opposition to properly engaging in program affairs. Given this context, combined with the ready to hand template of "all-or-nothing thinking" as a generic category of addicted thinking, the qualities-in-context that Clint's remarks exhibited for Norm strongly suggested the agency of Clint's putative alcohol addiction. The practical logic of the program's work gave Clint's putative addiction an empirical form distinct from Norm's categorical understanding of all-or-nothing thinking that became available for interpretation by way of that generic conceptual template. Thus, rather than originating in Norm's claims about it, Clint's addiction assumed a causal force as of the moral economy of program practice that Norm claimed to have witnessed. In this sense it was the *situation* defined rather than the *definition* of the situation that gave empirical form to Clint's alcohol addiction as a discrete causal agent.

19. I know of no formal nosology that specifies lighthearted irreverence as a symptom of mental illness or addiction.

Paula agreed with Edgar, "It's true Bob. I think you're real fast to look at things as a joke and not take them seriously. It's a way you have of stuffing your feelings. You could benefit from trying to get in touch with your feelings a little more."

In the following passage from a community meeting, even Sherry's "willfulness" is attributed to a putative *other inside* her! Paula had mentioned her surprise when she saw the list of people with three or more 6:15's because it was so long. She said she saw a lot of names she didn't expect to see on it, people who she had thought had been doing really well. Paula said,

"Let's start with you Sherry. I was surprised to see your name on this list. What's up?" Sherry said, "I'm surprised too, I don't know." Sherry mentioned what she thought she had gotten them for—things like not going to meetings and refusing to get to her kitchen assignment on time.

Paula said, "Sounds like a lot of 'em you got behind that willful behavior of yours..."

Sherry nodded, smiled, and said, "Yep, it does look like that. I think it is my being willful."

Paula said, "When you start having good ideas, when you start thinking that you know better than everybody else what's good for you, that's a good time to start getting suspicious and to check yourself. When you start saying 'I don't think I need to go to group.' or 'I don't think I need to get up and do my chore.' that's the kind of thing that's gonna get you kicked out of here and you'll be right back out there where you were. *That's your disease talkin' and tryin' to get you to relapse.* It's real important that when you start getting those willful feelings that you find somebody to talk to and check yourself." Sherry nodded sheepishly in agreement.

It was only thanks to Sherry's otherwise encouraging performance of late (coupled with a known history of putatively drug-related obstinance) that it became reasonable to attribute her recent and "willful" accumulation of 6:15's to an *other inside* her rather than to wrong living. If we view diagnosis as a strictly technical rational enterprise (see Kirk and Kutchins 1992, pp. 220–23), then clinical judgments like this may be considered aberrations—at best, mistakes, and at worst, deeply disturbing instances of personal oppression carried out under the auspices of clinical medicine (cf. Szasz 1961). However, if we view such diagnoses as grounded in the moral order of community living then things cease to appear quite so grave. Seen in this light, Sherry's "willfulness" was simply a departure from right living. This "willfulness" resisted being construed as an exhibit of her own human agency because it was inconsistent with the human agent Paula perceived Sherry to have become

("I was surprised to see your name on this list"). Given its inconsistency with Paula's current impressions of Sherry, Sherry's "willfulness" became eminently available for reading as an effect of her "disease" that was "tryin' to get [her] to relapse." While by strictly technical rational lights, "willfulness" may seem a very odd category of behavior to attribute to nonhuman causes, the practical circumstances in which Paula and Sherry found themselves allowed for this attribution without a hitch. Most fundamentally, these circumstances involved the production and sustenance of moral community between them.

Beyond their availability as empirically observable phenomena for Canyon House members, the causal effects had by *others inside* people were exhibited in the influence they exerted over the ongoing conduct of program affairs. People's perceptions of *others inside* themselves or one another changed the course of conversation and also informed nondiscursive changes in how people's recoveries were henceforth considered and pursued. In the following excerpt from a staff meeting, Doug testifies to the effect his recent recognition of Sheila's mental disorder has had on his interactions with her:

> That's like Sheila. She's sick too but I never knew a thing until I got her into voc. [vocational rehabilitation] . . . It took me getting her into voc. before I knew how sick that girl really was. When she was still in the program I couldn't have told you she was mentally ill at all. But right now it's all we're working on.

Once they became acquainted with the putative *others inside* themselves and their peers, program members did not simply acknowledge their presence, endeavor to formulate their features, or passively observe their actions. Instead, they initiated direct assaults upon these nonhuman agents in efforts to suppress the troubles they perceived them to be causing. If troubles were not effectively managed by virtue of being defined as the effects of a specific variety of disorder, they might be reformulated as the effects of another variety of that disorder, another disorder, or sometimes something else entirely—perhaps as the effects of organic brain damage. Alternatively though, they might also be reformulated as the effects of a human agent, adept at reproducing the local appearance of mental disorder for his or her own private, but eminently discoverable, human purposes. Thus the boundaries between those personal behaviors for which residents were held responsible and those that were attributed to *others inside* them were not decided on the basis of an ethically, ontologically, or otherwise fixed dichotomy between "the

human" and "the nonhuman." Instead, they were perpetually negotiated in and through the conduct of routine program practice.

CONCLUDING REMARKS

In Chapter 3 we saw how dramatic changes in the state-sponsored management of mental health, illicit drug abuse, and alcohol abuse occurred
as results of social forces both inside and outside these fields. Because
of pressures exerted by lay advocates, public officials, and the competing claims of various types of treatment professionals, alcoholism, drug
addiction, and mental illness each came to be known as notoriously multifaceted entities. They became widely regarded as entities that might
issue from diverse intrapersonal, interpersonal, and environmental antecedents and as entities that might manifest in a virtually infinite variety
of emotional, cognitive, perceptual, and behavioral forms. This legacy
was structurally manifest at Canyon House in the multiple modalities of
talk, behavioral, and pharmacological therapy in which residents were
asked to participate. It was practically manifest in the extremely wide
spectrum of experiential and behavioral troubles that could be properly
attributed to *others inside* Canyon House residents, and in the considerable discretion Canyon House members exercised in linking particular
troubles with particular types of disorder.

The fact that community advocates and officials at all levels of government had put pressure on both research and treatment professionals to
attend the needs of those judged least capable of community living had
profound effects on Canyon House practice as well. In the first instance
it catalyzed a more pervasive concern for dually diagnosed patients.
This eventually gave rise to the mandate shared by the Los Angeles
OAP, DAPO, and Department of Mental Health to produce a program
expressly for them. Secondly, it fostered a political climate conducive to
public funding for social model programs like Canyon House wherein
the treatment of insanities and addictions consists primarily in managing the social deficits attributed to them. Thirdly, it made comparatively
generous public subsidy a more obvious expectation, more justifiable,
more palatable to government agencies, and, thus, more probable. That
Canyon House was in fact quite generously funded during the period
of my fieldwork allowed the admission of more clients who could contribute nothing toward the cost of their treatment. The number of extremely impoverished clients at Canyon House was, of course, com-
plemented by the involvement of Rand as a client referral and funding

source during this period as well. No doubt, such an extremely impoverished clientele was more inclined to foster a therapeutic culture that was comparatively attentive to the profound mutual relevance of housing, tenable community living arrangements, and recovery from insanities and addictions.

The fact that Canyon House was residential and drew heavily from the twelve-step tradition fostered a pervasive emphasis on community, cooperation, peer insight, and personal responsibility in the recovery process. It thus reproduced at the local level many of the same issues of community identity, solidarity, and otherness that have played so prominently throughout the history of America's treatment of those judged addicted and/or insane. In much the same way that assessments of people's membership in the wider national, state, county, and municipal communities of America have historically governed whether their troubles and troublesome conduct were attributed to *others inside* them, assessments of people's standing as members of the local Canyon House community were also central considerations governing whether troubles were attributed to *others inside* them or to what I have been calling wrong living. Fostering right living and self empowerment through retrospection were the foundational modes of practice that linked the various modalities of therapy offered at Canyon House. Thus, for example, while participation in the thought or the mood disorder groups, the alcohol or drug groups, the women's or men's group, and so on somewhat altered the kinds of *templates* to which one was exposed and the kinds of expectations people developed regarding themselves, their peers in these groups, and the respective *others inside* that lurked within them, it did not alter the fundamental logic according to which these resources were acquired and employed.

Finally, the moral economy of program practice at Canyon House did more than simply inform how residents produced, sustained, and amended their *beliefs* about the respective *others inside* from which they were presumed to suffer. It actually gave empirical form to these *others inside* as causally influential things-in-the-world. These *others inside* were witnessed to exercise causal influences over people's perceptions and behaviors and, in doing so, altered not only people's beliefs but also the course of practice that constituted Canyon House community life itself. Rather than merely observing or describing their putative disorders, residents undertook strident campaigns to subdue the activities they attributed to those disorders. This work, in effect, *animated* these disorders as nonhuman agents, and engaged residents in interactional struggles with these disorders as collectively confirmed realities. Hence, the work of recovery at Canyon House amounted to a good deal more than a process of ideological transformation. Instead, it consisted in materially embodied struggles to overcome particular troubles conceived as the effects of consensually realized nonhuman entities.

Equally, though, the *others inside* them with which residents struggled were constituted *only* in and through the moral economy of program practice. Not only did the *others inside* program participants often take forms bearing no evident relationship to formally codified psychiatric nosologies, but assessments of both their presence and absence in residents' behavior were dictated *only* by the locally meaningful organization of program affairs and participants' expectations regarding themselves and one another as collaborators in those affairs. Thus it should be resolutely noted that genetic, neurological, and other forms of biological evidence that might be used to great advantage in other settings for the treatment of mental disorder had absolutely no part in it. The boundaries between the social and natural, human and nonhuman, causes of people's behavior and experiences were in no sense foreordained but were drawn by Canyon House members *in situ*, exclusively in response to the exigencies of Canyon House community life. Sociological explanations of this boundary work that would resort to objectivist assertions of biological or psychological processes occurring beneath or behind it are thus suspect both for their callousness to the profoundly moral character of this work and for their importation of explanatory resources that had no *evident* part in its accomplishment.

5   Twilights

The Origins of Twilights

Twilights was founded by behavioral scientists at the Rand Corporation to facilitate rigorous comparative research into the costs and benefits of residential and nonresidential care for dually diagnosed homeless adults. Toward that end, Twilights was designed to exactly replicate Canyon House in a nonresidential setting. Canyon House was itself included in the study because it had earned both local and national renown for offering high-quality care to dually diagnosed clients. But before moving further into the details of the research project itself, it will be useful to first briefly consider the broader sociopolitical crucible within which this project was forged.

Beginning in the early eighties, Americans came to view homelessness as one of the nation's most pressing domestic problems (Snow and Bradford 1994). As the magnitude of the problem grew more evident both on the streets and in the media, interest groups galvanized across the country to promote their respective solutions. The first two interest groups to achieve widespread notoriety were advocates for the homeless and spokespeople for local businesses and property owners. Their advocates cast homeless Americans as victims of a heartless society and demanded solutions to the various problems homeless people themselves suffered. Business and property owners cast homeless people as miscreants and a menace from which they deserved public protection (Stern 1984). Before long, politicians also weighed in. Conservative politicians claimed homelessness was a deviant lifestyle or symptomatic of personal pathology. Liberals blamed Republican welfare cuts, economic recession, and shrinking low-income housing markets. Scholarly experts from various disciplines echoed and elaborated upon these claims, but, in the early eighties, community mental health researchers were particularly well placed to claim expert authority.

The venerable history of sociological skid row research had abated in the seventies (Shlay and Rossi 1992), leaving sociologists to scramble back to the study of homelessness only after it began garnering greater public attention in the early eighties. Community mental health researchers were more advantageously disposed. To those with little understanding of the American job and low-income housing markets, it seemed reasonable to assume that rising rates of homelessness in the early eighties simply reflected the failure of deinstitutionalization and community mental health in the sixties and seventies. The demographically heterogeneous "new homeless" of the eighties also looked more like the mix of people now known to community mental health researchers as "young adult chronic patients" than they appeared to resemble the elderly white men featured in classic sociological skid row research (Bassuk and Lamb 1986).

But still more fundamentally from a public policy standpoint, community mental health research was well placed to facilitate a political compromise between those who looked to societal failings and those who looked to personal failings to explain rising homelessness in America. By the lights of community psychiatry, one could simultaneously emphasize the community's responsibility to more effectively look after homeless people *and* the putative personal deficits from which many homeless Americans were observed to suffer. Working to relieve homelessness could thus be cast as the noble works of a righteous society to meet the needs of its disabled citizens rather than meager and delinquent restitution for the country's political and economic assaults on the poor. This outlook proved congenial to a wide variety of stakeholders in the question of homelessness in America. And, hence, when public and private funding agencies began sponsoring research on homelessness, they overwhelmingly sought to know the numbers, personal characteristics, and disabilities of homeless people. Coincidentally, psychiatric epidemiology had grown prominent in the world of community mental health research during the early eighties and appeared perfectly suited to discovering the extent to which personal disability and homelessness overlapped.

The principal investigators on our study were proficient in state-of-the-art epidemiological research methods and the latest program evaluation methods. Long before they set to work on our study, they had established distinguished records of public policy research concerning community care. Their appointments at Rand had afforded them a variety of organizational resources that advantaged them in the pursuit of research funding as well. But, as noted in Chapter 3, the availability of research funding in the early eighties was shrinking and becoming tied ever more closely to the provision of services to politically conspicuous populations. Beholden, as they were, to funding agency initiatives, my eventual supervisors sought, and were awarded, a series of grants for research that attended primarily to the demographics and disabilities of homeless people (cf. Farr, Koegel, and Burnam 1986; Vernez et al. 1988). Their research designs were exceedingly rigorous and promised sound evidence regarding the characteristics of homeless people first in Los Angeles County and then throughout the state of California. Foremost among the findings these studies came to share was that a comparatively high proportion of homeless Californians suffered concurrently from psychiatric and substance use disorders (cf. Koegel and Burnam 1987, 1988; Koegel, Burnam, and Farr 1987, 1990; Vernez et al. 1988). By the late eighties, my supervisors had become leading figures in the newly revitalized field of homelessness research (known particularly for their methodological sophistication and findings of dual diagnoses among the homeless). They were, then, poised to effectively compete for the most coveted research grants offered by the National Institutes of Health to study homelessness in America.

In July of 1987, President Reagan reluctantly signed into law the Stuart B. McKinney Homeless Assistance Act. The McKinney Act was not the first federal response to the growing problem of homelessness in America but it marked a watershed in federal involvement. Prior to the McKinney Act, federal initiatives had largely focused on emergency food and housing and were handled primarily through the Federal Emergency Management Agency (FEMA) and the Department of Housing and Urban Development (HUD). The McKinney Act authorized an Interagency Council on the Homeless to coordinate programs across several federal agencies. It authorized federal subsidy not only for more emergency relief services, but also for the education and employment of homeless people, assistance to homeless veterans, and provision for the physical and mental health care of homeless Americans. One element of the McKinney Act mental health care provisions entailed support from the National Institute on Alcohol Abuse and Alcoholism (NIAAA) to "develop, implement, and evaluate innovative treatment interventions for homeless individuals with alcohol and/or other drug abuse problems" (NIAAA 1991).

After consultation with the National Institute on Drug Abuse (NIDA), the NIAAA responded to this mandate by publishing a document entitled *Request for Applications for Community Demonstration Grant Projects for Alcohol and Drug Abuse Treatment of Homeless Individuals* (NIAAA 1988). This Request did not seek a uniform treatment protocol from grant applicants because there was, as yet, little empirical evidence as to which programs worked with homeless clients (Huebner et al. 1993). It did, however, insist that at least 25 percent of each grant be devoted to program evaluation. In May of 1988, nine grants were awarded with a total federal outlay of $9.2 million in eight cities across the country. Though our study was not among them, its eventual form was heavily influenced by the lessons learned from this first round of studies. Several insights gathered during the first round were integrated into the design requirements of the second round of NIAAA-sponsored research projects (Huebner et al. 1993).

First, seven of the nine originally funded projects attempted experimental or quasi-experimental designs. These designs were often compromised, though, because of difficulties getting program components up and fully operational. Applicants for the second round of grants were expected to have devised explicit procedures for managing such difficulties. Second, the brevity of some of the first-round projects (e.g., outreach and detoxification services) had severely limited data collection. Applicants for the second round of studies were required to provide interventions of sufficient duration to afford meaningful outcome data. Third, methods for more rigorous and thoroughly standardized data collection were required. This was in large part due to NIAAA's effort to facilitate a more thorough national evaluation. Finally, applicants for the second round of studies were required to conduct quantitative, longitudinal evaluations of their interventions on individual clients and they were required to use comparison groups. In addition to spawning these design requirements, results of the first round of studies also strongly suggested the utility of social model and case management recovery approaches with homeless clients (Lubran 1990). This underscored the need for clinicians to attend to their clients' broader social circumstances. A variety of issues bearing on the tenability of clients' community living arrangements were thusly emphasized in the second round of NIAAA requests for proposals (NIAAA 1990).

These federally specified parameters were reflected in our own study's design in the following ways. Twilights was to be housed in a drop-in center for homeless mentally ill adults that was already an established fixture in the local community. This alleviated a number of the problems encountered in the first round of NIAAA studies. NIMBY (Not In My Back Yard) sentiments were dodged because no new setting was required. Regular visitors to the drop-in center also promised a rich catchment of people appropriate for the study, and a practical solution to the problem many first-round studies had in retaining clients.

Our study would only recruit people who had made five or more visits to the drop-in center and had thereby demonstrated their relative rootedness in the local community (and accessibility for longitudinal follow-up interviews). By designing Twilights as a nonresidential copy of Canyon House, we met the NIAAA requirements for both experimental comparison groups and for interventions of suitable duration to collect meaningful outcome data. Moreover, Canyon House was an ideal model insofar as (1) it was widely well regarded, (2) it was based on the social model approach in which NIAAA officials had expressed a particular interest, and (3) its dually diagnosed clientele was both politically salient and confluent with Rand research interests. Contrasting residential and nonresidential treatment outcomes was also a widely recognized research model among federally funded evaluation studies of mental health and drug treatment (cf. Hubbard et al. 1989).

Rand's was among the fourteen proposals NIAAA funded in its second round of demonstration projects for alcohol and drug abuse treatment of homeless individuals. The initial outlay for these projects totaled $16.4 million for fiscal year 1990 and $15.9 million for fiscal year 1991 (NIAAA 1991). Thanks primarily to the efforts of one Rand researcher (my eventual immediate supervisor, Paul Koegel), NIAAA provided a supplementary grant in 1991 for the purpose of adding an ethnographic component to the study. This component was to investigate similarities and differences between Canyon House and Twilights that were not readily discoverable by quantitative means. More specifically, the ethnographic component was to investigate how "treatment" was actually accomplished in each of the programs. It was hoped that this investigation would illuminate practical features of treatment that either facilitated or impeded successful outcomes. I became involved in this story as the field researcher on this ethnographic component of the "Evaluation of Treatment Options for the Dually Diagnosed" project at Rand.

THE STRUCTURE OF TWILIGHTS: SOME TRIALS OF IMPLEMENTATION

Because the Rand study was a quasi-experimental evaluation of residential and nonresidential treatment outcomes, it was methodologically essential to maximize design comparability between the two programs. Retaining maximum integrity in the *research* enterprise while at the same time remaining sensitive (and responsive) to the obdurate realities surrounding the *therapeutic* enterprise was the fundamental tension governing the implementation of the Twilights treatment program.

Some research design concessions were anticipated from the outset. As noted in Chapter 4, homeless candidates for admission into mental health and/or substance abuse treatment programs often count the alleviation of subsistence needs very highly among their incentives for participating (see also Drake, Osher, and Wallach 1991; Institute of Medicine 1988; Snow and Anderson 1993; Weinberg and Koegel 1995). Whereas the vast majority of clients' subsistence needs were met as matters of course at Canyon House, this was not to be true of Twilights. Therefore, as a nonresidential program, Twilights lacked much of the allure that Canyon House inevitably had for homeless people. Our principal investigators knew that some kind of alternative incentive structure would be essential to the viability of the nonresidential program (and indeed the study as a whole).[1] Furthermore, they were quite aware that Twilights clients' comparatively dire living conditions would present myriad obstacles to recovery that would not trouble their counterparts at Canyon House. Twilights clients would need ongoing assistance in finding access to such necessities as food, shelter, clothing, health care, entitlement benefits, legal aid, transportation, and companionship. Hence it was resolved that Twilights would provide a much more vigorous case management component than was provided at Canyon House. Twilights clients would also require assistance in stabilizing their mental health care routines beyond the boundaries of the program. Hence, establishing linkages with other long-term providers of community mental health care was made a basic component of case management at Twilights. Such interventions had no strong corollary at Canyon House. Though they did compromise the purity of the study's experimental design, they were nevertheless accepted as sorely needed incentives for participation, bulwarks to therapeutic success, and preservatives for a viable nonresidential program.

Similarly, the abstinence policy at Twilights was relaxed from the outset. Originally, it was felt that the Canyon House "one-strike-and-your-out" policy would prove too stringent. Twilights clients faced myriad

---

1. When I speak of the "viability" of the program, I am referring to the program's capacity to retain enough clients long enough to (1) preserve the therapeutic *community* basic to the social model approach, and (2) allow sound statistical comparisons between outcomes at Twilights and Canyon House.

threats to their abstinence that their peers at Canyon House were spared. Therefore, project leaders initially installed a "three-strikes-and-your-out" policy at Twilights. Before long, though, even this policy proved too difficult for many clients. To preserve the program's viability, the three-strike policy was eventually dropped in favor of setting specific goals for individual clients and enforcing those goals with behavioral contracts. A drift toward the personalization of treatment was also evident in the evolution of the attendance policy. Originally, Twilights clients had to attend everyday and an unauthorized absence of three consecutive days was grounds for termination. But this policy also proved far too demanding. Twilights was reduced to a five-day program, and the generic attendance policy was dropped in favor of a discretionary policy tailored to clients' unique circumstances. Finally, the emphasis on individual case management also contributed to a conspicuous movement away from generic treatment standards. Hence, even more than at Canyon House, sanctions up to, and including, termination from the program came to be predicated on discretionary assessments of an individual's commitment to recovery rather than conformity with generic standards.

But this personalization of services was not to be a panacea. Not only was it only partially effective in retaining those who were having trouble, but it ultimately triggered a backlash among clients who were performing better in the program. Those who attended Twilights regularly, accrued days of sobriety, and had achieved higher levels of psychiatric stability grew to know one another better and trust one another more as allies in recovery (see also Weinberg 1996). These clients resented what they viewed as the disruptive presence of clients who attended only intermittently, who continued to use drugs and/or alcohol, or whose levels of functioning they judged significantly lower than their own. Even worse, they plainly feared some of the more belligerent intermittent clients. Counselors learned that such complaints were discouraging a growing number of the more highly motivated clients from attending. It also became obvious that these problems were putting a considerable chill on those who did continue coming. Attendance fell well below the numbers necessary to sustain a viable program and the therapeutic milieu at Twilights, such as it was, suffered greatly.

The clinical staff came to regard disruptive clients as the primary obstacle to sustaining a viable program at Twilights and began a concerted campaign to reduce the damage these clients were held to be causing. Though they considered simply expelling troublemakers, the clinical staff knew this would threaten the study's validity. Ultimately, they approached the study's Executive Committee[2] about formulating some explicit guidelines regarding the management of very disruptive (violent and very low functioning) clients. In September 1991, realizing that Twilights was not performing adequately and was, indeed, in danger of total collapse, the study's principal investigators convened a "brainstorming session." The study's research staff (myself included), Twilights' clinical staff, the study's two psychiatric consultants, Brad Peterson from Canyon House, and the drop-in center director attended.

Outright expulsion was quickly marked as a last resort (to be used only in very serious cases of violence, threats of violence, or extremely low functioning clients). Various approaches to separating clients into higher and lower functioning tiers were reviewed. While the research staff recognized the critical importance of drawing the more motivated clients back into the program, they did not want to corrupt the study's results by retaining only the most manageable clients. They also expressed concern that a two-tier system might seriously threaten the comparability of Twilights and Canyon House. The director of the drop-in center passionately opposed excluding problem clients (or "creaming"), and an extremely emotional quarrel ensued between the director and the clinical staff. The drop-in center director accused staff of creaming and staff accused the director of an overtly hostile disregard for the tribulations of running a genuine treatment program.

Immediately after this meeting the clinical staff resigned en masse. The study's principal investigators then faced a harsh realization. There was, it appeared, a basic incompatibility between the strictly open-door policy enforced by the drop-in center director and the more conditionally inclusive policy that Twilights seemingly had to adopt to remain viable as a social model *treatment* program. It was resolved that if Twilights was to survive, it must somehow protect the sense of community that was its therapeutic core. This meant that, occasionally, client expulsions seemed unavoidable. All efforts to implement such a policy while Twilights remained housed in the drop-in center failed. Finally, on January 31, 1992, Rand's subcontract with the drop-in center was concluded and awarded to the Social Model Treatment Group. A new site was found, new staff hired, and Twilights assumed the organizational form it was to have during the bulk of my fieldwork.

2. The Executive Committee was made up of the study's four principal investigators, Brad Peterson, and the director of the drop-in center wherein the Twilights program was housed.

Needless to say, the search for a new site was rushed and constrained by a number of issues including affordability, districting codes, potential neighborhood opposition, client accessibility, and, of course, structural suitability for a social model program. The site that was found was remarkably suitable, given search constraints. It was in Venice Beach, California, close to bus routes. It was inconspicuous, on a street otherwise lined with small specialty shops, a coffeehouse, a small grocery store, and a local bar. It also had toilet and shower facilities, space for a washer and dryer, and a small kitchen. However, it was much smaller than the former space at the drop-in center. It consisted in two small meeting rooms, a kitchen, a small bathroom, and a patio. Regardless of referral volume and retention, the new facility had a maximum capacity of only about fifteen clients. Actual attendance fluctuated between four and fifteen, with an average of about ten. Staff (and some clients) often attributed this to the uncomfortable crowding clients felt when more than ten clients attended at once.

Twilights employed a staff of four recovery specialists, one of whom doubled as program director. Thus, the clinical staff/client ratio at Twilights (about 4/10) was rather more balanced than at Canyon House (about 6/35). No doubt, this fact alone exercised a strong influence on the dynamics of therapeutic practice. However, other factors also ensured that the staff exercised more influence over therapeutic practice at Twilights than at Canyon House. Twilights clients lacked many of the structural inducements that Canyon House clients had to invest in each other's recoveries. First, Twilights clients were together only five days a week, eight hours a day. Only rarely did they remain in contact beyond the confines of the program. In contrast, Canyon House residents were together all day, every day. Second, whereas Canyon House residents were forced to collaborate on chores teams and meal crews, this was not required at Twilights. Hence, there were far fewer opportunities at Twilights than at Canyon House for clients to get to know each other. As a result, clients were usually considerably less involved in fostering each other's recoveries. This comparatively low involvement between clients required that staff pick up the slack. Thus, group sessions at Twilights often looked more like formal classes, unlike the informal, and multivocal, discussions characteristic of Canyon House.[3]

---

3. That this was a consequence of the local social dynamics of the Twilights setting rather than staff personalities is indicated by two facts: (1) When Twilights recruited staff from Canyon House, these staff members relinquished the informal Canyon House style

The comparatively small number of clients, combined with the more dominant staff role, prompted a fusion of the drug and alcohol groups conducted at Canyon House into one "drug/alcohol class" and the mood and thought groups conducted at Canyon House into one "mood/thought class." The Canyon House stress and coping group became the "stress and coping class." Because of the fragility of the client peer group and/or time constraints, the resident council group convened at Canyon House was abandoned, as were the feeling good group, the men's and women's groups, outdoor recreational activities, and inspirational readings. In theory, the family systems group was to be retained and take place over dinner but it did not. Staff claimed that family issues were too emotionally charged to be effectively handled in their outpatient setting. Differentiation of clients' phases of treatment was retained but on a far less formal basis than at Canyon House. Individual counseling was folded into case management. Community meeting was divided into a fifteen-minute announcements session and two simultaneous forty-five-minute "problem solving" sessions wherein program newcomers and veterans convened separately (in deference to the complaints of veteran clients discussed earlier). Group discussions tended overwhelmingly to focus on the problems people were having outside the program rather than the problems of shared community living that tended to arise at Canyon House. Attendance of outside AA and NA meetings was required, and twelve-step language and activities were pervasive at Twilights. Added to the program were a formal relapse prevention class and a twelve-step reading and writing class respectively. As at Canyon House, all formal groups convened once weekly except community meeting, which convened daily.

THE DYNAMICS OF THERAPEUTIC PRACTICE

Therapeutic practice at Canyon House and at Twilights were in many ways quite similar. Just as at Canyon House, there was a basic preference at Twilights for finding human agency in people's actions and experiences. Likewise, there was evidence of efforts to enforce *right living*, to promote self-empowerment through retrospection, and other processes constitutive of therapeutic practice at Canyon House. My effort here,

---

and adopted the more formal style characteristic of Twilights, and (2) Twilights staff did make concerted efforts to foster the more informal Canyon House style, but met with very limited success.

however, is not to demonstrate these similarities but to show how the identification and management of insanities, addictions, and recoveries from them also systematically varied according to the local organization of therapeutic practice in each of these settings. Therefore this section should be read not as an exhaustive description of therapeutic practice at Twilights but as a set of analytically inspired descriptions of variations on themes specified in Chapter 4.

Promoting Recovery Through Tenable Community Living

At Canyon House, recovery was promoted primarily through *right living*. Given the usual meagerness of their prospects outside the program, clients generally tried, at least, to appear that they were contributing to the collective life of the house and affably abiding by the reasonable expectations of their peers. Because Twilights offered far less in the way of subsistence, clients had far fewer incentives to honor each other's expectations. For its part, the clinical staff was compelled for the sake of the study to retain sufficient clients to produce meaningful outcome data. Once people were assigned to Twilights, vigorous outreach campaigns were mounted to bring them into the program and to keep them participating. Instead of enforcing *right living* among clients, counselors were often compelled to cajole candidates to participate by stressing its tangible benefits. Suffice to say that most people didn't regard the promise of sobriety and enhanced psychiatric stability as particularly alluring incentives. Much more crucial to them were matters of immediate relevance to their day-to-day survival on the streets. Thus it was these matters that were emphasized in outreach efforts.

Prospective clients were told participation in the program entitled them to genial companionship, a free dinner every weeknight, a free bus pass, coupons for free meals at McDonalds, access to free laundry facilities, and use of the shower at no charge. They were informed of the vigorous case management services Twilights offered, and that Twilights could help them determine their eligibility and sign up for a variety of entitlement programs (e.g., General Relief, Aid to Families with Dependant Children, Supplemental Security Income, Social Security Disability Insurance). They were told they would get help finding temporary and/or permanent housing. And depending on a client's circumstances, staff also held out the possibility of assistance with other matters such as legal problems, medical problems, employment problems, clothing needs, storage needs, etc. These incentives for joining the program were, of course, also incentives for remaining in the program.

But rather than being incidental enticements to submit to clinical treatment, these services in fact comprised the bulk of the substance abuse and psychiatric treatment that Twilights clients received. Thus, instead of *right living*, recovery at Twilights was fostered primarily by promoting what I call *tenable community living*.

Analyzing psychiatric emergency teams (PET) and involuntary commitment hearings respectively, Emerson (1989) and Holstein (1993) have shown that decisions to release candidate mental patients often hinge upon judgments as to whether candidate patients' community living arrangements are *tenable*. They also showed that these judgments are intrinsically negotiated outcomes, subject to the discretionary assessments of a wide variety of contingencies specific to individual cases.[4] But in PET work and involuntary commitment hearings, candidate patients do not normally exercise much control over these negotiations. Their own actions figure primarily as raw material for *professional* assessments of tenability rather than direct contributions to the work of defining tenability. Defining and creating tenable community living arrangements also figured centrally at Twilights. However, at Twilights, clients were extremely influential in determining whether their own community living arrangements were tenable and how they might make them more tenable. In what follows I discuss some of the more routine aspects of defining and creating tenable community living arrangements at Twilights and demonstrate how this work was shared between clients themselves, Twilights staff members, and others.

I should emphasize that I am by no means arguing that concerns attendant to the clinical diagnosis and treatment of insanities and addictions were irrelevant to program practice at Twilights. It was indisputable among program participants that clients came to the program specifically to receive treatment for their addictions and psychiatric disorders. My point is that considerations of nosological issues were embedded in broader determinations of tenability. Furthermore, as I have said, despite their lack of professional training, clients were themselves integral players in the work of defining what in their lives was and was not an appropriate focus of therapy. This can be clearly seen in the

4. The defining characteristics of tenability vary widely from one case to the next. Holstein (1993, pp. 128–9) writes in this regard, "[a]s a practical matter, tenable living circumstances are established in terms of the fit between the particular *needs* and *demands* of the patient in question and the accommodations available in a proposed living situation. The adequacy of a proposed living situation can be interpreted only in light of its proposed occupant's needs and demands."

following exchange between Sean, a client, and Eve, a counselor, in a community meeting:

> "I don't think I've been that fucked up in the head since Maureen died." Eve asked, "You've been havin' a hard time off and on ever since then haven't you?" Sean nodded and Eve asked, "How often do you still think about her?" Sean said, "There ain't a day goes by I don't think about her. She's always with me." Sean turned to me, pointed to his prominent tattoo of her name on his neck and said, "She's always with me." He then turned to Eve and said, "I think things'd be a lot worse than they are if she wasn't."
>
> Eve asked if she ever talks to him and he said, "Yeah, I hear her voice sometimes but that's a blessing man. That's a blessing." Eve nodded and asked if he still mourned her death or if he was still depressed about her death and he answered, "I don't think I'll ever be as happy as I was when she was alive if that's what you mean. She was my everything and now she's gone. I don't think I'm as messed up about it as I used to be though. I've accepted it but I won't ever get over it." Eve nodded.

Here Eve speculated that Maureen's death triggered Sean's psychological breakdown and asked about Sean's experiences in a decidedly diagnostic tone. Sean seemed aware of Eve's agenda, but despite a general willingness to accept the reality of his mental illness ("I haven't been that fucked up in the head since Maureen died"), he declined to ratify Eve's diagnostic musings regarding hearing Maureen's voice and his current sadness about her absence. Sean offered that her voice is a "blessing" not a symptom and likewise refused to pathologize his missing her. In both cases Sean suggests he regards these candidate symptoms as tenable features of his life and hence not as symptoms of any mental disorder at all. Rather than interpreting his assessments as evidence of denial, Eve acquiesces. Clients were also empowered with respect to their use of medications. They were encouraged to negotiate with their psychiatrists about their medications and leave psychiatrists who resisted negotiation. Hence medications decisions, too, were not made according to strictly specified *professional* criteria but were embedded in more broadly negotiated determinations of tenability. This can be seen in the following discussion between Eve, a counselor, and Rachel, a client, in community meeting. Rachel said,

> "I got this fucking doctor who's prescribing me Stelazine and I told him that I nearly killed myself last time I was on Stelazine and if there was one drug I absolutely wasn't going to take it was Stelazine and that's what that motherfucker prescribed me. So I'm not taking it and that means I'm not taking anything . . ."
>
> Eve asked, "You told him you didn't want it?"
>
> Rachel replied, "Yeah, I told him but he didn't care."

Eve said, "What you gotta realize, Rachel, is that doctor was just pre-scribing you a medication that has worked for a lot of people and he thought it would work on you too. Psychiatry is not an exact science . . . If something doesn't work for you then it's your responsibility to tell the doctor that . . . "

Rachel angrily replied, "I did tell him!"

Eve said, "Well then maybe it's time to see about getting another psy-chiatrist if the one you have now isn't listening to you. But still you need to remember that it's up to you as much as it is up to the doctor to get the medication that's gonna be right for you. He might have to experiment .with a few things before you get on what's best for you. But nobody is gonna know what's best for you unless you tell 'em. It takes patience and it takes a little self-responsibility."

The same approach characterized recovery work aimed at overcom-ing addictions. At Twilights, recovery from addiction was not viewed merely in terms of professional ministrations nor merely in terms of re-maining drug free. Beyond abstinence, the work of recovery entailed tak-ing steps to change one's own life sufficiently so that drug use no longer seemed necessary. If people failed to cultivate lifestyles for themselves that they found satisfying and tenable without drugs, their sobriety was considered precarious. Stephen put it this way with respect to his own recovery,

Sometimes I get so bad off that I want to kick but after I'm clean for awhile I just think life is so boring, so awful without drugs why did I want to be clean anyway? It's not easy to kick for any amount of time when you don't have a life . . . I don't think I'm ever gonna get clean forever. I'll always relapse.

In the next excerpt two counselors emphasize the importance of recre-ating one's life so that it is *tenably* drug free. Several clients complained of boredom and Clarise, a counselor, replied,

"You know, what you all are saying right now is a very common feeling that people have early in their recovery. I know that when I first got clean I just about went out of my mind from boredom. It's very common. But what you all have to know is it does get better. What I used to think to myself is that the kind of excitement I got when I was drinking was not any kind of excitement I wanted to have again. Some of you might agree with me on that." People nodded and Clarise continued, "You know! I mean excitement is one thing, but havin' guns and knives put to your head, and bein' in car wrecks, and gettin' all torn up in fistfights, is that really what we want to get in our lives? I don't think so. I don't think you think so either. That being bored feeling does go away but part of it has to be you gettin' up off your butt and doin' things that can be fun to do sober."

Claire said, "That's why we have that thing on Fridays where we read about all the inexpensive things there are to do on weekends that don't take getting high to make 'em fun. I know that's been a little slow lately but a little creativity can go a long way sometimes. Go to more meetings. Call up your sponsor and see what she's doing, get out and see people you know in the program"

Both in the case of insanities and addictions, then, recovery work entailed the collaborative promotion of tenable community living rather than right living (or more narrowly focused efforts to subdue professionally specified biopsychological "symptoms"). Obviously, efforts to acquire shelter were among the most common ways in which Twilights members sought to foster tenable community living. Twilights clients very often viewed housing as their top priority. But affordable housing was extremely scarce on the west side of Los Angeles. Quite early on, the Executive Committee decided that Twilights should maintain a few apartment units and make them available to clients at a reduced rent once they had achieved thirty continuous days of sobriety. It was thought this would simultaneously encourage people to remain drug free, reduce the burden of a very difficult housing market, and bolster people by removing them from the streets. In principle, this was a perfectly sensible plan but for a variety of reasons only six of the forty-nine people who attended Twilights during my fieldwork ever actually used the Twilights apartments.

Many simply couldn't remain drug free long enough to become eligible in the first place. Others found even a subsidized rent more financially burdensome than they could, or cared to, manage. In the following excerpt Treanda expresses her preference for "a little spending money" over an apartment. Clarise, a counselor, said,

"Well one thing we all can be thankful for is that we're all in housing. That hasn't been true in this group for awhile has it?"

Treanda replied, "I ain't in housing."

Clarise, surprised, said, "You're not?"

Treanda said, "Naaaw."

Clarise said, "I thought you were gonna move into the [Twilights] apartment with Janet." Treanda shook her head. Clarise asked, "Well why don't you?"

Treanda answered, " 'Cause it's too damn expensive that's why!"

Many laughed. Clarise also smiled and said, "It's not so much."

Treanda asked, "How much is it then?" No one in the group was sure but a consensus emerged that it was just over three hundred dollars a month. Treanda said, "So I'd have to sell my foodstamps to live in there. If I sell my foodstamps I don't wanna spend it on no rent. I spend it on myself for somethin' nice. I'm the kinda person likes to have a little spendin' money in my pocket. A place is too expensive."

Others expressed concerns about the loneliness of an apartment. In community meeting, Claire, a counselor, turned to Richie and said,

"So you're happy to be back in the apartment huh?"
Richie said, "Yep."
Lee asked, "You never get lonely over there?"
Richie said, "No. Actually I'm real happy to have the privacy. I can sleep when I want without gettin' bothered. I really like that part of it. I couldn't ever get any privacy at Clare [a local shelter]."
Lee nodded and said, "I think I'd be lonely over there. I thought about it but I didn't think I would be happy by myself like that."
Claire asked, "Couldn't you go out and meet people? I mean you could still go down to Clare couldn't you?"
Lee said, "Yeah, I could but I ain't too good at meetin' new people you know? Maybe it's bein' a man or something but I never been too good at expressin' my feelings and tellin' people I like 'em or I wanna be friends. Right now it's more natural. I'll just be down there and smokin' a cigarette or watchin' T.V. and someone'll be there and we'll just start talkin'. It's more natural."

Sharing the Twilights apartment with other clients (like living in a board and care facility, or another sober living apartment) did not necessarily ease this problem. The difficulty was that these arrangements don't allow one to choose one's roommates. This can result in a loneliness born not of isolation but incompatibility. Beyond loneliness, personal incompatibility could itself render available housing arrangements untenable. Bob, an elderly veteran who had been living in the Twilights apartment, is exemplary:

Bob picked up the want ads and said, "I'm lookin' for a new place. They're pushin' me out of the apartment that they got here." I asked what happened and he said, "They're bringin' down this bastard from Canyon House to move in with us. I told 'em we don't like 'em. Mack [the other resident] feels the same way. But they don't care about that. All they care about is fillin' the place up. It's costin' 'em money when it ain't full up. So they'll put anybody they can get in there." I asked him what was wrong with the person they were moving in and he said, "Bastard tried to hustle me for my money up there. He ain't nothin' but a con artist drug addict hustler and I don't need that type in my own house." Bob looked at me over his glasses and said, "Another thing is this dude's queer. He's whadaya call, a homosexual. Now I ain't got nothin' against queers I just don't wanna live with one. You know what I'm sayin'?"

Though Twilights clients were virtually unanimous in sharing an abstract preference for housing over homelessness, in practice this preference depended on a variety of factors specific to people's circumstances. Several clients moved out of apartments and into temporary shelters because of roommates' drug or alcohol use. Others chose homelessness for other reasons. Ian, for example, described getting out of his abusive family's home and into a temporary shelter as indicative of progress in his recovery. I asked,

"Where you livin' now?"
Ian answered, "In the shelter for now." I asked him how that was and he said, "It's a little weird 'cause I'm not really used to livin' all cooped up with a bunch of strangers yet but it's a *lot* better than before. At least I ain't responsible for takin' care of all their shit in the shelter like I was at home. I think my gettin' my ass out of my home environment is a real good sign that I'm movin' in my recovery. I know I still got a lot to learn but I think that shows I'm gettin' somewhere. That was a big step for me."

Tenability also figured in decisions regarding work. Twilights clients generally looked at gainful employment as providing a more tenable livelihood than unemployment. Beyond simply needing the income, most Twilights clients felt that employment was also an important mark of recovery and was, at least in principle, something after which they should be striving. Eric told me about an interview his brother had arranged for him with an insulating company and said,

I'm sick of doing nothing all the time. To me, recovery is about getting back to work. I mean it's not like I don't appreciate Twilights. I do think I've gotten a lot out of coming here. But this isn't recovery, just coming to a program everyday. It makes me depressed just to come here everyday and do nothing to support myself. For some people this is enough, but not for me. I've worked before and I know I can do it.

On the other hand, clients often expressed concerns about their current capacity for work. People commonly shared that their psychiatrists and/or sponsors had advised them to avoid "unnecessary stressors" and that full-time employment had been unambiguously included in that category. Thus, while work was usually cast as a legitimate long-term goal, it was often dismissed as an unrealistic, or even harmful, short-term goal. After Ian was hospitalized for severe depression, staff generally agreed that his overzealous pursuit of employment and his many rejections by prospective employers was a major precipitating factor. Lee touched on similar themes in reflecting on his own recent relapse,

> It might have been that I was too busy. I was workin' a lot and maybe not spending enough time thinkin' about me. I think that's an important part of recovery, just allowin' yourself some time to think about yourself and how you're feelin'. I didn't do that enough. I was workin' a lot and not thinkin' too much about the effects it was havin' on my emotions, you know? I stopped comin' here and really I stopped workin' a program. Maybe that was it, I dunno. Maybe also havin' too much money in my pocket.

When Eric was finally offered the job with the insulating company, he became extremely anxious. This job entailed moving about fifty miles inland and hence giving up the support networks he had developed through Twilights, the local community mental health center, the health club where he swam and bathed, local AA meetings, and on the street. After a week of ambivalent deliberation, Eric decided not to take the job after all. He said,

> It was just too many hassles. I want to work but on the other hand maybe I'm not ready. I guess I wasn't ready yet. Maybe if a job came along that was closer or something like that but that one was just too many hassles. I also started thinkin' that if I was working and S.S.I. found out maybe my application wouldn't go through either and that was freakin' me out a little. I dunno. I think it's for the best. I relapsed this weekend and that is pretty good evidence that I still need more time. I'm sure not ready to go out and handle sobriety on my own.

In addition to the fear of losing one's support network and benefits, other factors served to make the search for work seem less tenable for Twilights clients. Layla was a legal assistant for fourteen years before her escalating cocaine use led to her dismissal. Now with a lengthy employment gap on her résumé, without good references, and without money for nice interview clothes, she found the job hunt deeply depressing. Bob and Mack were two war veterans in their mid-fifties who suffered physical disabilities that prevented their plying their former trades of ranching and automobile repair respectively. Charlie spoke for many of his peers when, in the following excerpt, he complained trenchantly regarding his own employment prospects.

> I'm totally unemployable. I'm over the hill, got no references, no appreciable skills, patchy work history at best, former alcoholic and addict, homeless. Whose gonna look at that and say, 'Oh, this guy's just what we need!'? I know I ain't marketable.

As a result of these many obstacles to employment, fostering clients' economic tenability usually meant securing and/or maintaining entitlement benefits. Chronic difficulties attended this work as well. People's efforts to secure entitlements were often thwarted by a multitude of problems including complicated application forms, extremely time-consuming application processes, spiteful staff, long processing delays, and suspiciously vexing policies regarding the maintenance of benefits. Mack told me his SSI benefits were contingent upon his participation in a treatment program and that most treatment programs required that clients either exhibit improvement or be discharged. If he exhibited too much improvement, however, he was liable to lose his benefits. Mack was convinced this was a catch-22 deliberately designed to prevent people like him from continuing to receive SSI. Beyond being deprived of the material sustenance entitlements made possible, Twilights clients were often tormented by their difficulties in obtaining benefits. One afternoon Eve asked Charlie how things had gone at the General Relief Office. Charlie sighed,

"I was there all day and they didn't get to me."

Disgusted, Eve asked, "What is this now, your third day down there and still nothing happening? That's really ridiculous!" She looked at me and said, "I hope this stuff will get into your report." I asked what stuff she meant and Eve replied, "The hassles people are put through just to get benefits that they're entitled to and that they need to survive. I mean it's really sad. How are people supposed to be able to focus on their programs when they have to spend literally all their time hassling with their benefits? It's so hard to get people to see that you can't expect people to get clean if they can't secure the basic necessities to survive."

Charlie said, "I'm powerless over it so there's no point in getting all worked up and relapsing behind it. I just gotta keep on tryin' and try not to lose my temper with any of those people 'cause that ain't gonna help the cause none neither."

Eve said, "Well I hope they get it together soon."

Charlie smiled, nodded, and said, "Me too."

As this passage begins to suggest, another important part of fostering tenable community living at Twilights consisted in the work of simply keeping spirits up. Twilights members often strove to help one another resist becoming despondent, to nourish a hope that things would get better, and, in the meantime, to sustain the sense that despite their terrible hardships, life is still worth living. Such efforts were pervasive both in and outside formal groups. As I have mentioned, unlike Canyon House members, Twilights members were poorly positioned to make or enforce moral demands of one another. Hence the maintenance of moral community was primarily accomplished through camaraderie and mutual encouragement. Though Twilights clients did not usually know each other very well, they nonetheless seemed to draw a level of sustenance from one another's company and to take seriously the work of imparting such sustenance to their peers. This dynamic can be seen in the following, rather lengthy, excerpt from a community meeting. Rachel said,

> "I dunno. I guess I could be a little more tuned into people and what their trips are. It's just that I can't relate to a lot of this stuff. It seems so unnatural for everyone to come here and talk like this, I mean our trips are all totally different, at least mine is. I don't have any friends here. I can't relate to what people are into. I guess I don't have *any* friends though right? That's why the fuck I'm in a program."
>
> Eve asked, "Why *are* you in the program?"
>
> Rachel answered, "I don't know. That's the honest to God truth."
>
> Eve said, "Well you must have *some* idea. Why'd you come in today instead of staying out there. It musta taken some effort to get here. Why'd you bother?"
>
> Rachel said, "I'm here 'cause I'm sick and tired of living the way I've been living. I mean it's sickening. I don't wash. All I do is drift all day long. I don't do anything. I come here 'cause I'm lonely, scattered, depressed, and hopeless. I mean I don't have anywhere else to go. I come here to get my ass off the street. And I figure coming here is better than nothing. Not much but it's a little better than just wallowing in my depression by myself."
>
> Ian said, "We don't know you too well Rachel but we are your friends. We're your friends 'cause we got the same problem you got. We're all addicts and we're all mentally ill. We can relate to what you're sayin'.... at least I can."
>
> Rachel said, "You're not my friends. I mean I come here 'cause I'm lonely and maybe I get a little companionship here. But you guys aren't my friends. We're too different. But beggars can't be choosers right? Heh, heh. I'm pathetic." Rachel looked down and shook her head on the verge of tears.
>
> Eric said, "I don't think you're pathetic. I think it took some courage to say what you just said and demand to talk like you did. I really respect that. Like when I got here I just kept my mouth shut all the time 'cause I was afraid people didn't care about my problems and I'd just be puttin' them through it all. I mean I've only been doin' this for 27 days and I feel like usin' every day so I'm not the answer guy by a longshot but I think..."
>
> Eve interrupted, "Yes you are. You're the answer guy. We're all the answer guys. Anybody that's workin' a program is an answer guy. I think you're bringin' a lot to these groups Eric."

Eric laughed shyly and said, "Well I don't know about that." He turned back to Rachel and said, "But I think it shows that you got a lot of hope that you insist on bein' heard instead of just sayin' 'fuck it.' and goin' back out there."

Ian said, "That's true. That takes guts to talk in these groups when you don't know nobody. Man, I know it takes guts."

Claire said, "He's right Rachel and you need to know that you are not the only person who's had these kinds of feelings. I think everyone in here was pretty confused and felt pretty isolated when they first got in here but it gets better right guys?" Everyone nodded. Claire continued, "Gene over here could tell you some stories about his first couple weeks in the program. He didn't think he was like anybody else and he didn't think anyone could relate to him and look at him now. He's a *graduate* and he's *still* comin' back! He can't get enough of this place . . . "

Eve teasingly flattered Gene, "Yep, Gene's our rags to riches success story. Now he's even got a job and is makin' some money."

Immediately after this group finished, I asked Eric how he thought it had gone. He said,

"Well it was pretty good I guess. I could relate to a lot of what Rachel was saying." I asked what he could relate to and he said, "Well, having problems with your psychiatrist, and feeling lonely and depressed and like you can't relate to anybody. I feel like that all the time. I mean it's getting a little better but it's a long way from bein' over, I know that. That's why I was sayin' there ain't no way I'm the answer guy. I'm probably the most fucked up person in there. But I could relate to what she was saying and I felt that way too when I first got here. So I just wanted to let her know that I could relate and it gets better. That's all I was really saying."

The vast majority of clients spoke of being estranged from their families. Likewise when they spoke more generally of their relationships with people outside the program they were overwhelmingly inclined to speak of loneliness, desolation, and their struggles to meet or relate to people. Thus, despite their precariousness, the relationships they had with each other were often the closest relationships Twilights clients had with anyone. Indeed some clients spoke of the Twilights program as the only "family" they had.

Tony came in looking very upbeat with another man about his own age and said to everyone, "I'd like y'all to meet my new sponsor. This is Fred. He's got four years." He then looked at Fred and said, "Fred, this here's my family. The Twilights family. I ain't got no other family than this (*laughs*) so this'll have to do." He looked at John and Eve and said, "No, in all seriousness though, that's true. I really do think of y'all as my family."

Twilights clients did manage to create and, for the most part, sustain a sense of moral community between themselves and, no doubt, this did enhance the tenability of their community living arrangements. But despite a strong sense of shared hardship and camaraderie, there was no ignoring the fact that Twilights clients often had very little else in common. Early on, clients were required to attend AA and NA meetings together. However, this policy was changed when clients began complaining that their favorite, or "home," meetings conflicted with the meetings Twilights made compulsory. Staff decided to foster clients' connections with their home meetings and dropped the requirement of attending meetings as a group. Hence, instead of enforcing an artificial level of solidarity among Twilights clients themselves, staff encouraged clients to find AA or NA sponsors with whom they more genuinely identified and a home AA or NA meeting attended by people to whom they "could relate." Clients had very interesting things to say in this regard.

Most preferred meetings that avoided long formal monologues. Twilights clients often grew impatient with the ritualistic stories, or "Drunk-a-logues," of how bad things were before sobriety and how good they are now that speakers were clean and sober. They yearned for interactions that fostered a "more natural" sense of community with other AA or NA members and for concrete advice about getting and staying clean. Additionally, clients preferred meetings attended by people like themselves.[5] Thus, clients sought out "stag" meetings convened exclusively by and for women or men, meetings geared toward specific ethnicities, gay men meetings and lesbian meetings, older meetings, younger meetings, singles meetings, meetings attended by friends, and "double trudger" meetings convened by and for people presumed to suffer from both mental illnesses and addictions. But the identity issue that came up most among Twilights clients concerned their level of personal identification with homelessness and/or "street culture." Various attitudes in this regard are evident in the following passage from a community meeting. Frank, a counselor, asked Janet,

> "What meetings you going to?" She mentioned several including a notorious local meeting widely known as the "snake pit."
> Frank asked, "What do you think of that meeting?"

---

5. People's interests in finding concrete practical advice *and* people to whom they could relate were intimately connected. Most clients believed the most useful advice would come from people who had similar life experiences, who approached life from a similar vantage, and hence people with whom clients identified.

Janet replied, "Oh, I love that meeting. Snake pit is like my home meeting. I know a lot of people in there."

Frank said, "So you like it huh?" and she said, "Oh yeah. Why? Don't you?"

Frank answered, "Nah, I like it alright. It's just that it's pretty wild in there sometimes and I've heard people sayin' it might not be the best meeting for people to go to early in their recoveries..."

David, a client, said, "No way. I disagree with that. The snake pit is the only meeting I really feel comfortable at. I don't mind the bikers and the gangbangers. That doesn't bother me. I mean you see those people out on the streets anyway. It's not like those are my kind of people or anything but the snake pit is better than some of those meetings where if a homeless person comes in they all kinda just spread out away from you, you know? At least the people at the pit have been around the block a couple times and they're not prejudiced against you if you're homeless."

Frank nodded and said, "So you like it too huh? What about other people?"

Dirk said, "I hate the pit." and Frank said, "You do? Why's that?"

Dirk replied, "Well it's like you said you know. It's just too hectic for me. I don't go in for all the crowds and the uh..." He smiled and continued, "criminal element."

This passage begins to convey the multiplicity of views people expressed regarding what, for lack of a better word, I will call "street culture." Janet claims the snake pit is "like [her] home meeting." David prefers the snake pit, despite "the gangbangers and bikers," specifically because he feels that homeless people are more accepted there. For his part, Dirk complains of its being "too hectic" and the "criminal element" in attendance. Most Twilights clients expressed mixed feelings regarding their comparative identification with the street "wildness" characteristic of the snake pit and the domesticity characteristic of more conventional meetings. While at different times struggling to belong to both worlds, Twilights clients tended toward a sense of social distance from both the kind of antiestablishment, affirmatively "bad," disposition valued by bearers of the convict culture or street culture *and* the punctilious courtesy they often ascribed to the various housed and working cultures constitutive of "mainstream America."

The following two fieldnote excerpts further exhibit this sense of cultural liminality (Turner 1969). The first exhibits the sense of distance many felt from the street culture in which they were generally immersed while homeless. The discussion had concerned how people distinguish good meetings and bad meetings. Charlie was the most vocal in his distaste for people who continue to embrace street culture after getting clean. John, a counselor, told Charlie that many meetings didn't have that kind of crowd. Charlie replied,

> "That's what I was thinking last week when Eve [a counselor] took us to that thug meeting in Hollywood. I just thought 'There are plenty of meetings that don't have this criminal element. What are we doing here?' I guess she's into those kinds of meetings. Maybe that's what turns her on. But I don't like 'em at all. It also makes me think Eve isn't too sensitive to the clients when she brings a bunch of people like us to a meeting like that. I mean what was she thinking? Did she really think we *would* be comfortable in there? I ain't scared of 'em I just don't like 'em. And it's not like I can't blend in if I wanted to either. I can blend in but I just can't relate to the kind of bad ass shit that's goin' on in those meetings."
>
> John asked, "What was it exactly that bothers you about these meetings?"
>
> Charlie said, "They're just full of gangbanger types and a bunch of people who get their jollies stompin' around goin' 'we're clean but don't fuck with us cause we're bad.' and I don't think that kind of shit is consistent with sobriety. I thought I was leavin' that shit behind but I guess they don't think so. That's fine but it just ain't for me . . .. I know a lot of people in AA have been in jail. I've been in jail. But some meetings have more of an ex-con feel to 'em than others. It doesn't mean they're still criminals it just means they go in for that kind of talk and dress and so forth. Some people dig that and I don't that's all I was sayin'. It's not a big deal."
>
> John asked, "Well what are the meetings you do like?"
>
> Charlie mentioned his regular meetings and mentioned that he preferred the smaller meetings and liked it when other homeless people were in them. Eric agreed that it was nice when other homeless people were in the meeting and said, "Some of the westside meetings can go in the other direction too. I don't like the prisoner meetings, like the snake pit. But I don't like the meetings where everybody looks really rich either. I like to see a few homeless people too."

This passage exhibits Charlie's and Eric's sense of social distance from street culture as well as Eric's equal sense of distance from the more affluent people who attended some AA and NA meetings on the west side of Los Angeles.[6] This later sense comes through even more powerfully below. Here both staff and clients joke at length about the social distance

6. I do not mean to suggest that Twilights clients looked at the world as dividing neatly into the dichotomous variables of "wild outside"/"domestic inside." The fact that Charlie and Eric didn't like "prisoner meetings" but did like to see other homeless people in the meetings they attended advises strongly against such rigid divisions. My point is that Twilights clients often claimed to feel alienated by both the wildness they found culturally hegemonic on the street and in "prisoner meetings" and by the sanctimony they found culturally hegemonic among housed and working Americans and in twelve-step meetings attended by more affluent recovering addicts.

between themselves and those who might attend an A.C.L.U. meeting
in Westwood or Beverly Hills.

> Community meeting began with a client reading from a local newspaper
> about various events available to attend over the weekend. Charlie told
> the group of an NA-sponsored blues festival, various movies that were
> playing, a local arts and crafts fair, and various twelve-step meetings. He
> then said, "For those that are interested, the A.C.L.U. is putting on a big
> meeting in 'Westwood slash Beverly Hills' and they'll have speakers 'from
> the community' speaking on quote 'The Homeless: What Can We Do for
> *Them?'"* Charlie made this announcement with more than a little irony
> and elicited hearty laughter and snickering from both clients and staff.
> Impressed with the positive reaction he continued, "You know what I'm
> sayin'? 'What can we do for *them?*' Isn't that nice? I'm sure they're all losin'
> sleep over that one. Those Beverly Hills A.C.L.U.ers gotta be real worried
> about *those* homeless, I tell ya." People laughed and carried on for several
> minutes about the concern housed and working people in Westwood and
> Beverly Hills surely felt for the plight of "the homeless."

For many different reasons, Twilights clients were fairly unsuccess-
ful in their bids for inclusion in the worlds of home and work. Hence,
they were forced to forge a livelihood, or what I have called tenable
community living arrangements, largely beyond the confines of those
worlds. Their material sustenance, such as it was, usually came from
state or charitable sources. Their sense of moral community, such as it
was, usually came either from those with whom they shared the streets
or from the recovery fellowships embodied in such groups as AA, NA,
and Twilights itself. Most claimed to have faired poorly in their search
for a tenable livelihood on the streets and felt "the program" was their
best available option. However, "the program" encompassed a very
wide spectrum of approaches to building community and empowering members. In the next section I discuss how, in contrast to their peers
at Canyon House, Twilights clients were usually empowered through
realistic planning rather than retrospection.

Self-Empowerment Through Realistic Planning

At Canyon House, self-empowerment was fostered primarily by retrospectively identifying the specific patterns in which people's putative
insanities and addictions had assailed them in the past. Given residents'
current enjoyment of room, board, and an extremely rarified social environment, there was little need to ensure one's own livelihood or to
fortify oneself against the kinds of obstacles to recovery that lurked beyond the confines of the program. These issues came to the surface as

residents approached graduation, but for the most part remained an-cillary to the bulk of therapeutic practice. Conversely, Twilights clients were not nearly so protected. They returned to their lives outside the program each evening at 9:00 P.M. And, of course, they remained deeply concerned with the exigencies of their outside lives throughout the time they spent at Twilights. John, who was a counselor at Canyon House for several years before becoming the director at Twilights, put it this way,

> We [at Twilights] tend to be more focused on what's going on for a person outside the program—finding housing, getting benefits, getting a sponsor, getting a relationship going with an outside psychiatrist, finding a home meeting, those kinds of things. Whereas in a program like Canyon House the focus tends to be a little more on internal issues like problems between residents, chores problems, and stuff like that. Our goal plans are more in terms of concrete practical issues that people need to address and the Canyon focuses a little more on feelings issues and patterns that residents have on dealing with people and their denial of responsibility for their problems. We deal with those things too but maybe not as much as an inpatient. I think that stuff comes up no matter what but for us it comes up in dealing with the more practical stuff.

At Twilights the work of empowering people focused less upon grasping the identities of the specific insanities and addictions that had presumably assailed clients in the past, than on the specific practical is-sues that emerged as obstacles to, or as opportunities for, the promotion of more tenable lives at present. The work of self-empowerment thus consisted more in looking forward than backward, more in the work of realistic planning than in the work of retrospection. This is not to say that realistic planning entailed no retrospective assessments of client's troubles. Rather it is to emphasize that in contrast to Canyon House, whatever retrospection took place was driven primarily by efforts to enhance the tenability of people's present community living arrange-ments and only secondarily by efforts to understand the *others inside* presumed to have afflicted them before. Furthermore, the work of real-istic planning did not necessarily implicate past troubles at all. Often it consisted in putting people in touch with emergent opportunities, or in addressing obstacles to recovery that loomed exclusively in the future rather than obstacles suggested by the patterns in one's past. In what follows I specify the work of promoting self-empowerment through re-alistic planning, indicating how it systematically differed from the work of promoting self-empowerment through retrospection.

Promoting recovery through realistic planning was distinct from promoting recovery through retrospection on both temporal and spatial[7] axes. More than anything else, Twilights clients' proximity to the circumstances of their suffering ensured that greater consideration would be given to people's *current* community living arrangements than to the patterns in their *past* personal actions and experiences. Certainly, one important feature of realistic planning entailed sensitizing people to the characteristic effects their community living arrangements were having on them. Though this was, in some sense, a retrospective project, it was decidedly less *intro*spective than the retrospective work done at Canyon House. This can be seen in the following excerpt from a community meeting. After acknowledging that many addicts resort to drug use only after terrible misfortune, John said,

> You need to recognize that those things are real issues for you and that they can overwhelm you at times but you need to take responsibility for the way you respond to the feelings those issues give you . . . We have a choice about how we're going to cope with those painful feelings. We can choose to go out and obliterate them and all our other feelings as well with drugs and alcohol or we can try and work it through and move on with our lives. You know in that sense it's just like any other disease. Once you know you have diabetes it's the same thing. You learn how the disease affects you and you take precautions to stay out of the situations that might be dangerous for you, like eating wrong or not having insulin handy. With alcoholism or drug addiction you work on discovering your triggers and what we call your slippery places and once you know what those are, it becomes your responsibility to avoid those places. Working a program is about living your life intelligently, given the knowledge you have about your disease.

Here John does focus attention specifically on the *others inside* presumed to afflict clients. And similarly to Canyon House, therapeutic practice is cast as in large part a matter of fostering knowledge about one's disease. However, John specifies that knowledge in distinctly situational terms ("You learn how the disease affects you and you take precautions to stay out of the *situations* that might be dangerous for you."). At Canyon House, fostering knowledge about one's disease consisted primarily in efforts to identify the characteristic personal patterns

7. I am using the concept spatial to indicate an axis between states internal to the person and states external to the person. My argument is that at Canyon House discussions of insanity and addiction more often focused on the intrapersonal or dispositional topics of behavioral patterns and "issues" whereas at Twilights such discussions more often focused on the environmental topics of "triggers" and "slippery places."

of action and reaction that created problems for people. At Twilights, it consisted primarily in efforts to identify the various *extrapersonal*, or environmental, "triggers" and "slippery places" that people needed to avoid if they were to sustain their recoveries. No doubt, the various intrapersonal and extrapersonal realities implicated in the work of recovery from insanities and addictions were often intimately related. Nevertheless, the greater emphasis placed on triggers and slippery places, rather than personal patterns, was a significant systematic difference between how insanities and addictions were identified and managed at Twilights as compared to Canyon House.

As at Canyon House, self-empowerment at Twilights often drew upon generic *templates* drawn from various lay and professional sources. However, the *templates* invoked at Twilights tended to refer to the realistic management of one's environmental circumstances rather than the retrospective understanding of one's personal patterns. This can be seen in the following passage from a community meeting. Janet said,

"Last night I had to go up to Hollywood and I had to walk right through some of my old areas I used to use at and it bothered me a little bit but not that much. It turned out bein' just fine."

Bob, another client, asked, "Why'd you have to go up there?"

Janet replied, "I had to get some papers from a friend who lives up there."

Clarise, a counselor, said, "I'm a little worried about you goin' up there like that all by yourself the night before your first birthday. That sounds a little too much like a set up."

Janet said, "What do you mean Clarise? Nothin' happened."

Clarise said, "Well maybe nothin' happened this time but addicts have a way of sabotaging their recovery—especially when they're about to hit a landmark like you are. I've seen that a million times and I'm just saying it's something to watch out for. Findin' some reason for goin' to your old usin' spots the night before your first birthday just sounds kind of fishy to me. I've had people who tell me, 'No, no, no. I am cured and there ain't no way I wanna use again. I just wanna go up there and show 'em all how good I look and maybe they'll see the light and start gettin' clean too. I care about 'em. That's why I gotta go back there.'"

Everyone laughed, including Janet.

Sean, a client, also said, "Clarise is right baby. Why even take the chance you know? Ain't no point in it. You can just as easily go up there with someone else who is clean as do it by yourself. You just don't need to take those kinds of risks."

Clarise said, "That's right. That's exactly what I'm saying. There just isn't a good reason to take risks like that when you don't have to."

Janet laughed and said, "Okay, okay, okay. Y'all are right."

In this passage Clarise interprets Janet's trip to Hollywood as "fishy" given what she, as a longtime AA member and professional recovery specialist, has learned about addicts in general. While Clarise's remarks are reminiscent of many I heard at Canyon House, they are different insofar as they focus more on helping Janet plan her movements through the community at large than on retrospectively assessing her own personal patterns. Twilights members tended to endorse the generic idea that insanities and addictions often strike suddenly and unexpectedly. Hence, beyond mapping and avoiding triggers and slippery places, *realistic* planning entailed staying focused on one's *immediate* future. Clients who spoke of long-term plans were often told that such plans were moot if their recoveries faltered in the short term. This can be seen below. Eve asked Sean,

> "So what do you think you can do now for your recovery?"
> Sean answered, "I don't know. I can't live like this no more. Livin' hand to mouth, one check at a time, blowin' 'em and livin' rough. I need to save up my checks and get myself a place is what I need to do. I'm gonna do it too. I can live out and not spend any money and just put all my checks away. I could get a couple of grand together, get a place and maybe then I could straighten myself out a little bit."
> Eve said, "That sounds like a good long-term plan but what about right now, like when you leave here tonight and this weekend?"
> Sean looked down, shook his head, and said, "I dunno man. I really don't." He looked up at Eve and said, "But that's the whole thing right there isn't it? The long-term shit don't make a damn bit of difference if I can't keep it somewhat together short term."

In addition to generic templates regarding addiction and insanity, generic templates regarding homelessness were also routinely used to inform Twilights clients' recovery efforts. This was much more common than at Canyon House for the obvious reason that people's homelessness was a much more immediately pressing matter at Twilights. It was generally assumed that Twilights clients had little structure in their lives beyond that which the program itself imposed. This, combined with the now centuries old idea that idleness enervates (Kusmer 2002), leaving one more prone to addictions and insanities, ensured that clients were routinely encouraged to devise structured and salutary pastimes for themselves. For example, Claire, a counselor, asked in community meeting,

> "What's up?" Nobody replied and she said, "Fridays are usually a pretty slow day. Everybody's pretty dead by the end of the week. A good thing to talk about on Fridays is what people plan on doing to get themselves

through the weekend. Weekends can be a hard time 'cause you guys are sort of left to your own devices and you have a lot of time on your hands . . . So why don't we start with that. What are people gonna do this weekend to stay clean and sober?" Many mumbled variations on "go to meetings."

Eric said, "I guess I gotta hit a lot of meetings this weekend 'cause it's exactly like you said Claire. I got too much time on my hands. Also I'm gonna see if I can get me some money together collectin' cans and bottles. For me it's a good way to occupy my time and get some pocket money. That might seem kinda low to you guys but that's just where I'm at."

Charlie said, "I've done it. If there ain't nothin' else that's a damn good way to get money."

The therapeutic use of generic templates regarding homelessness can also be seen in the following exchange. Claire asked,

"How's everybody feel about the holidays comin' up? What are people doin'? Anything?"

Replying to the first question, Del simply said, "Shitty."

Claire said, "Yeah, that's pretty common. The holidays can be a real hard time for a lot of people. It's pretty hard to watch everybody out there Christmas shopping and spending time with their families when you're broke and homeless and maybe don't have a family you can go to. That's why it's real important to keep yourself occupied with something. These marathon meetings are a real great thing to have if you start feelin' lonely or like you might wanna use. If you start feelin' that way just get yourself down to one of those meetings real fast. Who already plans on goin' to a marathon meeting this weekend?"

Drake raised his hand and Lee said, "I dunno. I might go down and check one out. I guess it depends on how I'm feelin'."

In this passage Claire predicates her promotion of realistic planning upon a generic *template* regarding how homeless people in general might react to being broke, homeless, and alone during the holidays. As at Canyon House, this *template* was invoked suggestively rather than co-ercively and clients were themselves allowed to decide whether it held in their particular cases. But also parallel to Canyon House, therapeutic practice at Twilights often transcended the use of generic *templates*. The following discussion took place a couple of days after Neil had relapsed into crack cocaine use. Eve asked,

"Well what do you think you can do to keep yourself out of trouble?"

Neil said, "Go to meetings."

Eve replied, "Well you were already going to a lot of meetings. What else do you think you can do?"

Neil said, "I hate to say it but I think what I need to do is keep hangin' out with the guy I'm hangin' with now. He is an *asshole* but I know if I stay with him I won't use."

Eve asked, "Is he in the program?"

Neil said, "No, he's a normie but he don't drink or use ..."

Janet said, "That's right. You can trust Paulie. He helped me out a lot of times when I was still out on the street and he don't use."

Charlie blurted out a laugh, looked at Neil and asked, "You talkin' about Paulie, Paulie?"

Neil said, "Yeah, you know him."

Charlie said, "Yeah, I know him, but don't be so sure he don't drink or use."

Janet objected, "He don't use! I know for a fact he don't use."

Charlie said, "Well he may not use but he drinks! I've seen him drink."

Eve asked Neil, "Why do you think he can keep you from using?"

Neil answered, "'Cause I won't use if I'm around him. If I'm around *him* I won't be around the people that I would use with."

Here we see Twilights members collaborating to devise a realistic plan to help Neil "keep [himself] out of trouble." These efforts begin with resort to a generic twelve-step remedy (go to meetings), but then move on to remedies more specifically tailored to the details of Neil's own life. Neil suggests that though Paulie may not be an ideal companion (insofar as he is an active drinker), he provides more tenable companionship than those with whom Neil routinely uses crack (his own drug of choice). As this discussion proceeded, Neil mentioned another important reason for associating with Paulie—he trusted Paulie with his things when he himself couldn't look after them. Neil claimed this was very important because losing his things might trigger another relapse. Charlie vehemently cautioned Neil against trusting Paulie with his belongings and proposed an alternative in the person of "old Bill." The discussion that ensued illustrates how self-empowerment through realistic planning sometimes transcended reliance on twelve-step or any other variety of generic conceptual *templates*. Charlie said,

"Neil if you need to have somebody look out for your stuff I suggest that it not be Paulie. But if you need someone like that, old Bill is an honest real decent human being. I known him for years and he wouldn't rip you off ..."

Janet said, "*Old* Bill?!! Old Bill is a fall down drunk! What you wanna give any of your stuff to him for? If he don't sell it he'll lose it" (*laughs*).

Charlie said, "That's not true Janet. I been out on those streets for five years and I know who you can trust and who you can't trust, believe me. If you wanna trust somebody, trust one of the older guys. They might be drunks but they ain't got the mind to rip anybody off. It's the young dudes who are the snakes."

Janet said, "Well the Big Book says stick with the winners and stay away from people that's still usin'. And old Bill is usin'."

Charlie said, "Neil don't pay no attention to what the Big Book says. The Big Book doesn't know you and doesn't know what you personally are gonna have to do to keep sober. We are. The people right here in this room are the people who know who *you* are."

Janet shook her head in lighthearted disapproval of Charlie's blasphemy against the Big Book. Eve noticed this, laughed, and said, "Don't forget about the Big Book Neil."

Smiling, Charlie emphatically said, "Forget about it."

Eve laughingly said, "Okay Neil, you got this written down? You got the best advice money can buy. Experts sittin' in this room ... "

Neil smiled and said, "Yeah, I got it."

This passage vividly demonstrates that while Twilights members may have regarded the AA "Big Book" as a very useful resource, they did not regard it as inviolable. More important than honoring AA dictates like "stick with the winners" was to realistically assess the details of people's unique circumstances and devise realistic methods for coping with them. The Big Book was not a sacred proclamation of commandments but a resource to be utilized or disregarded on a *discretionary* basis in light of people's unique circumstances. This kind of local, and / or personal, discretion was also evident in people's efforts to avert putative psychiatric problems. Rather than being bound by expert theories regarding the nature and management of mental diseases, these theories figured only as candidate resources alongside myriad other conceptual and technical resources. Sometimes such resources bore no resemblance whatsoever to generic, professionally authorized, therapeutic resources. The dialogue below followed a film about living with schizophrenia. Tony, who was himself diagnosed with schizophrenia, said he particularly related to the person in the film who found that brushing his teeth helped him to forestall episodes of paranoia or delusional thought. Tony said this reminded him of his own approach. He said,

"I always make sure my shoes are clean because when things start to get bad I always feel that it comes up from the dirt on the ground through my shoes into my legs and then up into my head. And if I always make sure that my shoes are clean then I know it won't start movin' on up."

Bill, a counselor, said, "That's really interesting Tony. Why do you think you think of your episodes as coming up from the dirt on the ground?"

Tony said, "Because I start getting dirty myself. When I get sick I don't care about my physical appearance and I don't wash myself or my clothes, or brush my teeth or any of that. That's why I could relate to his wanting to brush his teeth and feeling like that kept him in control. I think washing my shoes is the same kind of thing. If the shoes stay clean I know I got the rest of it under control."

The work of self-empowerment through realistic planning entailed efforts to help clients enhance the tenability of their particular community living arrangements. This primarily entailed planning ways to avoid and/or endure the various "triggers" and "slippery places" that threatened their recoveries. This work was often informed by generic *templates* drawn from the twelve-step fellowships, psychiatry, social work, and other sources. However, it was frequently undertaken at a level of specificity quite beyond the scope of any received body of generic wisdom. On such occasions, Twilights members drew upon their knowledge of particular individuals, their circumstances, and the unique array of resources available to them. The decidedly prospective and environmental emphases of realistic planning at Twilights distinguished it from the manner in which self-empowerment was fostered at Canyon House. In contrast to self-empowerment through retrospection, self-empowerment through realistic planning did not so consistently entail efforts to grasp the identities of the specific insanities and addictions presumed to have assailed clients in the past. This, in turn, systematically affected how *others inside* were made to figure as embodied causal agents at Twilights.

The Social Reality of Others Inside: A Contrast with Canyon House

In Chapter 4 I showed that invocations of *others inside* Canyon House residents were particularly likely when those who had exhibited a commitment to the program and to their own recoveries were found to have lapsed from *right living* in some way. This was also true at Twilights. However, the distinctive organizational logic of therapeutic practice at Twilights gave rise to several important variations on the Canyon House theme. To begin with, unlike Canyon House residents, Twilights clients had to make an effort to attend the program each day. Attendance often required a good deal of personal initiative insofar as people were forced to walk long distances, catch buses, and remain until rather late in the evening. Douglas was a Canyon House resident who had been homeless on the west side for several years. He described what his homeless friends had said about Twilights,

> People say it's an alright program but the big problem was that it let you out too late at night. What'd it go to? It went until like ten or something

and that's too late. If you live on the street you wanna be in your spot by sundown. That's just common knowledge. It's not safe after dark and I heard that a lot of people didn't like coming out of there that late. It's also a pretty demanding schedule. It's everyday, eight hours a day or something. That's almost like a full time job. I don't think most people were invested enough to spend that kind of time in a program. Especially if they aren't gettin' a place to sleep out of it, you know? Most people just don't think it's worth their while. Whadaya expect though, right?

Twilights members were themselves well aware of these issues and tended to give people a lot of credit just for turning up regularly. Hence, a client's mere presence was generally taken as good prima facie evidence of a commitment to recovery. Furthermore, as I noted earlier, Twilights counselors were under significant pressure to keep people in the program long enough to produce meaningful outcome data. This had two important effects. First, the demands placed on clients were comparatively minimal. This meant that the number and variety of opportunities for Twilights clients to "come up short," as it were, were also minimal compared to the opportunities for doing so at Canyon House. Second, even when clients did appear to be coming up short, staff tended to indulge them. Clients routinely arrived late and left early without any sanction from staff. They sometimes refused to engage in program activities despite staff requests that they participate. A few clients were overtly hostile to staff but were in no way criticized. In the following exemplary exchange, Rachel verbally attacks Claire in a stress and coping class. Rather than insisting that Rachel calm down or leave (as would almost certainly have occurred at Canyon House), Claire virtually apologizes for the content of her own remarks. Midway through Claire's presentation on "signs of stress," Rachel interrupted,

"So what?! I mean what difference does this shit make?! Why do we want to know this stuff?! How does it help us deal with our problems?!"

Claire answered, "To get a little knowledge on what's going on for you when you're experiencing stress. Maybe learn some tools for dealing with it."

Rachel complained, "But what's stressing me is I don't have anywhere to live and I don't have a job!! If I could get those things I wouldn't be stressed! I don't see how this stuff helps me with that at all! It seems totally pointless!"

Claire replied, "I'm not up here saying that learning this stuff is going to be the answer to all your problems. This isn't the whole program though either. We do try and help people get into housing and get into work too. This is the stress and coping class and what we try and do in here is show you guys some ways to deal with stress in more positive ways than just freaking out or going out and using. But you're right to say this isn't the whole story."

Likewise in the following excerpt, Bill, a counselor, normalizes Bob's many hostile dealings with Claire by pointing to his age and life experience. He thereby conspicuously avoids finding any manner of wrong living or disability in Bob's actions,

> Bill said Bob had been saying some very hostile things about Claire in group after she left. Bill said, "I knew he didn't like her but he's been saying some real vicious stuff." I asked, "Like what?" and he said, "Like she didn't know what she was doing and that paying her was a waste of money. Basically stuff like that, that she was incompetent. I think, bottom line, is that Bob's in his mid-fifties, he's been in the military and been all over the world. He's got like five kids. He's done a hundred different jobs in his life and he has a real hard time being told what to do by a thirty year old woman. I think he saw Claire as a little girl, somebody young enough to be his daughter and he hated the idea of her telling him what to do. He's just too proud for that."

Compare the two excerpts above with the assessment another client made of Bob's hostility. After group, Bob snapped at Eve for not holding the door for him. Roland remarked,

> That guy has a real problem. He's just lookin' for things to send him off. Now I ain't sayin' he's goin' out but that kinda behavior has addict written all over it. He wants to blow up and have his going out be somebody else's problem. That's text book shit he's pullin'.

While Bill attributed Bob's hostility to pride, Roland attributes it to addiction. Twilights staff were routinely inclined to let a lot more contentious conduct pass than were Canyon House staff because, compared to their colleagues at Canyon House, their clientele was a good deal more precariously invested in the program. In addition to being more impressed by mere attendance, Twilights staff were also more concerned to avoid alienating clients. Whereas Canyon House staff could safely assume residents wanted very much to remain in the program, Twilights staff felt a constant need to encourage clients to remain. Twilights clients were themselves rather less forgiving of one another but they were also less likely to know one another or to bother getting involved. The result was that *right living* was a good deal more crudely defined and loosely enforced at Twilights than it was at Canyon House. Departures from *right living* were likewise more ambiguous and less often registered in the course of therapeutic practice. This meant that distinctions between *wrong living* and *moral derangement* were also much rarer at Twilights than they were at Canyon House.

As at Canyon House, when this distinction did arise it was often invoked to excuse apparent lapses from *right living* as in the following exchange from a community meeting. The group had been discussing Claire's plan to move when someone told a joke. Roger had been staring blankly into space until the burst of laughter reawakened his attention. He looked up at Claire bleary eyed and asked,

"Where you goin'?"

People laughed and Charlie, a client, said, "Hey, Roger you're right onto all of this stuff. We need you to take the minutes to these meetings I think."

Ian, another client, said, "She's going to Denver. Where have you been?!"

Roger looked down and said, "I don't know I guess I wasn't listening."

Claire, a counselor, asked him if he was okay.

Roger shook his head and said, "Not really."

Claire asked, "What's wrong?"

He replied, "I just don't feel that great lately."

Eve, a counselor, asked, "How do you feel, kinda blue? What?"

Roger said, "Yeah, I guess kinda blue. I just feel depressed."

Eve asked, "How long have you been depressed Roger?"

He answered, "About a week I guess."

Eve asked, "What's getting you down do you think?"

Roger said, "Nothin' really. I just feel blue. I don't think anything brought it on. It's just sometimes I get blue."

Eve asked, "Nothing really goin' on for you right now?"

Roger shook his head and said, "Nothin' out of the ordinary. Just normal frustration. Sometimes it just creeps up on me and it seems like I can't take it anymore."

Claire asked Roger, "Is there anything else goin' on other than the feeling blue?"

Roger said, "Yeah, I feel a lot of anger and my voices come back when I get depressed."

Claire asked, "What are they saying?"

Roger replied, "That I should kill myself or kill somebody."

Claire said, "So your voices are putting those kinds of thoughts in your head? It's not that you feel like killing somebody but your voices are telling you you should?" Roger nodded and Claire nodded back.

Roger was first chastised for his inattention. After his dejected response provoked Claire to ask how he was, Roger reported having been depressed for "about a week." His claim was taken seriously despite the facts that (1) it arose as an excuse for his inattention in group, and (2) no one else had noticed any signs of his depression until now. At Twilights, it was much more common for clients' reports of personal affliction to be accepted at face value rather than being submitted to the program community's collective evaluation as at Canyon House (recall the Ricky exchange in the previous chapter). This pattern reflected both the comparative lack of knowledge and the lack of moral control that Twilights members had of one another. Thus therapeutic practice tended to consist in personally reported problems followed by collectively rendered advice. The collective rendering of both problems and advice was much less common at Twilights than it was at Canyon House.

Because departures from *right living* were registered with comparative rarity at Twilights, the bulk of the evidence for people's insanities and addictions was not found in such departures. The causal effects of *others inside* Twilights clients were far more often found in events that occurred *between* the periods clients were present in the program. That is, such evidence was drawn primarily from events that took place outside the program setting itself. For example, in the next excerpt Wes recounts with pride how he had overcome the call of his addiction in Highland Park. He said he had routinely used crack in the park before joining the program and when he was there again recently he felt powerful urges to "hang out for awhile."

> "I mean I could feel it. I wanted to stay and see if any of the old fellas were around but I knew what would happen if I saw any of them. So I just got my check and left." The others on the patio gave Wes a round of applause for leaving the park quickly.

In the following excerpt Eric describes his recent struggles to abstain from alcohol:

> "I've been drinkin' a lot and then drinkin' because I drank. And I'll be doin' totally crazy shit. Shit even *I* think is crazy!"
> Eve asked, "Like what?" and he said, "Well like arguin' with myself about whether to take the next sip of beer or whether to pour it out. And that's happened more than once. I bought myself a six pack of Rainer Ales today and I was walkin' in one of those alleys in Santa Monica. I had already drank three of 'em and I had three left. And I just cracked open the fourth one and I didn't want to drink it but I just busted it open anyway just like I always do and I was tellin' myself to drink it and then tellin' myself just to pour it out, back and forth like that. It was ridiculous. If someone had seen me back there they woulda thought I was crazy for sure (*laughs*). Finally I did pour it out I'm happy to say. But I'm sick."

In both of these excerpts clients describe the trials their addictions had recently caused them outside the program context. In the following excerpt Layla speaks to her experience while present in the program but links her present condition to her personal activities outside the program as well:

> I'm doin' real, real bad right now. I'm feelin' real depressed. I'm havin' trouble right now stayin' clean for more than two days at a time and I'm in so deep with the dope man that I gotta get me a job, and I mean fast, to get him the money for what I *already* smoked. I mean I am a mess and I just don't know what to do about it at all. I hate myself for goin' out and I don't know if there's anything that can save me anymore. I'm feeling very disillusioned because I feel like I worked this program good. I worked it real hard. I came every day without fail and I wrote and I went to step studies and called my sponsor every day. If anybody worked this program I did and it still didn't work for me. I'm feelin' real desperate right now. Even right now all I can think about is I really want a hit. Even now, and right here, I still feel that way. I don't know if I'm gonna make it back this time around. This last relapse was the worst I ever had and I still feel like I just want more. I think I'm gonna die out there. But one thing I hope is that the other people in this room right now can look at me and see what it's like when we go out. I'm miserable. I really am and if that can put some sense into somebody's head I hope it does. Another thing I want to tell you is I love a lot of people in this room and it makes me cry to think how much you all cared (*she started to cry*), I mean *really* cared about me and I feel ashamed that I let y'all down. I missed everybody while I was out but I just don't know if I can hang on. I feel real low right now. That's all I really have to say. Thank y'all for lettin' me share.

Layla expresses feelings of being torn between the moral community and sense of belonging she shares with her peers in the Twilights program and her compulsion to use crack cocaine. She describes her investment in recovery in terms of "working" the program, in terms of coming everyday "without fail," and also in terms of her love and sense of responsibility to her peers in the program. In contrast to the combination of personal industry, emotional connection, and moral accountability she found constitutive of her recovery, she describes her yearning to use cocaine as occurring despite herself. Her addiction, she claims, is something from which she is not sure she can be saved. It makes her "a mess," makes her "hate herself," makes her "miserable," and otherwise alienates her from her sense of self-esteem and self-governance. But even further, she describes her addiction as alienating her from her sense of moral community and connection. It is something that may prevent her from "mak[ing] it back," and may, indeed, kill her.

In Chapter 4 I argued that the perceived effects of *others inside* Canyon House residents often changed the course of program practice there.

Once people became acquainted with the putative *others inside* themselves and one another, they mounted campaigns aimed to eradicate the influences these troublesome intrapersonal agents had on people. But because of the remote location of the facility, people almost never went AWOL from the program at Canyon House. Hence the putative *others inside* Canyon House residents were almost never found to have proximally caused the removal of residents from the program setting. They were instead found to provoke various human agents to take specific courses of remedial action. If and when a person's disorder was found too severe to be effectively managed with resort to locally available remedies, *human agents* undertook the work of removing residents from the program and placing them in settings more appropriate to their needs and capabilities. In contrast, more than merely changing the course of practice within the program, the insanities and addictions presumed to dwell within Twilights clients were often held to have caused clients' literal disappearance. This can be seen in the following discussion between Clarise and Bob regarding Bob's roommate, Mack. Clarise said,

> "Mack relapsed." I asked what happened and she said, "Well Mack finally got his retroactive SSI check. I guess they owed him several thousand dollars or something . . . Bob, how much was it for?"
>
> Bob shrugged and said, "I dunno. I never saw it. A lot though."
>
> Clarise said, "Anyway as soon as he got it he took off, disappeared as soon as he got it."
>
> Bob laughed sarcastically and said, "Figures, don't it? He left me holdin' the bill to the cable too. He's got all this money all the sudden and he goes off leavin' me with the bill for the cable."
>
> Clarise asked, "It was his turn?"
>
> Bob said, "Think he'd leave when it was my turn? No way. That motherfucker was goin' for all he could get. Dope fiend motherfucker is all he is."
>
> Clarise said, "We've all done things like this but that doesn't mean it ain't a shame. I thought Mack was doin' real good. I guess it just goes to show you doesn't it, how destructive this disease can be?"
>
> Bob said, "Yep."

Such disappearances were not always as complete as in this case. Often disappearances took the less complete form of mere absence or disengagement from the shared recovery work of the program. This can be seen in the following excerpt wherein Bill describes Stephen's failures to return to the program. When I asked Bill about Stephen and his friend Alicia, he replied,

They haven't been back for about a week and a half. I was supposed to bring Stephen to the doctor on Monday but I went to his apartment and he wasn't there. We went by on Tuesday too and he wasn't there...Stephen is a very sick guy. He is very paranoid, very delusional and he won't stay on his meds. I don't think he's the kind of person that can make it in a program like this one. It's just too much for him. When I was supposed to pick him up on Monday we were going to see the doctor about getting him placed in a residential program. I think he needs more than Twilights can give him. Stephen was one of those people who would come in for a day or two days and quit. The only reason he came back was because Alicia was coming and we physically went and brought him back in. He doesn't have much commitment to this program at all. The last time a Rand interviewer knocked on his door he wouldn't open it. He just yelled to them to leave him alone and go away. I mean what are you supposed to do about someone like that? There's not a lot you can do short of kidnapping them.

While Bill does speak to Stephen's lack of commitment, he also emphasizes the severity of Stephen's disorder and his having greater "needs" than Twilights can meet. Hence, Stephen's absence from the program is explained as a product of both his lack of resolve (as a morally accountable human agent) and the severity of his affliction (by the nonhuman agency of his mental disorder). As was the case at Canyon House, being found to be governed by one's insanity or addiction did not entail being found to have been completely deprived of one's humanity, or human agency. Instead, it entailed being found afflicted to an extent precluding adequate participation in the collaborative recovery work of the program. It is in light of the relationships people routinely found between their own and one another's human agency, accountability, and participation in a shared moral community that the analytic value of conceiving insanities and addictions as collaboratively realized *others inside* people becomes clearest.

In different ways, Canyon House and Twilights members always construed their insanities and addictions as intrapersonal afflictions that troubled and sometimes destroyed the moral community they otherwise shared with other people. When the putatively afflicted were found accountable for these troubles, they were not found to have decisively rejected their communities but to have lacked the resolve to remain connected despite their disorders. Thus it was that the proximal cause of their troubles were held to be *others inside* them over which they could not, or would not, rise rather than their own intrinsic moral deficiencies. Therefore, we must resist understanding the social construction of insanities and addiction in such settings to consist in processes through which people's human identities, or selves, are transformed. Canyon House and Twilights clients were often simultaneously found accountable for their lack of resolve and not accountable for the specific behavioral and experiential manifestations of their putative afflictions. This fact cannot be explained unless we accept that at least two distinct types of intrapersonal agency were held capable of governing their personal behavior and experience—the first, a morally accountable human agent, or self, and the second, some type of amoral *other* with which clients in both programs remained pitted in equally chronic but very different kinds of practical struggle.

CONCLUDING REMARKS

Twilights is best understood as the product of several social processes that began with the rise of homelessness as a public problem in the eighties. Various claimsmakers emerged and competed for ownership of this problem. But more than any other faction, community mental health professionals were able to effectively capture the imaginations of American public officials with their claims regarding the nature of, and proper remedies for, homelessness. This resulted, in part, from the historical contingency of simply being in the right place at the right time—studying young adult chronic patients just when more and more of them appeared to be streaming onto the streets. But I have argued that there was also a moral and political component to their success. Community mental health professionals were uniquely poised to forge a middle road between those on the right who held homelessness to reflect the poor personal choices of a relatively small number of reprobates, and those on the left who held it to reflect a colossal fallout from the cruel political economy of the times. Community mental health professionals cast homelessness as a largely technical problem of improving the "interactive fit" between those with intrapersonal problems and the public services designated to manage those problems (cf. GAP 1987). Hence, they could advocate renovation and expansion of state-sponsored services and still avoid broad indictments of recent housing, labor, and public welfare policies. This imagery and the course of intervention it suggested proved expedient to a comparatively wide range of public officials, policy makers, and private stakeholders.

In the wake of the McKinney Act, a variety of federally sponsored programs to reclaim homeless Americans were initiated. Among these were several studies initiated by the NIAAA to develop new and innovative methods for treating homeless Americans with alcohol and/or other drug abuse problems. This federal response to homelessness in the United States is clearly amenable to interpretation as a gesture of outreach and inclusion to those who once might have been viewed as irreconcilably *other*, and hence unworthy of state assistance. From a clinical point of view, one might applaud the enlightened vision embodied in the federal government's attention to the mental health of homeless Americans, and the insight that led NIAAA to embrace more expansive definitions of treatment for homeless people. But these programs often also created powerful incentives for people, including sufferers themselves, to regard the troubles presented and endured by impoverished and socially marginalized Americans in particular kinds of ways. Rather than viewing their troubles as products of the architectonic rumblings of the global economy or the shrinking compassion of the American public welfare system, many people were certainly incited by these programs to construe the troubles of homeless Americans as symptomatic of mental health problems. One might very reasonably hesitate to endorse the enticement these programs present for people to systematically pathologize the troubles attendant to homelessness in the United States.[8]

The enticement Twilights presented to homeless people themselves to address their troubles in mental health terms certainly proved less compelling than the enticements to do so presented by residential programs like Canyon House. In the interest of preserving the viability of the program and the study, Twilights administrators were compelled to alter the program's basic design in a variety of ways to make it both more appealing and more manageable to prospective participants. Thus Twilights was compelled to offer a more vigorous case management component than was offered at Canyon House, to reduce attendance and abstinence

---

8. While this is a very real and serious consequence of managing the diverse troubles of homeless people under clinical auspices, it should not be overstated. What, if any, tangibly negative effects such enticements have had on peoples' actual lives is not self-evident. Some research suggests that the stigma of homelessness is already itself as serious as the stigma of mental disorder (cf. Phelan et al. 1997). Thus attributing people's homelessness exclusively to their poverty rather than their putative mental disability may not seriously alter their social status in the community at large. Furthermore, reducing the tendency to pathologize the troubles of homeless people could easily eliminate their entitlement to the higher welfare benefits that accompany putative disability. In light of these points, those who object in principle to the "medicalization of poverty" because it seemingly blames victims should probably tread cautiously if their primary interest is to improve the lives of socially disadvantaged Americans.

requirements to levels below those demanded at Canyon House, to ini-tiate an ancillary housing component, and to partially concede to the demands of more motivated clients to be segregated from newcomers and episodic attendees. These trials of implementing the Twilights pro-gram ultimately became so severe as to require a transfer of management responsibilities to the Social Model Treatment Group and a relocation of the program to a smaller setting. This, in turn, placed a cap on the number of clients who could attend Twilights, which itself altered the dynamics of therapeutic practice in a variety of important ways.

Because Twilights clients were offered less in the way of meeting immediate subsistence needs, they had fewer incentives to hold them-selves accountable to other program members. This, in addition to other factors, caused Twilights clients to be more precariously invested in the collective recovery work of the program than were Canyon House clients. Thus, rather than enforcing *right living* among clients, Twilights staff were often compelled to undertake vigorous campaigns to bring clients into the program and to keep them there. This usually entailed highlighting how Twilights could help clients manage their community living arrangements and fostered a general orientation to "treatment" cast very much in terms of enhancing the tenability of those arrange-ments. Clients were themselves extremely influential contributors to the work of determining whether their own community living arrange-ments were tenable and how they might go about making them more tenable. Hence, treatment at Twilights came to consist in the collabo-rations of Twilights staff, clients, and their various significant others to realistically formulate, and carry out, the work of improving the ten-ability of clients' unique community living arrangements.

For a variety of reasons, Twilights clients tended to be relatively un-successful in their quests for inclusion in the worlds of home and work. Therefore they were forced to seek whatever livelihood they might hope to find largely outside the confines of those worlds. The best hope most Twilights clients had for material sustenance usually came from public or charitable provisions of one variety or another. The best hope they had for moral community usually came from the recovery fellowships embodied in such groups as AA, NA, and Twilights itself. Under these general auspices, however, there existed a rather wide spectrum of ap-proaches to the practice of recovery and moral community. Clients often pursued very different approaches to achieving and sustaining tenable community living arrangements depending upon their own personal likes, dislikes, and resources. This was perfectly acceptable at Twilights so long as people's various approaches to improving their respective lots ostensibly included efforts to manage their putative insanities and addictions.

Self-empowerment at Twilights consisted primarily in the shared work of formulating plans through which particular clients might enhance their own unique community living arrangements. As a feature of this work, Twilights members strove to formulate ways to help clients avoid and/or endure the events and places held to constitute their distinctive "triggers" and "slippery places." As at Canyon House, this work was often informed by generic *templates* drawn from the twelve-step fellowships, psychiatry, psychology, social work, and elsewhere. However, it was also frequently undertaken at a level of specificity quite beyond the scope of any received body of generic wisdom. On such occasions, Twilights members drew upon their knowledge of particular individuals, their circumstances, and the unique array of resources available to them. Compared to Canyon House residents, Twilights clients had little time or freedom to contemplate the patterns their troubles had taken in the past. Thus, in contrast to self-empowerment through retrospection, self-empowerment through realistic planning did not so directly entail distinguishing those personal patterns for which clients should be held morally accountable and those attributable to the characteristic *others inside* presumed to lurk within them.

Unlike staff at Canyon House who worked with the benefit of clients who very much wanted to remain in the program and a waiting list of prospective clients clamoring to get in, Twilights staff worked under a constant pressure to keep sufficient clients in the program long enough to produce meaningful outcome data. For their part, Twilights clients had fewer incentives and many more obstacles to their continued participation in the program than did Canyon House clients. Thus, as opposed to their peers at Canyon House, the mere fact of Twilights clients' attendance was taken as a sounder indicator of their commitment to recovery. They were also subject to far fewer demands after showing up. Additionally, Twilights clients tended to know one another more superficially than did Canyon House clients and were less inclined to overtly sanction one another's behavior if and when they found it transgressive. For all these reasons, *right living* was a good deal more crudely defined and loosely enforced at Twilights than it was at Canyon House. Hence, departures from *right living* were likewise more ambiguous and less often registered in the course of therapeutic practice. This meant that distinctions between wrong living and moral derangement were also rarer at Twilights than they were at Canyon House.

If and when such distinctions were made they tended to be initiated by clients themselves. Thus the dynamic of therapeutic practice at Twilights tended to assume the form of personally reported problems followed by collectively rendered advice, rather than the collective rendering of both problems and advice that was more commonly in evidence at Canyon House. Whether it was found by clients themselves or by their peers, the bulk of evidence for the respective *others inside* presumed to afflict Twilights clients was found in events that took place outside the program setting itself. Indeed, Twilights members tended to draw a very close affinity between absence from the program setting and the causal effects of *others inside* them. Because of the remoteness of the facility, people almost never went AWOL from the program at Canyon House. Hence the putative *others inside* Canyon House residents were almost never found to have proximally caused residents to depart from the setting. They were instead found to provoke human agents to take specific courses of remedial action. More than merely changing the course of practice within the program, the *others inside* presumed to dwell within Twilights clients were often held to have caused clients' literal disappearance or complete estrangement from the Twilights moral community.

6   Conclusion

ASCENDANT ACCOUNTS of the genesis of the modern Western self are aligned in suggesting profound transformations in human self-conceptions arising concomitant with the broader social changes that embodied the Enlightenment and the transition to modernity (cf. Elias 1978; Foucault 1970; Sennett 1976; Taylor 1989). Though they differ in their details, these accounts uniformly tell of an unprecedented increase in self-scrutiny, a collective turn inward and eclectic efforts to grasp the newly mysterious essence of personal being beginning in the early eighteenth century. They recount an epochal transition from a period wherein the reality of the self was largely settled (consisting almost wholly in terms of social station, loyalty, and reliability) to a later period that has borne revolutionary new problematics for self-understanding that continue to hold enormous influence to this day. Though there is fierce debate regarding the relative importance of the events that anteceded and embodied this transition, there is widespread agreement on at least one of its consequences. The transition to modernity introduced a profound crisis of meaning, leaving many people deeply unsure of their identities, their circumstances, their values, and the purpose of their lives. My own narrative begins with a time when this uncertainty, this crisis of meaning, was already widely evident in America, but collective techniques for its management were only beginning to take form.

One of the most important features of this uncertainty concerned the boundaries of moral community in colonial North America. As the Puritan commonwealths gave way to an industrializing nation, the techniques by which lines of social inclusion and exclusion had traditionally been drawn broke down. As the methods for defining community broke down, traditional methods for socially locating one's self and the selves of one's countrymen inevitably broke down as well. This breakdown was caused by both a decline in religious consensus regarding the boundaries of moral community and an increase in population density, migration, and comparatively impersonal dealings between

Americans.[1] Essentially derivative, as they were, from religious and preindustrial conceptions of the relationship between moral inclusion, exclusion, and human identity, traditional conceptualizations of madness began to crumble during this period as well. Naturalistic orientations began to supplant religious and classical conceptions of "moral derangement" more by the attrition of the latter than the effective exposition of the former. Suspicions grew to the effect that troubled and troublesome actions and experiences once held to flow from supernatural sources, and to designate a body wholly divested of reason, humanity, and moral identity, must actually indicate definite organic pathogens to which human bodies (and hence their minds) are heir. Despite the fact that scientific evidence supporting these suspicions remained elusive, wider political economic processes ensured their entrenchment both in the structures of American public government and in the American popular imagination.

Advertising, and claiming professional credit for, the putative efficacy of moral treatment, physicians lobbied public officials to establish facilities for the medical management of morally deranged Americans. Though their therapeutic regimen amounted to little more than fostering moral community and enforcing what I have called *right living* among their charges, medical men successfully touted its merits to decisively establish themselves as the ultimate arbiters of the *nature* of madness. For their part, public officials saw in the claims of these ambitious physicians a politically expedient avenue for the containment of Americans whose manner of community living they judged chronically untenable. Medical doctors became the proprietors of publicly funded institutions whose mandate was none other than to contain those who,

1. Charles Taylor (1989), among others, argues persuasively that the modern self is intrinsically both a morally oriented and a socially located agent. He writes, "one cannot be a self on one's own. I am a self only in relation to certain interlocutors: in one way in relation to those conversation partners who were essential to my achieving self-definition; in another in relation to those who are now crucial to my continuing grasp of languages of self-understanding . . . It is this original situation which gives its sense to our concept of "identity", offering an answer to the question of who I am through a definition of where I am speaking from and to whom. The full definition of someone's identity thus usually involves not only his stand on moral and spiritual matters but also some reference to a defining community" (Taylor 1989, p. 36).

If one generally accepts this proposition, as I do, then one can begin to imagine how deeply disruptive the simultaneous breakdown of colonial Americans' moral/spiritual and social structural moorings would have been to their reflexive regard for their own personal identities. Moreover, the fundamental interdependence between social and personal being falls into much sharper focus (Cahill 1998).

for one reason or another, had become personae non grata most everywhere else. Hence it was that medical and political leaders colluded to promote somatic concepts of the *nature* of insanity while specifying *right living* and *tenable community living* as the fundamental measures of recovery from insanity. In this way, mental illnesses took on the extraordinary guise of natural intrapersonal pathogens for which the only evidence lay in one's moral and practical displacement from a communal order. While in practice madness vexed the moral and practical inclusion of the afflicted, in theory it was no longer held to completely extinguish their humanity. No longer held to render sufferers themselves wholly *other*, insanities came to be viewed as nonhuman *others inside* beings who themselves remained essentially human and, as such, entitled to human rights and potential collaborators in their own redemption.

These ideas originated in settings established to provide treatment to well-to-do patients, people who, if not for their putative diseases, would have held respectable standing in their communities. It was indeed patients' possession of such credentials that gave credence and impetus to the notion of their redemption. However, the establishment of state-sponsored programs based on the potentialities of moral treatment was driven by a political economic interest in containing people who had quite likely never held anything close to respectable standing in American society. Some physicians, inspired by an evangelical Christian faith, were moved to hold out the possibility of moral redemption to *others*, but their patrons tended to be less sanguinely invested in such missionary projects. Public officials were concerned to diffuse the threats to civil order they perceived in the growing numbers of dangerous, disruptive, and dependent individuals crowding into their communities and overwhelming the traditional institutions intended for their management. Their patrons' interest in social control had the effect of pushing psychiatrists' attentions further and further to the margins of American society. Begrudgingly, psychiatrists were transformed during the nineteenth century from missionaries into mercenaries and their conceptual armamentaria evolved accordingly.

At the same time that psychiatrists were being swept into the public management of America's most marginal classes, a growing collection of wellborn Americans were proclaiming the notion that habitual alcohol use produced a "disease of the will" that wreaked havoc upon people's lives and communities. Like the medicalization of moral derangement, this campaign was born of the growing existential anxiety that attended the urbanization and industrialization of American society. The idea that a growing number of city dwellers were enslaving themselves to liquor proved a compelling account of poverty and urban disorder for progressive and conservative social commentators alike. Progressives found in the notion of addiction a credible *environmental* explanation for the deficiencies they observed among the urban poor. Alcohol addiction was construed as a pestilence akin to cholera or typhus that germinated in the squalid conditions under which the urban poor were forced to live. If urban disorder was symptomatic of an epidemic brought on by the contagion of liquor, then sufferers of the contagion themselves might still be held up as deserving members of the American moral community, victims of calamitous circumstance, and entitled to the largesse of their more fortunate countrymen. The opposing view held that alcohol use was a vice and that those who overindulged reaped the harvest they had sown. Addiction and its attendant hardships were thus construed as the just deserts of those who had failed to live a prudent and industrious life. By these lights, alcohol addicts were lumped among the undeserving poor who bore no entitlement to the hard-won prosperity of their more conscientious neighbors. Originally, it was the progressives who made most of the idea of addiction, using it to mount a campaign to recover putative alcohol addicts from their sad plight. They thereby popularized the view that addictions, too, were intrapersonal pathogens, menacing nonhuman *others inside* beings who were themselves essentially human, deserving, and capable of collaborating in their own redemption.

In Chapter 2, I recounted how three distinct social fields emerged and developed around insanities, alcohol addictions, and eventually "narcotic" drug addictions in the nineteenth century. Each of these fields began optimistically with efforts to recover and empower the humanity of those who suffered. In each case the notion that insanities or addictions exist as *others inside* the afflicted was originally propagated as a resource for mitigating the spite that might otherwise have fallen on putative sufferers and to guide efforts aimed at their recovery. In each case these social fields institutionalized specific technologies for the therapeutic redemption of sufferers that were eventually found inadequate for the state agendas for which they became enlisted. With growing public pressures to turn these technologies on the populations presumed most dangerous, disruptive, and dependent (and growing tendencies to measure their efficacy exclusively in terms of social control), therapeutic efforts to foster recovery were progressively transformed into coercive efforts to permanently exclude putative sufferers from the mainstream of American life. Scientific concepts of the disorders themselves followed suit. By the early twentieth century, insanities and addictions, when they were found among members of the lower and marginalized classes, were widely thought to suggest one suffered not from a temporary and remediable affliction, but from an essentially and irremediably flawed personal being. Now conceived in terms of degeneracy and psychopathy, insanities and addictions were again widely viewed as effectively dehumanizing people held to be afflicted by them, rendering them wholly and irretrievably *other*. As such, findings of insanity and/or addiction were much more likely to entitle sufferers to confinement and neglect than to empathy or therapeutic assistance.

Over the course of the twentieth century, the state-sponsored mental health, alcohol, and drug addiction fields grew into more or less discrete nationally organized systems. Though largely separate, these social fields developed parallel to one another, often competing for public funding, for clients, and for the authority to name, explain, and manage the afflictions to which they consensually, and with widespread popular support, insist human beings are heir. In each case, the legitimation and spread of therapeutic interventions was spearheaded by collective efforts to resurrect the reputations of putative sufferers as deserving members of our national, state, and local communities. To the extent they have been regarded "one of our own," attributions of the troubles people present and endure to *others inside* them rather than to their own intrinsic moral depravity have been that much more likely. Perceptions of undeserved suffering among those with whom we have assumed a sense of community solidarity have tended to catalyze the production and growth of publicly subsidized efforts to promote their recovery. Likewise, the perceived probability of sufferers actually achieving some level of recovery from their respective disorders has retained its inverse relation to their economic and cultural marginality. These facts strongly suggest that despite the increasingly technical language used to articulate the nature and consequences of insanities and addictions, our approaches to understanding and managing these phenomena remain fundamentally tied to issues of moral community and belonging. Despite the fervent efforts of clinicians and clinical researchers to cloak the diagnoses of insanities and addictions in a scientistic language devoid of moral content, these assessments remain essentially collateral to judgments of sociocultural compatibility and collective identity.

The enduring relationship between findings of moral community and findings of insanity, alcohol addiction, and illicit drug addiction is further confirmed when we examine the specific ways in which each of the three fields (and their phenomena) have evolved over the course of the twentieth century. In each case, tensions between the agendas of professionals in these respective fields and their public funding agencies continue to dictate the general character of the clients served within a system, the kinds of problems addressed, and hence the nature of services proffered. Whereas funding agencies have been inclined to push professionals in the fields of mental health and the addictions to focus their attentions on socially integrating (or at least domesticating) people whose adjustments to community living they judge the poorest, treatment professionals have themselves been inclined to confine their attention to less aberrant clienteles. Public agencies have been primarily concerned to preserve civil order but they have also been occasionally responsive to well-mobilized private interest groups who lobby for public programs to address the burdens they, their friends, and/or their family members suffer because of the putative ravages of insanity and addiction. For their part, though they remain largely beholden to the agendas of their sponsors, publicly funded researchers and service providers are primarily concerned to preserve their own safety, to preserve their livelihood, to enjoy their work, and to resist strictly mercenary definitions of their mandates.

These dynamics were seen in the community mental health era when treatment professionals pushed for more inclusive definitions of their public mandate and proceeded to neglect the needs of prospective clients who might once have been candidates for hospitalization. The federal government responded first with the Community Support Program, and then with funding cuts and insistences that public funding for treatment be restricted to the "severely disabled." Mental health professionals reliant on public funding were cowed. The enlistment of putative alcohol addicts as collaborators in their own recoveries was driven in the first instance by unpaid members of Alcoholics Anonymous—former addicts who personally identified with them. When the publicly funded alcoholism treatment industry emerged, treatment professionals pervasively favored more compliant and less deviant clients, while public funding agencies continually pressed them to admit the more troubled and troublesome "chronic public inebriates." Once again, if they intended to secure public funding for their work, treatment professionals had to at least present the appearance of attending to more troublesome or politically salient categories of clientele.

Like alcohol addicts, the enlistment of illicit drug addicts as collaborators in their own recoveries has been spearheaded primarily by former addicts who personally identified with them. In the field of publicly

sponsored illicit drug control, public officials capitulated to more inclusive and empowering approaches to the management of addicts
only when leaders in the field of corrections complained of being overwhelmed, and evidence suggested that control might be more effectively
achieved by making addicts themselves "therapeutic agents." Ironically,
improvement of public provisions for illicit drug addicts has also been
fostered by the advent of block grants, funding reductions in the alcohol
and mental health fields, and the war on drugs. The funding opportunities provided by the war on drugs promoted a pervasive fusion of alcohol and drug addiction treatment that in turn resulted in a large-scale
commingling of illicit drug addicts with the less stigmatized personae
of alcoholics in publicly funded treatment settings. As an unintended
result of these fundamentally exclusionary trends in public policy, poor
Americans presumed to suffer from illicit drug addictions may now
catch glimpses of a level of inclusion in the American moral community
they have not seen for more than a century.

The relationship between findings of moral community and findings
of insanities and addictions is also clearly evident in the rise of dual diagnoses as an American public problem. In the interest of defining some of
their most troublesome clients out of their own areas of professed expertise and professional responsibility, practitioners in the mental health,
alcohol, and illicit drug addiction fields historically diagnosed these
clients as suffering from *both* mental illnesses and addictions. This diagnosis rendered its recipient ineligible for admission into most publicly funded programs and was therefore an effective technique for
dispensing with people one considered beyond the pale, too aberrant,
or "treatment-resistant." Thusly, clients whom treatment professionals
judged too troublesome were routinely expelled beyond the domain
of public provision. When groups like NAMI (National Alliance for the
Mentally Ill) began effectively lobbying on behalf of their disabled family
members and friends, and Republican welfare reforms put a premium
on treating only those who were severely disordered, treatment professionals were pressured to reintegrate those they had formerly been
happy to assess as incorrigible others and system "misfits." Once again,
the reach of public services was extended to those presumed to suffer
from dual diagnoses by a combination of private efforts to resurrect
the reputations of putative sufferers as deserving members of their national, state, and local communities and governmental concerns to limit
the scope of public welfare provision but preserve civil order.

The programs in which I did ethnographic fieldwork were established in response to the pressures exerted by community advocates

and public officials to reintegrate the dually diagnosed into the public mental health and addiction treatment systems. Responding to political pressures exerted by NAMI and their allies, the Los Angeles Board of Supervisors ordered the County Office of Alcohol Programs, the Drug Abuse Program Office, and the County Department of Mental Health to collaborate on a program to deal specifically with the dually diagnosed. In response to this initiative, Canyon House took its place in the Los Angeles County human services system with the all but explicit mandate to absorb those clients, many of whom were chronically homeless, who had proven troublesome to the treatment routines in other more traditional settings. These clients were designated less by the nature of their specific diagnoses than by the fact that they had been found "resistant" to the extant panoply of publicly sponsored interventions available for them. Likewise, public funding for Twilights emerged from federal initiatives devised specifically to more effectively manage homelessness. Hence, a concern to maintain civil order and to reintegrate or domesticate a population that had fallen outside the American moral community was once again the original source of interest in sponsoring a clinically specified agenda.

The intimate relationship between findings of moral community and findings of insanities, addictions, and recoveries from them were not only evident in the macroscopic processes that motivated the establishment of Canyon House and Twilights. Indeed, this relationship proved absolutely central to the quotidian routines of therapeutic practice in each of these programs as well. In both programs a fundamental emphasis was placed on motivating clients to personally pledge themselves to the collective work of maintaining the program. Clients were told that their recoveries would come through their own conscientious participation in the program—that is, through a simultaneously moral and practical investment in the program's common life. Thus, contrary to the expectations one might derive from the extant clinical literature, program practice was not in the first instance concerned with the technical detection and repression of pathognomonic *personal disorder* but with the mundane production and maintenance of *communal order*. The bulk of my discussion in Chapters 4 and 5 was taken up with describing the specific details of this work at Canyon House and at Twilights. At Canyon House this work consisted primarily in the enforcement of right living among program members. At Twilights it consisted primarily in the collective cultivation of tenable community living. In both cases, insanity and addiction were invoked only as collateral resources in the more basic work of fostering and maintaining clients' effective inclusion as participants in their respective moral communities.

Likewise, in both cases the empowerment of clients was not only an explicitly sought outcome of treatment but also an explicitly avowed resource for treatment. In this aspect, treatment at Canyon House and at Twilights perpetuated a manner of realizing the relationship between particular insanities, addictions, and human selves that originated in the therapeutic regimens developed by Tuke and Pinel. Like the earliest instances of moral treatment, therapeutic practice at Canyon House and at Twilights was fundamentally concerned with equipping clients to become the primary ministers of their own recoveries. This required that distinctions be made between the actions and identities of the various human agents who collaborated in the therapeutic enterprise and the actions and identities of the putative disorders held to occasionally compromise their respective contributions to that enterprise. It was only by distinguishing sufferers and their afflictions as separate intrapersonal agents that people could be simultaneously held morally accountable to manage their putative disorders, and exonerated from moral accountability for the specific manifestations of those disorders. Invocations of others inside program participants in the guise of insanities or addictions were particularly likely when clients who had generally demonstrated a commitment to the program and to their own recoveries were found to have somehow lapsed from right living.

Though I found no strict formulae for distinguishing the symptoms of specific mental illnesses and addictions as such, disparate tendencies in the ways others inside were designated at Canyon House and at Twilights were very plainly evident. In both cases these tendencies were informed by the distinctive ways in which efforts were made to foster moral community and empower program clients. I've already noted that moral community was fostered primarily through the enforcement of right living at Canyon House and the promotion of tenable community living at Twilights. Likewise, the work of self-empowerment occurred in distinctly different ways in the two settings. At Canyon House, self-empowerment was a primarily retrospective enterprise, while the self-empowerment of Twilights clients consisted primarily in fostering realistic planning for the immediate future. Insofar as they were presently spared most of the trials of securing their own immediate subsistence, Canyon House residents were relatively free to contemplate their pasts. Thus the work of self-empowerment at Canyon House consisted primarily in formulating the particular patterns one's own and each other's troubles had taken, and parsing these troubles into those for which people should be held personally accountable and those that had been foisted upon people by others inside them. Empowerment thus consisted in developing residents' sensibilities regarding their own and each other's respective personal temperaments and personal "issues." This retrospective work informed the ways in which emergent actions and events were differentially construed as indicative of particular people's selves or their respective disorders.

In contrast, Twilights clients were usually overwhelmed with the immediate demands of securing their own subsistence. Therapeutic activities consisted largely in helping clients manage the particular circumstances under which they were presently living rather than altering the particular patterns according to which they had developed their problems. This dynamic did not put as much emphasis on formulating the specific identities of the others inside presumed to afflict clients. Furthermore, given the precariousness of clients' investment in the program, the weight given mere attendance as an indicator of investment, staff's concern to retain clients, and the comparative superficiality of clients' relationships with one another, departures from right living were more ambiguous and less often registered at Twilights than at Canyon House. If and when a departure from right living was registered at Twilights, it was generally individual clients themselves who determined whether their putative departures were symptomatic of others inside them or not. When collective efforts were made to formulate the identities of others inside program clients, these efforts consisted primarily in discovering the specific "triggers" and "slippery places" that posed threats to clients' recoveries. Thus, at Twilights, others inside were formulated more in terms of the environmental circumstances that provoked their reoccurrence in people's lives than in terms of their characteristic patterns of action as such (see also Weinberg 2000).

Insofar as departures from right living were registered with comparative rarity at Twilights, the bulk of evidence for the others inside presumed to lurk within Twilights clients was not found in such departures. The causal effects of others inside Twilights clients were far more often found in events that took place *between* the periods they were present in the program. That is, such evidence was drawn primarily from outside the program setting itself. Indeed, Twilights members tended to draw a very close affinity between absence from the program setting and the causal effects of others inside them. Because of the remoteness of the facility, people almost never went AWOL from the program at Canyon

House. Hence the putative others inside Canyon House residents were almost never found to have proximally caused residents to part from the setting. They were instead found to provoke human agents to take specific courses of remedial action. More than merely changing the course of practice within the program, the others inside presumed to dwell within Twilights clients were often held to have caused clients' literal disappearance or complete estrangement from the Twilights moral community.

One of the more important analytic tasks I have hoped to accomplish in this book is to demonstrate that the therapeutic work performed at Canyon House and at Twilights was by no means wholly determined by one therapeutic idiom or another, or even a collection of idioms artfully patched together. Though Twilights was intended to exactly replicate the Canyon House program design in a nonresidential setting, obdurate practical exigencies forced a variety of significant changes in how therapeutic practice was actually conducted. These changes did not occur at an idiomatic level but at the level of embodied organizational practice itself. No doubt, various generic forms of knowledge including those found in discourse among participants in the twelve-step fellowship, psychiatry, and clinical social work were widely evident and valuable resources in both settings. However, program participants often transcended generic forms of knowledge by incorporating what they knew of people's unique personal histories and personal circumstances into their formulations of both their problems and the remedies appropriate for them. In both settings, therapeutic activities were generally geared toward fostering moral community and the self-empowerment of clients and it was the distinctly practical logic of these activities that governed if, when, and how recourse was made to the conceptual resources program participants inherited from extant expert, or otherwise therapeutic, knowledge.

It is facts like these that ground the analytic priority I have given in this book to institutionalized and embodied practice over ideas (see also Bourdieu 1990). My focus has remained trained on the logic of practice itself rather than the ideographic dynamics that might define the idioms, theories, conceptual schemes, ideologies, narratives, or other such varieties of symbolic structure and constraint social scientists have so often presumed to dictate mental health and substance abuse treatment practice. Though various identifiable idiomatic conventions were certainly used to great effect on occasion, it was decidedly not these conventions themselves that in the first instance structured therapeutic practice at Canyon House and Twilights. And if therapeutic practice is not in the first instance structured by its idiomatic inheritances, then we must avoid conceptualizing therapeutic successes in terms that confer undue importance on solely *ideological* conversions or the acquisition of idiomatic fluency in local therapeutic discourses. Fostering recovery in these settings was not simply a matter of training clients to "talk the talk" that indicated conversion to a locally endorsed therapeutic ideology. It was much more fundamentally concerned with ensuring that clients learn to "walk the walk," whatever that walk might happen to be, that enhanced their inclusion in their respective moral communities and empowered them to sustain the tenability of their unique community living arrangements. Furthermore, the putative capacities of insanities and addictions themselves to actively intervene in people's lives, and to obstinately resist people's efforts to prevent them from doing so, was a central focus of the social activities that comprised these settings. Wholly discursive accounts of therapeutic practice systematically elide from view the extent to which therapeutic activities are directly responsive not only to human discursive practices but also to the actions people attribute to their respective disorders as materially embodied causal agents.

But if it is a mistake to regard insanities, addictions, and recoveries from them as wholly *discursive* constructions, it is no doubt equally mistaken to confer a reality on these phenomena that is independent of the ongoing conduct of meaningful human affairs (cf. Barrett 1996; Currie 1993; Frank and Frank 1991; Gubrium 1992; Holstein 1993; Klienman 1988; Ray 1961; Rudy 1986; Snow et al. 1986; B. Turner 1996; V. Turner 1967; Wiley 1991). Ascendant conceptions of mental disorder and recovery err not in their refusal to confer upon them a more than discursive reality, but in completely removing these phenomena from the province of social history and socially situated human activity. Throughout this book I have been at pains to demonstrate the deficiencies in this approach to understanding insanities, addictions, and recoveries as well. At the epistemological level, orthodox biological and psychological approaches to mental illness, addiction, and recovery suffer for their total lack of reflexive regard for the conditions of their own production. This disregard for their own epistemological bearings prevents the majority of biological and psychological researchers from linking their insights regarding insanities, addictions, and recoveries to the worldly contexts that give them their distinctive sense and value. This, in turn, promotes a profoundly myopic regard for the defining characteristics of these disorders and a theoretical blindness to the diversity of forms that they actually take in human affairs (not to mention the diverse empirical realities that condition those forms). I earnestly hope that this analysis has demonstrated some of the more serious problems that attend this approach to understanding insanities, addictions, and recoveries from them as well.

Far from affirming any manner of fixed conceptual gulf between mental disorder and social difference, my analysis suggests a certain continuity between the human variations of otherness embodied by economically and culturally marginalized Americans and the nonhuman otherness embodied by their putative insanities and addictions. But this is decidedly not simply another sociologically or politically partisan reduction. I have not argued that insanities and addictions are conceptually reducible to cultural difference. Rather, I have argued that in the temporal course of human practice evidence of cultural difference is often literally transformed into evidence of insanities and/or addictions and vice versa. Likewise, in response to specific practical contingencies, evidence of social integration and assimilation is often literally transformed into evidence of recovery from insanities and addictions. Historical and ethnographic investigation of insanities and addictions among homeless and impoverished Americans advises strongly against fixed categorical distinctions between assessments of sociocultural marginality and diagnoses of insanities and addictions. Instead of construing these assessments as completely different in kind, my analysis suggests they be viewed on a continuum and in light of their often intimate relationships with one another.

Historically, human others and nonhuman others in the guise of insanities and addictions have both been cast in terms of the viciousness, savagery, brutality, artlessness, ineptitude, vulgarity, stupidity, and/or irrationality of the events they are said to have caused. But though they have often been found capable producing the same sorts of effects, human and nonhuman others have normally been managed in distinct sorts of ways. At the most general level, human and nonhuman varieties of others are distinguishable with respect to local assessments of the practical value in holding an agent accountable for the events that he or she or it is said to have caused. My research suggests that the issue of moral accountability has figured absolutely centrally (but in a variety of ways) in the historical evolution and contemporary construal of insanities, addictions, and recoveries among homeless and otherwise marginalized Americans.

When we have not been concerned with preserving moral solidarity or compatibility we have not been particularly concerned to avoid attributing people's troublesome, distasteful, or unintelligible actions to their own intrinsic viciousness or deficiency. But when we have been concerned to preserve or establish solidarity, invocations of others inside as scapegoats for people's putative transgressions or deficiencies have proven a deeply compelling and historically enduring practical resource. More ominously, though, insanities and addictions have not always been cast as others inside people. Concepts of insanity and addiction have often been used to literally and completely dehumanize the evident otherness of certain categories of Americans. Rather than mitigating the spite their differences inspired, or indicating methods for easing the problems attributed to those differences, concepts of insanity and addiction have often become favored resources for absolving ourselves from our own accountability to those presumed afflicted. By orienting to the troubles *others* presented and endured as evidence of degeneracy and psychopathy (and thus rendering them wholly and irretrievably subhuman), we have effectively preempted all but the most cursory and superficial interrogations of our own moral accountability to them.

Thirty-five years ago, Erving Goffman (1971, p. 335) wrote,

> For more than 200 years now the doctrine has been increasingly held that there is such a thing as mental illness, that it is a sickness like any other, and those who suffer from it should be dealt with medically: they should be treated by doctors, if necessary in a hospital, and not blamed for what has befallen them. This belief has social uses. Were there no such notion, we would probably have to invent it.

Though these remarks are no doubt overly schematic, I agree with the essential point I believe Goffman is making. This point holds equally true for the notions insanity and addiction. Quite obviously, concepts of insanity and addiction have myriad social uses and, in some respects, they may very well be practically indispensable. I also think investigation of the social uses of these concepts (and their attendant practical technologies) is an immensely fruitful and yet hitherto underappreciated aspect of scientific research regarding these phenomena. As I noted earlier, theorists who attend to only the biological or psychological causes and characteristics of insanities and addictions fail to appreciate the myriad social uses to which the notions of insanity and addiction are put. Furthermore, they systematically overlook the profoundly consequential ways in which the temporally emergent contingencies of social history and socially situated human activity govern these uses. For this reason, I have suggested that biologically and psychologically essentialist

understandings of insanities, addictions, and recoveries are rather fallow grounds for sociological cultivation.

Likewise, though, much of the received sociological literature has
underappreciated the rich practical complexities attendant to the invocation, discovery, and management of insanities and addictions. While
it is no doubt seminal in many important respects, Goffman's classic
work (Goffman 1961) on the dehumanizing consequences of asylum life
exemplifies one of the more serious limitations of received sociological
work in this regard. For Goffman, and for many others, placement in a
treatment setting effectively ended the efforts of a patient's community
to normalize his or her behavior and experiences (see also Foucault 1965;
Rosenhan 1973). Regardless of whatever a person might have done or
been prior to admission, he or she was now a mental patient and all
that he or she did or said was construed with respect to its relevance
to that new and eminently stigmatizing "master status." In my view,
this outlook on treatment practice has been profoundly overstated and
prevents us from appreciating the complexities of the work I have considered here. That is, it prevents us from fully grasping the practical
dynamics whereby personal actions and experiences are differentially
attributed to human and to nonhuman causes even within the context
of treatment settings.[2]

It is quite possible that the source of this distinction between mine and
Goffman's findings is empirical. Goffman did his fieldwork in settings
that were a good deal more custodial than those in which I did mine.
The fact that members of my ethnographic research settings placed a
premium on lay assessments of mental disorder, on distinguishing nonhuman disorders from the human clients who suffer from them, and on
eliciting the collaboration of human clients in the work of overcoming
their own putative disorders no doubt placed the work of distinguishing human from nonhuman agency in a good deal more dramatic relief
than was likely the case in Goffman's settings. But beyond these empirical issues, extant sociological research regarding insanity, addiction,
and recovery has also been theoretically constrained. Research that has
focused on the myriad social uses to which concepts of insanity and
addiction are put, and/or the profoundly consequential ways in which

2. Though Goffman (1961) was alert to the fact that mental patients, despite their
diagnoses, remained largely responsible, as human agents, to comply with institutional
protocol within the confines of total institutions, he was not attentive to the ways in which
mental disorders and human selves *differentially* figured in the work of the institution, nor
to the ways in which members of these settings variably discerned the *actions* of patients
and the *effects* of patients' putative disorders.

the contingencies of social history and socially situated human activity govern those uses, has failed to provide an adequate account for how these putative disorders might come to be experienced as causally influential agents in their own right. In other words, they have not been able to tell us how insanities and addictions, once assembled as meaningful objects of discourse and practice, might in turn come to exercise their own causal influences upon people's experiences and upon the practical activities that comprise their social worlds. The analysis that I have outlined here overcomes this long-standing theoretical impasse in the received social scientific literature.

Finally, this analysis has demonstrated, both historically and ethnographically, that the relationship between social exclusion and mental disability is absolutely intrinsic to the social reality of the latter. My analysis lends no manner of support to the antipsychiatric argument that mental illnesses and addictions are not real. I have argued that in fact they are quite real indeed. However, their reality cannot be meaningfully extricated from the social contexts within which they come to be perceived as such. These social contexts profoundly influence whether mental disabilities are perceived at all, how they are perceived, and how efforts to manage them are formulated and undertaken. The fact that I have focused on the relationship between homelessness and mental disability should be seen as only an extreme case study of the relationship between social exclusion and mental disability (Flyvbjerg 2001, p. 78). The dynamics of social inclusion and exclusion take various forms, some of which very clearly implicate more obvious categories of exclusion like housing status, race, class, gender, and sexuality, but some of which very clearly do not do so. Nonetheless, the fact that some modes of social inclusion and exclusion rely on more subtle or idiosyncratic patterns of judgment must not count as evidence of the irrelevance of social difference and community solidarity to the diagnosis and treatment of putative mental disability. The goal of social scientists must instead be to grasp the details of both extreme and more subtle or idiosyncratic patterns of inclusion and exclusion and their relationship to the precise ways in which categories of mental disability are put to practical use. It is only by this kind of careful and discerning social research that we might produce sound assessments of whether mental health interventions are genuinely empowering or repressive to those who undergo them in any particular case.

References

Alcoholics Anonymous. 1976. *Alcoholics Anonymous*. New York: Alcoholics Anonymous World Services, Inc.

American Psychiatric Association. 1980. *Diagnostic and statistical manual of mental disorders*. 3rd ed. Washington, DC: American Psychiatric Association.

———. 1987. *Diagnostic and statistical manual of mental disorders*. 3rd ed., rev. Washington, DC: American Psychiatric Association.

———. 1994. *Diagnostic and statistical manual of mental disorders*. 4th ed. Washington, DC: American Psychiatric Association.

Anderson, Dwight. 1945. Analysis of wet and dry propaganda. *Journal of Studies on Alcohol*, 355–69.

Anglin, M. Douglas. 1988. The efficacy of civil commitment in treating narcotic addiction. *Journal of Drug Issues* 18(4):527–45.

Ashmore, Malcolm, Robin Wooffitt, and Stella Harding, eds. 1994. Humans and others: The concept of "agency" and its attribution. *American Behavioral Scientist* (special issue) 37(6).

Bachrach, Leona L. 1982. Program planning for young adult chronic patients. In *The young adult chronic patient*. Edited by Bert Pepper and Hilary Ryglewicz. San Francisco: Jossey-Bass, pp. 99–110.

———. 1987. The chronic mental patient with substance abuse problems. In *Leona Bachrach speaks: Selected speeches and lectures*. San Francisco: Jossey-Bass, pp. 29–41.

Bader, Michael J. 1989. Is psychiatry going out of its mind? *Tikkun* 4:43–48.

Barrett, Robert. 1996. *The psychiatric team and the social definition of Schizophrenia*. Cambridge: Cambridge University Press.

Barrows, Susanna, and Robin Room. 1991. Introduction. In *Drinking behavior and belief in modern history*. Edited by Susanna Barrows and Robin Room. Berkeley: University of California Press, pp. 1–25.

Bassuk, Ellen L., and H. Richard Lamb. 1986. Homelessness and the implementation of deinstitutionalization. In *The mental health needs of homeless persons*. Edited by Ellen L. Bassuk. San Francisco: Jossey-Bass, pp. 7–14.

Bateson, Gregory. 1972. *Steps to an ecology of mind*. New York: Ballentine Books.

Baum, Alice S., and Donald W. Burnes. 1993. *A nation in denial*. Boulder, CO: Westview Press.

Baumohl, Jim. 1986. On asylums, homes, and moral treatment: The case of the San Francisco Home for the Care of the Inebriate, 1859–1870. *Contemporary Drug Problems* Fall:395–445.

———. 1990. Inebriate institutions in North America, 1840–1920. *British Journal of Addiction* 85:1187–1204.

Baumohl, Jim, and Robin Room. 1987. Inebriety, doctors, and the state: Alcoholism treatment institutions before 1940. In *Recent developments in alcoholism,* vol. 5. Edited by Marc Galanter. New York: Plenum Press, pp. 135–74.

Beard, George M. 1871. *Stimulants and narcotics: Medically, philosophically, and morally considered.* New York: G.P. Putnam & Sons.

Beauchamp, Dan E. 1980. *Beyond alcoholism.* Philadelphia: Temple University Press.

Becker, Howard S. 1953. Becoming a marijuana user. *American Journal of Sociology* 59:235–42.

———. 1967. History, culture, and subjective experience: An exploration of the social bases of drug-induced experiences. *Journal of Health and Social Behavior* 8:162–76.

Belknap, Ivan. 1956. *Human problems of a state mental hospital.* New York: McGraw-Hill.

Bloor, David. 1991. *Knowledge and social imagery.* 2nd ed. Chicago: University of Chicago Press.

Bloor, Michael, Neal McKeganey, and Dick Fonkert. 1988. *One foot in Eden.* London: Routledge.

Blumer, Herbert. 1969. *Symbolic interactionism.* Berkeley: University of California Press.

Bogdan, Robert, and Steven J. Taylor. 1989. Relationships with severely disabled people: The social construction of humanness. *Social Problems* 36:135–48.

Bourdieu, Pierre. 1990. *The logic of practice.* Stanford: Stanford University Press.

Boyer, Paul. 1978. *Urban masses and moral order in America, 1820–1920.* Cambridge, MA: Harvard University Press.

Brecher, Edward M. 1972. *Licit and illicit drugs.* Boston: Little, Brown and Company.

Brown, Phil. 1987. Diagnostic conflict and contradiction in psychiatry. *Journal of Health and Social Behavior* 28:37–50.

Burnham, John C. 1993. *Bad habits.* New York: New York University Press.

Burt, Martha R. 1992. *Over the edge.* New York: Russell Sage Foundation.

Cahill, Spencer E. 1998. Toward a sociology of the person. *Sociological Theory* 16(2):131–48.

Cain, Carole. 1991. Personal stories: Identity acquisition and self-understanding in Alcoholics Anonymous. *Ethos* 19:210–53.

Callon, Michel, and Bruno Latour. 1992. Don't throw the baby out with the Bath school! A reply to Collins and Yearley. In *Science as practice and culture.* Edited by Andrew Pickering. Chicago: University of Chicago Press, pp. 343–68.

Caudill, William. 1958. *The psychiatric hospital as a small society.* Cambridge, MA: Harvard University Press.

Chodorow, Nancy J. 1999. *The power of feelings.* New Haven, CT: Yale University Press.

Cohen, Jacqueline, and Stephen Jay Levy. 1992. *The mentally ill chemical abuser: Whose client?* New York: Lexington Books.

Collins, Randall. 1994. *Four sociological traditions.* Oxford: Oxford University Press.

Conrad, Peter, and Joseph W. Schneider. 1992. *Deviance and medicalization.* Philadelphia: Temple University Press.

Coulter, Jeff. 1973. *Approaches to insanity.* New York: John Wiley & Sons.

———. 1979. *The social construction of mind.* London: MacMillan.

Courtwright, David T. 2001. *Dark paradise.* Cambridge, MA: Harvard University Press.

Currie, Elliot. 1993. *Reckoning.* New York: Hill and Wang.

Dain, Norman. 1964. *Concepts of insanity in the United States, 1789–1865.* New Brunswick, NJ: Rutgers University Press.

Davies, John B. 1997. *The myth of addiction.* Reading, MA: Harwood Press.

Dear, Michael J., and Jennifer R. Wolch. 1987. *Landscapes of despair.* Princeton, NJ: Princeton University Press.

Denzin, Norman K. 1991. The AA group. In *Society, culture, and drinking patterns reexamined.* Edited by David J. Pittman and Helen Raskin White. New Brunswick, NJ: Rutgers Center of Alcohol Studies, pp. 702–15.

———. 1993. *The alcoholic society.* New Brunswick, NJ: Transaction Publishers.

Desjarlais, Robert. 1997. *Shelter blues.* Philadelphia: University of Pennsylvania Press.

Deutsch, Albert. 1948. *The shame of the states.* New York: Harcourt, Brace.

Dohrenwend, Bruce P., and Barbara S. Dohrenwend. 1975. Sociocultural and social factors in the genesis of mental disorders. *Journal of Health and Social Behavior* 16:365–92.

Drake, Robert E., Fred C. Osher, and Michael A. Wallach. 1991. Homelessness and dual diagnosis. *American Psychologist* 46:1149–58.

Dunham, H. Warren. 1976. *Social realities and community psychiatry.* New York: Human Sciences Press.

Dunham, H. Warren, and S. Kirson Weinberg. 1960. *The culture of the state mental hospital.* Detroit: Wayne State University Press.

Durkheim, Emile. 1982. *The rules of sociological method.* London: MacMillan Press.

Duster, Troy. 1970. *The legislation of morality.* New York: The Free Press.

Eaton, William W., and Carlos Muntaner. 1999. Socioeconomic stratification and mental disorder. In *A handbook for the study of mental health.* Edited by Allan V. Horwitz and Teresa L. Scheid. Cambridge: Cambridge University Press, pp. 259–83.

Elias, Norbert. 1978. *The civilizing process,* vol. 1. New York: Pantheon Books.

Emerson, Robert M. 1989. Tenability and troubles: The construction of accommodative relations by psychiatric emergency teams. In *Perspectives on social problems,* vol. 1. Edited by Gale Miller and James A. Holstein. Greenwich, CT: Jai Press, pp. 215–37.

Emerson, Robert M., E. Burke Rochford, Jr., and Linda L. Shaw. 1981. Economics and enterprise in board and care homes for the mentally ill. *American Behavioral Scientist* 24(6):771–85.

Erikson, Kai T. 1966. *Wayward Puritans.* New York: MacMillan.

Estroff, Sue E. 1981. *Making it crazy.* Berkeley: University of California Press.

Faris, Robert L., and E. Warren Dunham. 1939. *Mental disorders in urban areas.* Chicago: University of Chicago Press.

Farr, Rodger K., Paul Koegel, and Audrey Burnam. 1986. *A study of homelessness and mental illness in the skid row area of Los Angeles*. Los Angeles: Los Angeles County Department of Mental Health.

Fingarette, Herbert. 1989. *Heavy drinking*. Berkeley: University of California Press.

Flyvbjerg, Bent. 2001. *Making social science matter*. Cambridge: Cambridge University Press.

Foucault, Michel. 1965. *Madness and civilization*. Translated by Richard Howard. New York: Vintage Books.

———. 1970. *The order of things*. New York: Random House.

———. 1977. Nietzche, genealogy, history. In *Language, counter-memory, practice*. Edited by Donald F. Bouchard. Ithaca, NY: Cornell University Press, pp. 139–64.

———. 1978. *The history of sexuality*, vol. 1. New York: Random House.

Frank, Arthur. 1997. Narrative witness to bodies: A response to Alan Radley. *Body & Society* 3(3):103–9.

Frank, Jerome D., and Julia B. Frank. 1991. *Persuasion and healing*. 3rd ed. Baltimore, MD: Johns Hopkins University Press.

Frye, Robert V. 1986. Editor's Introduction. A special issue, "The therapeutic community: The third decade." *Journal of Psychoactive Drugs* 18(3): 191–97.

Garfinkel, Harold. 1963. A conception of, and experiments with, "trust" as a condition of stable concerted actions. In *Motivation and social interaction*. Edited by O. J. Harvey. New York: Ronald Press, pp. 197–238.

———. [1967] 1984. *Studies in ethnomethodology*. Cambridge: Polity Press.

Garfinkel, Harold, Michael Lynch, and Eric Livingston. 1981. The work of a discovering science construed with materials from the optically discovered pulsar. *Philosophy of the Social Sciences* 11:131–58.

Giddens, Anthony. 1993. *New rules of sociological method*. Stanford: Stanford University Press.

Glass, James. 1982. The young adult chronic patient: ADM Working Conference. Washington, DC: NIDA.

Goffman, Erving. 1961. *Asylums*. New York: Anchor Books.

———. 1971. The insanity of place. In *Relations in public*. New York: Harper & Row Publishers, pp. 335–90.

Goode, David. 1994. *A world without words*. Philadelphia: Temple University Press.

Goode, Erich. 1993. *Drugs in American society*. 4th ed. New York: McGraw-Hill, Inc.

Greenblatt, Milton, Richard H. York, and Esther Lucile Brown. 1955. *From custodial to therapeutic patient care in mental hospitals*. New York: Russell Sage Foundation.

Grob, Gerald N. 1983. *Mental illness and American society: 1875–1940*. Princeton, NJ: Princeton University Press.

———. 1991a. Origins of DSM-I: A study in appearance and reality. *American Journal of Psychiatry* 148:421–31.

———. 1991b. *From asylum to community: Mental health policy in modern America*. Princeton, NJ: Princeton University Press.

———. 1994. *The mad among us*. New York: The Free Press.

Gronfein, William. 1985a. Incentives and intentions in mental health policy: A comparison of the Medicaid and community mental health programs. *Journal of Health and Social Behavior* 26:192–206.

———. 1985b. Psychotropic drugs and the origins of deinstitutionalization. *Social Problems* 32(5):437–54.

Group for Advancement of Psychiatry (GAP). 1978. *The chronic mental patient in the community*. New York: Group for Advancement of Psychiatry.

———. 1987. *Interactive fit*. New York: Brunner Mazel.

Grusky, Oscar, Kathleen Tierney, James Holstein, Renee Anspach, David Davis, David Unruh, Stephen Webster, Steven Vandewater, and Harris Allen. 1985. Models of local mental health delivery systems. *American Behavioral Scientist* 28(5):685–703.

Gubrium, Jaber F. 1986. The social preservation of mind: The Alzheimer's disease experience. *Symbolic Interaction* 6:37–51.

———. 1992. *Out of control*. Newbury Park, NJ: Sage.

Gurwitch, Aron. 1964. *The field of consciousness*. Pittsburgh, PA: Duquesne University Press.

Gusfield, Joseph R. 1981. *The culture of public problems*. Chicago: University of Chicago Press.

———. 1982. Deviance and the welfare state: The alcoholism profession and the entitlements of stigma. *Research in Social Problems and Public Policy* 2:1–20.

———. 1986. *Symbolic crusade*. 2nd ed. Urbana: University of Illinois Press.

———. 1989. Constructing the ownership of social problems: Fun and profit in the welfare state. *Social Problems* 36(5):431–41.

Hacking, Ian. 1983. *Representing and intervening*. Cambridge: Cambridge University Press.

———. 1986. Making up people. In *Reconstructing individualism*. Edited by Thomas C. Heller, Morton Sosna, and David E. Wellbery. Stanford: Stanford University Press, pp. 222–36.

———. 1995. *Rewriting the soul*. Princeton, NJ: Princeton University Press.

———. 1999. *The social construction of what?* Cambridge, MA: Harvard University Press.

Haraway, Donna J. 1991. *Symians, cyborgs, and women*. New York: Routledge.

Harre, Rom. 1987. The social construction of selves. In *Self and identity*. Edited by K. Yardley and T. Honess. New York: John Wiley & Sons, pp. 41–52.

Hazelrigg, Lawrence E. 1986. Is there a choice between "Constructionism" and "Objectivism?" *Social Problems* 33:s1–s13.

Herd, Denise. 1991. The paradox of temperance: Blacks and the alcohol question in nineteenth-century America. In *Drinking behavior and belief in modern history*. Edited by Susanna Barrows and Robin Room. Berkeley: University of California Press, pp. 354–75.

Heritage, John. 1984. *Garfinkel and ethnomethodology*. Cambridge: Polity Press.

Hollingshead, August B., and Frederick C. Redlich. 1958. *Social class and mental illness*. New York: Academic Press.

Holstein, James A. 1987. Producing gender effects on involuntary mental hospitalization. *Social Problems* 34(2):141–55.

———. 1993. *Court-ordered insanity*. New York: Aldine de Gruyter.

Hopper, Kim. 1991. A poor apart: The distancing of homeless men in New York's history. *Social Research* 58(1):107–32.

Hopper, Kim, Ellen Baxter, and Stuart Cox. 1982. Not making it crazy: The young homeless patients in New York City. In *The young adult chronic patient*. Edited by Bert Pepper and Hilary Ryglewicz. San Francisco: Jossey-Bass, pp. 33–42.

Horwitz, Allan V. 2002. *Creating mental illness*. Chicago: University of Chicago Press.

Hubbard, Robert L., Mary Ellen Marsden, J. Valley Rachel, Henrick J. Harwood, Elizabeth R. Cavanaugh, and Harold M. Ginzburg. 1989. *Drug abuse treatment*. Chapel Hill: University of North Carolina Press.

Huebner, Robert B., Harold I. Perl, Peggy M. Murray, Jack E. Scott, and Beth Ann Tutunjian. 1993. The NIAAA cooperative agreement program for homeless personas with alcohol and other drug problems: An overview. *Alcoholism Treatment Quarterly* 10(3/4):5–20.

Hughes, Patrick H. 1966. Patients as therapeutic agents. In *Rehabilitating the narcotic addict*. Edited by S. Sells. New York: Arno Press.

Hume, David. [1739] 1978. *A treatise of human nature*. Oxford: Oxford University Press.

Ingleby, David. 1982. The social construction of mental illness. In *The problem of medical knowledge*. Edited by Peter Wright and Andrew Treacher. Edinburgh: Edinburgh University Press, pp. 123–43.

Institute of Medicine. 1988. *Homelessness, health, and human needs*. Washington, DC: National Academy Press.

———. 1990. *Treating drug problems*, vol. I. Washington, DC: National Academy Press.

Irwin, John. 1985. *The jail*. Berkeley: University of California Press.

Isaac, Rael Jean, and Virginia C. Armat. 1990. *Madness in the streets*. New York: The Free Press.

Jaffe, A. 1978. Reform in American medical science: The inebriety movement and the origins of the psychological disease theory of addiction, 1870–1920. *British Journal of Addiction* 73:139–47.

Jansen, Martin H. 1966. Paramedical group counseling of hospitalized addicts. In *Rehabilitating the narcotic addict*. Edited by S. Sells. New York: Arno Press.

Jaspers, Karl. 1963. *General psychopathology*. Translated by J. Hoenig and M. Hamilton. Chicago: University of Chicago Press.

Jellinek, E. M. 1942. An outline of basic policies for a research program on problems of alcohol. *Quarterly Journal of Studies on Alcohol* 3:103–24.

Jencks, Christopher. 1994. *The homeless*. Cambridge, MA: Harvard University Press.

Jimenez, Mary Ann. 1987. *Changing faces of madness*. Hanover, NH: Published for Brandeis University Press by University Press of New England.

Jones, Maxwell. 1952. *Social psychiatry*. London: Tavistock.

Kane, H. H. 1881. *Drugs that enslave*. Philadelphia: Presley Blakiston.

Kanter, Rosabeth Moss. 1972. *Commitment and community*. Cambridge, MA: Harvard University Press.

Karp, David A. 1996. *Speaking of sadness*. New York: Oxford University Press.

Katz, Michael B. 1986. *In the shadow of the poorhouse*. New York: Basic Books.

———. 1989. *The undeserving poor*. New York: Pantheon Books.

Keller, Mark. 1976. Problems with alcohol: An historical perspective. In *Alcohol and alcohol problems*. Edited by William J. Filstead, Jean J. Rossi, and Mark Keller. Cambridge, MA: Ballinger Publishing Company, pp. 5–28.

Kirk, Stuart A., and Herb Kutchins. 1992. *The selling of DSM*. New York: Aldine de Gruyter.

Kirk, Stuart A., and Mark E. Therrien. 1975. Community mental health myths and the fate of former hospitalized mental patients. *Psychiatry* 38(3):209–17.

Klerman, Gerald L. 1989. Psychiatric diagnostic categories: Issues of validity and measurement. *Journal of Health and Social Behavior* 30:26–32.

Klien, Dorie. 1983. Ill and against the law: The social and medical control of heroin users. *Journal of Drug Issues*. Winter:31–55.

Klienman, Arthur. 1988. *Rethinking psychiatry*. New York: Free Press.

Koegel, Paul, and M. Audrey Burnam. 1987. Traditional and non-traditional homeless alcoholics. *Alcohol Health and Research World* 11:28–33.

———. 1988. Alcoholism among homeless adults in the inner city of Los Angeles. *Archives of General Psychiatry* 45:1011–18.

Koegel, Paul, M. Audrey Burnam, and Rodger K. Farr. 1987. The prevalence of specific psychiatric disorders among homeless individuals in the inner city of Los Angeles. *Archives of General Psychiatry* 45:1985–92.

———. 1990. Subsistence adaptation among homeless adults in the inner city of Los Angeles. *Journal of Social Issues* 46(4):83–107.

Kramer, Peter D. 1993. *Listening to Prozac*. New York: Viking.

Kurtz, Norman R., and Marilyn Regier. 1975. The Uniform Alcoholism and Intoxication Treatment Act: The compromising process of social policy formulation. *Journal of Studies on Alcohol* 36(11):1421–41.

Kusmer, Kenneth L. 2002. *Down and out, on the road*. Oxford: Oxford University Press.

Laing, Ronald D. 1969. *The divided self*. London: Penguin Books.

Latour, Bruno, and Steve Woolgar. 1979. *Laboratory life*. Beverly Hills, CA: Sage.

Levine, Harold G. 1978. The discovery of addiction: Changing conceptions of habitual drunkenness in America. *Journal of Studies on Alcohol* 39(1):143–74.

———. 1984. The alcohol problem in America: From temperance to alcoholism. *British Journal of Addiction* 79:109–19.

———. 1985. The birth of American alcohol control: Prohibition, the power elite, and the problem of lawlessness. *Contemporary Drug Problems* 12:63–115.

Lidz, Theodore, Alice Cornelison, Dorothy Terry Carlson, and Stephen Fleck. 1958. Intrafamilial environment of the schizophrenic patient: The transmission of irrationality. *Archives of Neurology and Psychiatry* 79(3):305–16.

Lindesmith, Alfred R. 1938. A sociological theory of drug addiction. *American Journal of Sociology* 43:593–609.

———. 1940. The drug addict as psychopath. *American Sociological Review* 5: 914–20.

———. 1947. *Opiate addiction*. Bloomington: Principia Press.

———. 1961. *Drug addiction*. Bloomington: Indiana University Press.

———. 1968. *Addiction and opiates*. Chicago: Aldine.

Love, Robert E. 1984. The community support program: Strategy for reform? In *The chronic mental patient: Five years later*. Edited by John A. Talbott. Orlando, FL: Grune & Stratton, Inc., pp. 195–214.

Lubran, Barbara. 1990. Alcohol and drug abuse among the homeless population: A national response. *Alcoholism Treatment Quarterly* 7(1):11–23.

Lynch, Michael. 1984. "Turning up signs" in neurobehavioral diagnosis. *Symbolic Interaction* 7:67–86.

———. 1993. *Scientific practice and ordinary action*. Cambridge: Cambridge University Press.

Maddux, James F. 1978. History of the hospital treatment programs, 1935–1974. In *Drug addiction and the U.S. Public Health Service*. Edited by William R. Martin and Harris Isbell. Rockville, MD: U.S. Department of Health, Education, and Welfare, pp. 217–50.

Maisel, Albert Q. 1946. Bedlam 1946. *Life* 20:103–18.

Matza, David. 1966. The disreputable poor. In *Class, status, & power*. 2nd ed. Edited by Reinhard Bendix and Seymour Martin Lipset. New York: The Free Press, pp. 289–302.

McGlothlin, William H. 1976. California civil commitment: A decade later. *Journal of Drug Issues* Fall:368–79.

McGovern, Constance M. 1985. *Masters of madness*. Hanover, NH: Published for University of Vermont by University Press of England.

McGrane, Bernard. 1989. *Beyond anthropology*. New York: Columbia University Press.

Mechanic, David. 1989. *Mental health and social policy*. 3rd ed. Englewood Cliffs, NJ: Prentice Hall.

Mechanic, David, and David A. Rochefort. 1990. Deinstitutionalization: An appraisal of reform. *Annual Review of Sociology* 16:301–27.

Menninger W. Walter, and Gerald T. Hannah, eds. 1987. *The chronic mental patient II*. Washington, DC: American Psychiatric Association.

Menninger, William C. 1948. *Psychiatry in a troubled world*. New York: Macmillan.

Meyerson, Arthur T., ed. 1987. *Barriers to treating the chronic mentally ill*. San Francisco: Jossey-Bass.

Mirowsky, John, and Catherine E. Ross. 1989. Psychiatric diagnosis as reified measurement. *Journal of Health and Social Behavior* 30:11–25.

———. 1999. Well-being across the life course. In *A handbook for the study of mental health*. Edited by Allan V. Horwitz and Teresa L. Scheid. Cambridge: Cambridge University Press, pp. 328–47.

Monkkonen, Eric H. 1993. Nineteenth century institutions: Dealing with the urban "underclass." In *The "underclass" debate: Views from history*. Edited by Michael B. Katz. Princeton, NJ: Princeton University Press, pp. 334–65.

Morgan, H. Wayne, ed. 1974. *Yesterday's addicts*. Norman: University of Oklahoma Press.

———. 1981. *Drugs in America*. New York: Syracuse University Press.

Morgan, Patricia. 1980. The state as mediator: Alcohol problem management in the post-war period. *Contemporary Drug Problems* Spring:107–40.

———. 1981. Systems in crisis: Social welfare and the state's management of alcohol problems. *Contemporary Drug Problems*. Summer:243–61.

Morrissey, Joseph P. 1982. Deinstitutionalizing the mentally ill: Process, outcomes, and new directions. In *Deviance and mental illness*. Edited by Walter R. Gove. Beverley Hills, CA: Sage, pp. 147–76.

Musto, David F. 1987. *The American disease*, exp. ed. New York: Oxford University Press.

National Institute on Alcohol Abuse and Alcoholism (NIAAA). 1988. *Synopsis of community demonstration grant projects for alcohol and drug abuse treatment of homeless individuals*. Rockville, MD: U. S. Department of Health and Human Services.

———. 1990. *Cooperative agreements for research demonstration projects on alcohol and other drug abuse treatment for homeless persons: Request for applications*. Rockville, MD: NIAAA.

———. 1991. *Synopses of cooperative agreements for research demonstration projects on alcohol and other drug abuse treatment for homeless persons*. Rockville, MD: U. S. Department of Health and Human Services.

Patterson, James T. 1981. *America's struggle against poverty, 1900–1980*. Cambridge, MA: Harvard University Press.

Peele, Stanton. 1989. *Diseasing of America*. Boston: Houghton-Mifflin Company.

Pepper, Bert, and Hilary Ryglewicz, eds. 1982. *The young adult chronic patient*. San Francisco: Jossey-Bass.

———. 1984. Treating the young adult chronic patient: An update. In *Advances in treating the young adult chronic patient*. Edited by Bert Pepper and Hilary Ryglewicz. San Francisco: Jossey-Bass, pp. 5–15.

Peyrot, Mark. 1984. Cycles of social problem development: The case of drug abuse. *Sociological Quarterly* 25:83–96.

———. 1991. Institutional and organizational dynamics in community-based drug abuse treatment. *Social Problems* 38(1):20–33.

———. 1995. Psychological testing and forensic decision-making: The properties-in-use of the MMPI. *Social Problems* 42(4):574–86.

Phelan, Jo, Bruce G. Link, Robert E. Moore, and Ann Stueve. 1997. The stigma of homelessness: The impact of the label "homeless" on attitudes toward poor persons. *Social Psychology Quarterly* 60(4):322–36.

Pickering, Andrew. 1995. *The mangle of practice*. Chicago: University of Chicago Press.

Pittman, Bill. 1988. *AA the way it began*. Seattle, WA: Glen Abbey Books.

Pittman, David J., and C. Wayne Gordon 1958. *The revolving door*. Glencoe, IL: Free Press.

Piven, Francis Fox, and Richard A. Cloward. 1993. *Regulating the poor*, updated edition. New York: Vintage Books.

Pollner, Melvin. 1987. *Mundane reason*. Cambridge: Cambridge University Press.

Pollner, Melvin, and Lynn McDonald-Wikler. 1985. The social construction of unreality: A case study of a family's attribution of competence to a severely retarded child. *Family Process* 24(2):241–54.

Pollner, Melvin, and Jill Stein. 1996. Narrative mapping of social worlds: The voice of experience in Alcoholics Anonymous. *Symbolic Interaction* 19:203–24.

Polsky, Andrew J. 1991. *The rise of the therapeutic state*. Princeton, NJ: Princeton University Press.

Porter, Roy. 1985. The drinking man's disease: The "pre-history" of alcoholism in Georgian Britain. *British Journal of Addictions* 80:385–96.

Putnam, Hilary. 1987. *The many faces of realism*. La Salle, IL: Open Court.

Quadagno, Jill. 1987. Theories of the welfare state. *Annual Review of Sociology* 13:109–28.

Ray, Marsh. 1961. The cycle of abstinence and relapse among heroin addicts. *Social Problems* 9(2):132–40.

Reinarman, Craig. 1979. Moral entrepreneurs and political economy: Historical and ethnographic notes on the construction of the cocaine menace. *Contemporary Crises* 3:225–54.

———. 1994. The social construction of drug scares. In *Constructions of deviance*. Edited by Patricia and Peter Adler. Belmont, CA: Wadsworth, pp. 92–104.

Rhodes, Lorna A. 1991. *Emptying beds*. Berkeley: University of California Press.

Robertson, Nan. 1988. *Getting better*. New York: William Morrow and Company, Inc.

Rochefort, David A. 1993. *From poorhouses to homelessness*. Westport, CT: Auburn House.

Roizen, Ron. 1994. Norman Jolliffe, the Rockefeller Foundation, and the origins of the modern Alcoholism Movement. *Journal of Studies on Alcohol* 55: 391–400.

Roman, Paul M. 1991. Problem definitions and social movement strategies: The disease concept and the hidden alcoholic revisited. In *Alcohol*. Edited by Paul M. Roman. New Brunswick, NJ: Rutgers Center of Alcohol Studies, pp. 235–53.

Room, Robin. 1972. Drinking and disease: Comment on "The Alcohologist's Addiction." *Quarterly Journal of Studies on Alcohol* 33:1049–59.

———. 1976. Comment on "The Uniform Alcoholism and Intoxication Act." *Journal of Studies on Alcohol* 37(1):113–44.

———. 1978. *Governing images of alcohol and drug problems*. Ph.D. Dissertation, Department of Sociology, University of California, Berkeley.

———. 1982. Alcohol, science, and social control. In *Alcohol, science and society revisited*. Edited by Edith L. Gomberg, Helen Raskin White, and John Carpenter. Ann Arbor: University of Michigan Press, pp. 371–84.

———. 1983. Sociological aspects of the disease concept of alcoholism. *Research Advances in Alcohol and Drug Problems* 7:47–91.

———. 1985. Alcohol as cause: Empirical links and social definitions. In *Currents in alcohol research and the prevention of alcohol problems*. Edited by Jean-Pierre von Wartburg, Pierre Magnenat, Richard Muller, and Sonja Wyss. Berne: Hans Huber Press, pp. 11–19.

Rosenfield, Sarah. 1999. Gender and mental health: Do women have more psychopathology, men more, or both the same (and why)? In *A handbook for the study of mental health*. Edited by Allan V. Horwitz and Teresa L. Scheid. Cambridge: Cambridge University Press, pp. 348–60.

Rosenhan, David L. 1973. On being sane in insane places. *Science* 179:250–8.

Rossi, Peter. 1989. *Down and out in America*. Chicago: University of Chicago Press.

Rothman, David J. 1980. *Conscience and convenience*. Boston: Little, Brown and Company.

————. 1990. *The discovery of the asylum*, rev. ed. Boston: Little, Brown, & Company.

Rubington, Earl. 1977. The role of the halfway house in the rehabilitation of alcoholics. In *The biology of alcoholism*, vol. 5. Edited by B. Kissin and H. Beglieter. New York: Plenum Press, pp. 351–83.

Rudy, David R. 1986. *Becoming alcoholic*. Carbondalle: Southern Illinois University Press.

Sass, Louis. 1992. *Madness and modernism*. New York: Basic Books.

Schacter, Stanley, and Jerome E. Singer. 1962. Cognitive, social, and physiological determinants of emotional state. *Psychological Review* 69(5):379–99.

Scheff, Thomas J. 1984. *Being mentally ill*. 2nd ed. New York: Aldine.

Schmidt, Laura. 1991. Specialization in alcoholism and mental health residential treatment: The "dual diagnosis" problem. *Journal of Drug Issues* 21(4):859–74.

————. 1995. "A battle not man's but God's": Origins of the American temperance crusade in the struggle for religious authority. *Journal of Studies on Alcohol* 56:110–21.

Schmidt, Laura, and Constance Weisner. 1993. Developments in alcoholism treatment: A ten-year review. In *Recent developments in alcoholism*, vol. 11. Edited by Marc Galanter. New York: Plenum Press, pp. 369–96.

Schneider, Joseph W. 1978. Deviant drinking as disease: Alcoholism as a social accomplishment. *Social Problems* 25(4):361–72.

Scull, Andrew. 1977. Madness and segregative control: The rise of the insane asylum. *Social Problems* 24:338–51.

————. 1981. A new trade in lunacy: The recommodification of the mental patient. *American Behavioral Scientist* 224(6):741–54.

————. 1984. *Decarceration—A radical view*. 2nd ed. New Brunswick, NJ: Rutgers University Press.

————. 1989. *Social order/mental disorder*. Berkeley: University of California Press.

Segal, Steven P., and Uri Aviram. 1978. *The mentally ill in community-based sheltered care*. New York: John Wiley & Sons.

Segal, Steven P., and Jim Baumohl. 1980. Engaging the disengaged: Proposals on madness and vagrancy. *Social Work* 25:358–65.

Segal, Steven P., Jim Baumohl, and Elsie Johnson. 1977. Falling through the cracks: Mental disorder and social margin in a young vagrant population. *Social Problems* 24(3):387–400.

Sennett, Richard. 1976. *The fall of public man*. New York: Vintage Books.

Shapin, Steven. 1994. *A social history of truth*. Chicago: University of Chicago Press.

Shelly, Joseph A. 1966. Daytop Lodge—A two year report. In *Rehabilitating the narcotic addict*. Edited by S. Sells. New York: Arno Press.

Shlay, Anne B., and Peter H. Rossi. 1992. Social science research and contemporary studies of homelessness. *Annual Review of Sociology* 18:129–60.

Simon, Jonathan. 1993. *Poor discipline*. Chicago: University of Chicago Press.

Skoll, Geoffrey R. 1992. *Walk the walk and talk the talk*. Philadelphia: Temple University Press.

Snow, David A., and Leon Anderson. 1993. *Down on their luck*. Berkeley: University of California Press.

Snow, David A., Susan G. Baker, Leon Anderson, and Michael Martin. 1986. The myth of pervasive mental illness among the homeless. *Social Problems* 33:407–23.

Snow, David A., and M. Gerald Bradford. 1994. Broadening perspectives on homelessness: An introduction. *American Behavioral Scientist* 37(4):454–60.

Spitzer, Robert L., and Janet B.W. Williams. 1982. The definition and diagnosis of mental disorder. In *Deviance and mental illness*. Edited by Walter R. Gove. Beverley Hills, CA: Sage, pp. 15–31.

Stanton, Alfred H., and Morris S. Schwartz. 1954. *The mental hospital*. New York: Basic Books.

Starr, Paul. 1982. *The social transformation of American medicine*. New York: Basic Books.

Stephens, Richard C. 1991. *The street addict role*. Albany, NY: SUNY Press.

Stern, Mark J. 1984. The emergence of the homeless as a public problem. *Social Services Review* 58:291–301.

Stienberg, James B., David W. Lyon, and Mary E. Vaiana, eds. 1992. *Urban America*. Santa Monica, CA: Rand.

Straus, Robert. 1976. Problem drinking in the perspective of social change, 1940–73. In *Alcohol and alcohol problems*. Edited by William J. Filstead, Jean J. Rossi, and Mark Keller. Cambridge, MA: Ballinger Publishing Company, pp. 29–56.

———. 1991. Seldon D. Bacon as a teacher, colleague, scholar, and founder of modern alcohol studies. In *Alcohol*. Edited by Paul M. Roman. New Brunswick, NJ: Rutgers Center of Alcohol Studies, pp. 113–23.

Sugarman, Barry. 1974. *Daytop Village*. New York: Holt, Rinehardt and Winston.

Swazey, Judith. 1974. *Chlorpromazine in psychiatry*. Cambridge, MA: MIT Press.

Szasz, Thomas. 1961. *The myth of mental illness*. New York: Hoeber-Harper.

Talbott, John A., ed. 1978. *The chronic mental patient*. Washington, DC: American Psychiatric Association.

———. 1980. Toward a public policy on the chronic mentally ill patient. *American Journal of Orthopsychiatry* 50(1):43–53.

———. 1984. *The chronic mental patient: Five years later*. Orlando, FL: Grune & Stratton, Inc.

Taylor, Charles. 1989. *Sources of the self*. Cambridge, MA: Harvard University Press.

Thoits, Peggy A. 1985. Self-labeling processes in mental illness: The role of emotional deviance. *American Journal of Sociology* 91:221–49.

———. 1990. Emotional deviance: Research agendas. In *Research agendas in the sociology of emotions*. Edited by Theodore D. Kemper. Albany, NY: SUNY Press, pp. 180–203.

Thompson, E. P. 1967. Time, work-discipline and industrial capitalism. *Past and Present* 38:56–97.

Tittle, C., and D. Tittle. 1963. Structural handicaps to therapeutic participation: A case study. *Social Problems* 13:129–42.

Tomes, Nancy. 1984. *A generous confidence*. Cambridge: Cambridge University Press.

Torrey, E. Fuller. 1988. *Nowhere to go*. New York: Harper & Row.

Trice, Harrison M., and William J. Staudenmeier, Jr. 1989. A sociocultural history of Alcoholics Anonymous. In *Recent developments in alcoholism*, vol. 7. Edited by Marc Galanter Williams and Harris-Reid. New York: Plenum Press, pp. 295–314.

Tuke, Samuel. 1813. *Description of the retreat: An institution near York for insane persons of the society of friends*. York: Thomas Wilson & Sons.

Turner, Bryan S. 1996. *The body & society*. 2nd ed. London: Sage.

Turner, Victor. 1967. *The forest of symbols*. Ithaca, NY: Cornell University Press.

———. 1969. *The ritual process*. Ithaca, NY: Cornell University Press.

U. S. Court of Appeals. 1966. *Driver v. Hinnant*, 356 F. 2d 50.

———. 1966. *Easter v. District of Columbia*, 361 F 2d 761.

U. S. General Accounting Office (GAO). 1977. *Returning the mentally disabled to the community: The government needs to do much more*. Washington, DC: U.S. Government Printing Office.

U. S. Supreme Court. 1962. *Robinson v. California*, 370 U.S. 660.

———. 1968. *Powell v. State of Texas*, 392 U.S. 514.

Valverde, Mariana. 1998. *Diseases of the will*. Cambridge: Cambridge University Press.

van Steenbergen, Bart, ed. 1994. *The condition of citizenship*. London: Sage.

Vernez, Goerges, M. Audrey Burnam, Elizabeth A. McGlynn, Sally Trude, and Brian Mittman. 1988. *Review of California's program for the homeless mentally disabled*. Santa Monica, CA: Rand.

Wagner, David. 1993. *Checkerboard square*. Boulder, CO: Westview Press.

Waldorf, Dan, Craig Reinarman, and Sheigla Murphy. 1991. *Cocaine changes*. Philadelphia, PA: Temple University Press.

Wallace, John. 1990. Controlled drinking, treatment effectiveness, and the disease model of addiction: A commentary on the ideological wishes of Stanton Peele. *Journal of Psychoactive Drugs* 22(3):261–84.

Wallace, Samuel E. 1965. *Skid row as a way of life*. New York: Harper & Row Publishers.

Warner, Jessica. 1994. "Resolv'd to drink no more": Addiction as a preindustrial construct. *Journal of Studies on Alcohol* 55:685–91.

Warren, Carol A.B. 1981. New forms of social control: The myth of deinstitutionalization. *American Behavioral Scientist* 24(6):724–40.

Weber, Max. 1958. *The protestant ethic and the spirit of capitalism*. New York: Charles Scribner's Sons.

———. 1978. *Economy and society*. Berkeley: University of California Press.

Weinberg, Darin. 1996. The enactment and appraisal of authenticity in a skid row therapeutic community. *Symbolic Interaction* 19(2):137–62.

———. 1997a. The social construction of nonhuman agency: The case of mental disorder. *Social Problems* 44(2):217–34.

———. 1997b. Lindesmith on addiction: A critical history of a classic theory. *Sociological Theory* 15(2):150–61.

———. 1998. Praxis and addiction: A reply to Galliher. *Sociological Theory* 16(2):207–8.

———. 2000. "Out there": The ecology of addiction in drug abuse treatment discourse. *Social Problems* 47(4):606–21.

———. 2002. On the embodiment of addiction. *Body & Society* 8(4):1–19.

Weinberg, Darin, and Paul Koegel. 1995. Impediments to recovery in treatment programs for dually diagnosed homeless adults: An ethnographic analysis. *Contemporary Drug Problems* 12(2):193–236.

Weisner, Constance. 1983. The alcohol treatment system and social control: A study in institutional change. *Journal of Drug Issues* Winter: 117–33.

———. 1992. The merging of alcohol and drug treatment: A policy review. *Journal of Public Health Policy* 13(1):66–80.

Weisner, Constance, and Robin Room. 1984. Financing and ideology in alcohol treatment. *Social Problems* 32(2):167–84.

Weppner, Robert S. 1983. *The untherapeutic community*. Lincoln: University of Nebraska Press.

Wieder, D. Lawrence. 1988. *Language and social reality*. Washington, DC: University Press of America.

Wiener, Carolyn L. 1981. *The politics of alcoholism*. New Brunswick, NJ: Transaction Books.

Wiley, Juniper. 1991. A refracted reality of everyday life: The constructed culture of a therapeutic community. *Symbolic Interaction* 14:139–63.

Williams, David R., and Michelle Harris-Reid. 1999. Race and mental health: Emerging patterns and promising approaches. In *A handbook for the study of mental health*. Edited by Allan V. Horwitz and Teresa L. Scheid. Cambridge: Cambridge University Press.

Wiseman, Jacqueline P. 1970. *Stations of the lost*. Chicago: University of Chicago Press.

Wolch, Jennifer, and Michael Dear. 1993. *Malign neglect*. San Francisco: Jossey-Bass.

Woolgar, Steve, and Dorothy Pawluch. 1985. Ontological gerrymandering: The anatomy of social problems explanations. *Social Problems* 32:214–27.

Wright, James D. 1989. *Address unknown*. New York: Aldine.

Yablonsky, Lewis. 1965. *The tunnel back*. New York: Macmillan.

———. 1989. *The therapeutic community*. New York: Garner Press.

Yarrow, Marion R., Charlotte G. Schwartz, Harriet S. Murphy, and Liela C. Deasy. 1955. The psychological meaning of mental illness in the family. *Journal of Social Issues* 11:12–24.

Young, Allan. 1995. *The harmony of illusions*. Princeton, NJ: Princeton University Press.

Index

AA. *See* Alcoholics Anonymous, twelve step

AACI. *See* American Association for the Cure of Inebriates

activists, 61, 72, 76; *see also* liberals, progressives, reformers

actor-network theory; human agents, 8; nonhuman agents, 8; symmetry between human and nonhuman agents, 8; *see also* Pickering's approach

addiction, xi, xii, xiv, xv, xvi, 1–4, 6, 9–11, 15–17, 20–21, 23–24, 26, 28, 37, 39–45, 47–52, 55–62, 64–65, 67, 70, 72–74, 84, 90–92, 96, 97, 99–102, 119–121, 124, 126, 127, 129, 130, 133, 136–138, 139, 141, 154, 155, 157, 170, 171–172, 178, 180, 181, 182, 183, 192–196, 200–204; and generic conceptual templates, 119–121, 136–138, 171–172; as complex and versatile causal agent, 65, 72–3, 92, 127, 136–138, 141; as disease, 24, 39, 40, 42, 55–62, 64–65, 67, 90, 192–196; as *other inside*, xvi, 9–11, 28, 39, 44, 47, 55–56, 60, 65, 70, 74, 90, 91, 92, 112, 127, 137, 139, 183, 192; as particular not generic affliction, 124, 127, 136, 136–140; as socially negotiated outcome, 3, 127, 136–141; as threat to moral community, 11, 22, 26, 44–45, 51, 65, 72–73, 84, 92, 136–141, 155, 157, 181, 192–196; at Canyon House, 99–102, 119–121, 124, 126, 127, 129, 130, 133, 136–138, 139, 141, 200; at Twilights, 154, 155, 157, 170, 171–172, 178, 180, 181, 182, 183, 200; critique of objectivist biological concept of, 4–5, 143, 200–201; critique of objectivist psychological concept of, 4–5, 143, 200–201; critique of psychosocial approaches to, 5–6; Enlightenment and, 23–24; medicalization of, 2, 3, 24, 39–44, 53–66, 67; Synanon, concept of, 70; *see also* alcoholism

Alcohol, Drug Abuse, and Mental Health Administration (ADAMHA), 89–90

Alcoholics Anonymous (AA), 53–66, 70, 95, 97, 98, 102, 103, 118–121, 153, 165–168, 175, 194; and cultural diversity of meetings, 103, 121, 165–167; and moral community, 54, 56, 165–167, 194; as source of generic conceptual templates, 118–121, 172; "Big Book", 55, 175; funding accountability, 64; "hidden alcoholics", 59; in Canyon House, 98, 102, 103, 104–107, 118–121; in Twilights, 153, 165–168, 172, 175; limits of, 56, 61; National Council on Alcoholism (NCA), 60–62; National Institute on Alcoholism and Alcohol Abuse (NIAAA), 62; *others inside* and, 55–56, 65; Research Council on Problems of Alcohol (RCPA), 57; Silkworth, William, 55; Smith, Dr. Bob, 54; Synanon, 70; Wilson, Bill, 54; *see also* Alcoholism Movement; twelve step

alcoholism, xii, 1, 16, 49, 53–66, 73, 74, 95, 96, 97, 141, 170, 194; allergy theory, 58; as complex and versatile causal agent, 65; as disease, 24, 39–44, 53–66, 170; treatment, 39–44, 53–66, 73, 74, 95, 96, 97, 170, 194

Alcoholism Movement, 53–66; and science, 56–60; and the state, 60–66; and the temperance movement, 59; and the Yale Center of Alcohol Studies, 58–60

American Association for the Cure of Inebriates (AACI), 43

American Psychiatric Association (APA), 4, 74, 76, 85, 86, 127

Anderson, Dwight, 60

Anderson's four-pronged credo, 60

Anglin, M. Douglas, 69, 205

Anti-Drug Abuse Act, 73

Anti-Saloon League, 56

Ashmore, Malcolm, 7, 205

Association of Medical Superintendents of American Institutions for the Insane (AMSAII), 34

DARIN WEINBERG teaches in the Department of Sociology at Cambridge University and is a Fellow of King's College, Cambridge.